KU-222-126

Prepare for IELTS
THE IELTS PREPARATION COURSE

Penny Cameron

A comprehensive coursebook for candidates preparing
for the Academic Modules and General Training Modules
of the International English Language Testing System (IELTS)

Insearch Language Centre
and
International Programs,
University of Technology, Sydney

Insearch Language Centre
and
International Programs
University of Technology, Sydney

10 Quay Street
Sydney NSW 2000
Australia

Copyright © 1999 Insearch Language Centre and International Programs,
University of Technology, Sydney
Reprinted 2000

Produced by Insearch Language Centre

This publication is copyright. Apart from any fair dealing for the purposes of private study,
research, criticism or review as permitted under the Copyright Act, no part of this publication,
book and cassette tape, may be reproduced or transmitted in any form or by any means,
electronic, mechanical, photocopying, recording or otherwise, nor stored in a database
or retrieval system, without the written permission of the copyright holders.

Where copying is made for educational purposes, the Copyright Act requires that
due procedures be followed. This includes those parts of this publication marked:
'This activity may be photocopied'.

National Library of Australia
Cataloguing-in-Publication data

Cameron, Penny.
Prepare for IELTS. The IELTS Preparation Course

ISBN 1 86365 801 7

1. International English Language Testing System.
2. English language - Study and teaching - Australia - Foreign speakers.
3. Education - Australia - Curricula.
I. University of Technology, Sydney. Insearch Language Centre.
II. Title.
III. Title: Prepare for International English Language Testing System.

428.0076

Edited by Mary Jane Hogan, mjh Editorial & Language Services.
Cover and layout by Simon Leong Design, Sydney.
Illustrations on pages 17, 21, 35, 37, 48, 71, 110, 111, 114, 115,
118, 119, 120, 129, 130 by Pam Horsnell, Juno Creative Services.
All other diagrams by Simon Leong.
Printed by Southwood Press Pty Ltd, Marrickville NSW Australia.

Preface

The manifest purpose of a preparation course for a specific test is to give students the background knowledge and practice materials in the prescribed format to enable them to obtain acceptable scores on the test itself. The author of this course has fulfilled this requirement admirably, with clear and appropriate explanations of what is expected of the students, along with practical exercises that guide students to the achievement of their goals. A very important characteristic of these materials is that they are interesting. Boredom will not cloud students' minds, causing loss of effectiveness due to inattention.

The comprehensive coverage of various forms of the language, with American, British, and Australian sources, makes this text, like the IELTS test for which it is designed, usable in all English-speaking countries, as well as for all students around the globe, regardless of the form of English that their previous study has stressed.

Perhaps the greatest value of this text is to be found in its teaching potential. Many test preparation materials, designed for various university entrance examinations, accomplish nothing beyond acquainting students with the form of the test and various techniques for producing correct answers. Courses which prepare students solely to 'get around' a placement test do them a great disservice, leaving them unable to cope with their university courses. *The IELTS Preparation Course* does much more than train students in test-taking strategies: it teaches language. Anyone satisfactorily completing this course must have gained knowledge of form and technique for the test by learning the language and skills that are required, not by learning the 'tricks of the trade' for taking a specific test. They will have the knowledge of and skills in the language which will be essential after they are enrolled.

Joyce Merrill Valdes
Professor Emeritus in English
University of Houston, Texas

November 1998

Contents

Map of book

Map of book

Unit 1
Introduction

To the teacher

The International English Language System (IELTS) test is used to assess the language proficiency of students from a non-English-speaking background who want to live and study in an English-speaking country. The IELTS test is divided into two Modules, Academic and General Training. The Academic Module is for candidates who wish to study at tertiary level in English-speaking countries and the General Training Module is for candidates who wish to pursue high school studies or less linguistically demanding courses. The General Training Module is also taken by candidates wishing to immigrate to Australia or New Zealand.

On the day of the test, all candidates take the same Listening and Speaking modules, or subtests. Academic Module candidates take the Academic Reading module and the Academic Writing module, while General Training candidates take the General Training Reading module and the General Training Writing module. The order in which the modules are taken is: Listening, Reading, Writing, Speaking. All modules must be taken.

All candidates are scored on a band scale of 1 to 9. Generally speaking a score greater than 6 in the Academic Module is required for university entry. The General Training Module is not acceptable for university entry. Candidates should find out the entrance requirements for the institution at which they propose to study before applying to sit for the IELTS test.

More detailed information about the IELTS test can be found in a reading skills exercise in Unit 3: The Reading Test.

Description of this book and its companion titles

Prepare for IELTS: The IELTS Preparation Course focuses on the language skills and strategies candidates will need in order to complete the four modules of the IELTS test, and will be referred to as *The IELTS Preparation Course* for the rest of this introduction. It aims to consolidate the skills which will be needed to perform well in the test and to familiarize the candidates with specific question types. The companion titles, *Prepare for IELTS: Academic Modules* and *Prepare for IELTS: General Training Modules*, contain sample tests. All three titles are published by Insearch Language Centre and International Programs, University of Technology, Sydney.

Organization of The IELTS Preparation Course

The IELTS Preparation Course has been organized to parallel the test in the four areas of Listening, Reading (both Academic and General Training), Writing (both Academic and General Training), and Speaking. These areas are not mutually exclusive, and skills learned in one area will pass to others. Similarly, candidates can do extra practice by borrowing from exercises in the module they will not be attempting. The teacher will know what is best for any particular class, and will decide on the degree of emphasis to be given to each skill. There is no need to complete the work in one skill area before passing to another.

A detailed description of each test is at the beginning of each skill area. Candidates are then given exercises designed to develop their skills in each area of the test. These exercises are not sample tests.

Each boxed number in the margin indicates the beginning of a new activity. In the answer key the answers are arranged according to the numbers within each Unit, and the accompanying teacher's notes may make suggestions for exploiting different exercises in the book. The tapescript of the listening exercises is at the back of the book.

The tape symbol indicates that students should listen to a taped passage. There are hints for the students in shaded boxes.

Content focus

The IELTS test assesses all four skills both functionally and structurally and requires candidates to demonstrate the ability to understand, produce and manipulate discourse. To meet these needs *The IELTS Preparation Course* focuses on learning and communication strategies which will assist the student in developing both the productive skills of writing and speaking and the receptive skills of reading and listening. These strategies are continually emphasized and developed throughout the course.

The IELTS Preparation Course emphasizes the importance of interpreting the question and of correctly reading instructions. It practises essential reading and writing skills employable in the different tasks encountered in the test; it helps candidates to learn from their own errors and analyse their own errors and their own difficulties. It is intended to give candidates the confidence to face an examination task knowing that they can interpret it and fulfil its requirements.

Topics of general interest have been chosen, in keeping with the test. The materials used in the reading sections of the book reflect the vocabulary used daily by native speakers.

The course includes model essays written by experienced teachers familiar with the performance standards required for IELTS. Learners are expected to analyse and compare their efforts with the models. By the end of the course learners should have a clear idea of the criteria for evaluating their abilities. It is not recommended to assess or predict candidates' actual performance scores, as no amount of simulated exam practice is a valid basis for accurate prediction of a real test result, which is decided by real test performance under exam conditions.

International English materials

The IELTS test is a test of international English, and the range of materials used in this book reflects this. The reading passages come from publications in Singapore, New Zealand, South Africa, the United States, Britain, Australia and Canada. The listening passages are recorded in the accents of different places in the English-speaking world.

Please be sure the candidates read the passage 'The language of the test' in the section: 'To the student'.

Pages which may be photocopied

We have tried to keep this book to a reasonable size, so students should write their answers on a separate sheet of paper, or on one of the photocopiable answer sheets. Where the students need to write on the page, photocopying is permitted. These pages are marked *This activity may be photocopied*.

Candidate profile

The IELTS Preparation Course is designed as the final stage of preparation immediately before a candidate takes the exam, and therefore requires a very high Upper Intermediate or Advanced level of proficiency. There is more detailed information under the heading: 'Student entry profile'.

Course development

The IELTS Preparation Course was developed at Insearch Language Centre at the University of Technology, Sydney, with candidates intending to undertake tertiary study, and it incorporates their feedback and experiences. It was used in the classroom by teachers with experience in IELTS preparation and testing.

Course duration

This course is designed to fit a minimum 100 hours of instruction for advanced students. Many of the activities can be set for homework or self-study.

Student entry profile

Before students begin *The IELTS Preparation Course* they should demonstrate the ability to perform the tasks set out here. Profiles for all four skills, as well as ability in learning-how-to-learn, are given. However, if time is limited, it is probably most effective to test a student's writing skills; if a satisfactory performance in writing is achieved, competence in the other skill areas for the purpose of entry to *The IELTS Preparation Course* can usually be assumed.

Writing performance

A student should have good control of written language at paragraph level, with a demonstrated understanding of correct tense and time markers and of active and passive mood. The organization of text, for example the use of cohesive devices and essay structure, will be taught in the course.

In the written discourse produced, a student should show familiarity with:

- complex sentence structure (main clause + subordinate clause, some use of v+ing in the subordinate clause)
- preposition phrases (temporal and location)
- noun phrases
- nominalization for thematic purposes ('to immigrate - immigration')
- temporal markers for sequencing
- referencing with pronouns
- existentials (there is/are)
- modality (can/can't, will/won't, should/shouldn't, could/couldn't, must/mustn't, need to/needn't, would/wouldn't)
- modifying and intensifying adverbs (still, very)
- verbs as adjectives ('In developing countries')
- compound verbs (verb + infinitive: 'We have to stop')
- causal relationships expressing reasons or argument (because)
- relative clauses (who, whom, which, that, whose)
- conjunctions: of comparison and contrast, exemplification, concession, addition
- thematization ('It was fun to go out with friends')
- gerund as theme ('Spending the weekend at home is boring')
- projected clauses ('We felt that we were a family', 'He believed that it was true').

Reading performance
The student should be able to demonstrate the ability to:

- identify and retrieve information from authentic texts
- predict the content of various authentic texts based on familiar topics
- extract main ideas and understand the writer's intention using texts based on familiar topics
- analyse texts for alternative points of view
- critically evaluate the contents of texts for relevance to a particular writing task
- understand the main points of a passage by recognizing ways of linking ideas, sentences and paragraphs, e.g. cause and effect, addition, contrast and time
- reach a detailed comprehension of an authentic text without needing to understand every word.

Oral communication
The student should be able to demonstrate the ability to:

- initiate, maintain and terminate a conversation with native speakers, demonstrating a high degree of fluency
- call on a vocabulary wide enough to communicate confidently and effectively on a variety of common interest topics and general knowledge areas
- respond to main changes of topic and tone and show flexibility with register
- make and respond to statements of fact and opinion confidently, and to define and evaluate attitudes and events
- express and justify points of view
- relate a sequence of events in detail
- recognize and reproduce stress and intonation patterns with a degree of accuracy.

Listening skills
The student should be able to demonstrate the ability to:

- comprehend most speech directed at him/her, delivered at normal speed, without requiring repetition or explanation
- understand complicated telephone messages
- follow reports presented in the media
- listen to authentic speech and recognize examples of register and tone in relation to the speakers and the context.

Learning-how-to-learn
As well as being able to demonstrate the performance skills described in these profiles, a student using *The IELTS Preparation Course* ideally should have achieved a high degree of maturity as a language learner, that is, in 'learning-how-to-learn'. (This comment applies particularly to candidates who wish to take the Academic Module.) A student should have developed some ability to:

- develop conversation techniques and strategies in order to keep an interaction going
- find, analyse and correct errors in written discourse
- monitor and evaluate his/her own oral performance and show a capacity to use self-correction strategies in conversation
- apply language skills and strategies learnt in the classroom to everyday situations
- develop greater autonomy by making use of community resources and by completing projects outside the classroom
- consider the value of new words before learning them
- use an English-English dictionary
- evaluate his/her own learning.

To the student

Organization of the book

This book has been written to help increase your skills so you can approach the test confidently. It is not a workbook, and we suggest you write the answers on a separate piece of paper or on one of the photocopiable answer sheets similar to those used in the listening and reading tests.

Each boxed number in the margin indicates the beginning of a new activity. When you look in the answer key you will find the answers according to the numbers within each Unit. The tape symbol indicates that you should listen to a taped passage. You will occasionally find helpful hints in shaded boxes.

There are different strategies which will help you understand the requirements of the different question types; the passages and exercises are designed to develop your skills in using English, and they may be shorter or longer than the passages you would encounter in an IELTS test. There are no actual sample test papers in this book: these are available in our companion volumes *Prepare for IELTS: Academic Modules* and *Prepare for IELTS: General Training Modules*.

The language of the test

In this book you will find reading passages which come from publications in Canada, Australia, the United States, the United Kingdom, New Zealand, South Africa, in fact anywhere where English is used as a first language. This reflects the fact that English is an international language.

The IELTS examiners will accept answers given in, for instance, American English if this is the form of the language the student uses consistently. If you need to write the word *center*, this spelling is as acceptable as the British spelling *centre*. The examiners do expect that you will use either one form or the other, and not switch between them, so if you also have to write the word *honor* you must use the American spelling *honor* if you used *center* before, and the British spelling *honour* if you used *centre*.

Similarly, the listening passages come in different varieties of English and are recorded in the accents of the different places in the English-speaking world. In the speaking test, candidates need not sound like speakers of any particular variety of English; the test assesses how fluently and effectively you communicate.

You will find some differences in vocabulary between British and American English. As with any other unknown vocabulary, look at the context of the word to understand its meaning.

Different scales of measurement are used in different parts of the world. For example:

1 centimetre (cm) = 0.3937 inches   1 gram = 0.035274 ounces
1 metre (m) = 39.37 inches   1 kilogram = 2.2046 pounds
1 kilometre (km) = 0.621 miles or 3280.8 feet   1 metric tonne =2204.6 pounds

The IELTS test is difficult, but the skills you learn as you prepare for the test will stand you in good stead when you are working or studying in an English-speaking environment. Good luck!

Unit 2
The Listening Test

Introduction to the Listening test

This unit contains information about the Listening module of the IELTS test. The information can be found by listening to the audio tape for the first listening exercise **1** below.

The unit also covers listening skills and skills practice, as well as providing practice in the question types to be found in the IELTS Listening module. Please note that the exercises in this book are designed to teach students the skills needed to answer the questions but they are not necessarily sample questions.

Listening skills

Anticipation

It is very important to anticipate what information the task requires for a correct answer.

1 Look at the notes you will have to fill in below. What is likely to go in each gap? Work with your partner and try to anticipate the sort of information you will hear. Write your answers on a sheet of paper.

About the Listening Test

Example:

The test is about _____ long and contains about _____ questions.

Suggestions for the gaps:

The test is about *number and word concerned with time* long and contains about *number* questions.

1. There are _____ sections.

2. One section might be divided into several short parts of _____ minutes, or it could be one topic which goes on for _____.

3. You have _____ seconds to read over the questions, and _____ to check your answers. You have to listen carefully because _____.

4. One example of a 'survival situation' is _____. One example of an 'academic situation' is _____.

5. Accents heard in the test could be _____ or _____ or _____.

6. A monologue is _____. A dialogue is _____.

7. Types of questions include _____ (Name at least 3 types of questions used in the test.)

8. You can't always copy down the exact words you hear but you must show that you understand the _____ of what you hear.

9. You have to transfer your answers to the _____.

 Now listen to the conversation about the listening test and answer Questions 1 to 9 above. From the information in the conversation complete the sentences with a word or phrase. On this occasion you may hear the tape more than once. Write your answers on a sheet of paper.

Example:

The test is about _30 minutes_ long and contains about ____40____ questions.

2　Look at the table below. Work with a partner, and try to anticipate what the speaker or speakers will say.

Ask:　what is the topic?
　　　what do I know about this topic?
　　　what clues does the table give me?

Allow about 30 seconds to look at the survey. Then discuss the questions with your partner.

This activity may be photocopied

PASSENGER SURVEY

1. Today's date: _____　　　　　Bus Route: 440

2. How often does the passenger travel on this bus route? Check ✓ the box:

   ☐ less than once a month　　☐ daily

   ☐ twice a day　　　　　　　☐ more than twice a day

3. Purpose of this journey. Check ✓ the box:

   ☐ work　　　　　　☐ recreation

   ☐ education　　　　☐ other

   How do you rate the bus service? Check ✓ the box:
   (1 is very bad, 4 is very good)

	very bad			*very good*
	1	**2**	**3**	**4**
4. punctuality	☐	☐	☐	☐
5. comfort	☐	☐	☐	☐
6. cost	☐	☐	☐	☐
7. cleanliness of the bus	☐	☐	☐	☐
8. service from the staff	☐	☐	☐	☐

Listen to the interview and fill in the survey while you listen.

After you have listened once only, discuss these issues with your partner or group:

What were the most difficult parts to understand?
What did you predict correctly by looking at the survey?

Listening situations

The listening situations in the IELTS test will be of general interest. They will involve either social situations or study-related situations.

3 Think of listening situations which might arise:

Accuracy

Word endings

Students often find it difficult to distinguish the end of words.

This activity may be photocopied

4 You will hear 10 sets of three words. Circle the word which you hear twice.

For example, if you hear '18 80 18', you will circle '18'.

Example (18) 80

1.	15	50
2.	bend	bent
3.	led	let
4.	word	work
5.	16	60
6.	dish	ditch
7.	bed	bet
8.	13	30
9.	seal	seam
10.	slim	slip

Numbers

There are differences in the way numbers are said in British and American English. The British will often say 'double' when a number occurs twice, or 'triple' when it occurs three times.

Thus the number 973 1277 could be said:

nine seven three one two double seven   (British English) OR
nine seven three one two seven seven   (American English)

Both are correct.

The figure zero is often spoken as 'O' *(oh)*.

Candidates need to be able to recognize various ways of saying numbers.

 5 You will hear ten numbers in these conversations. Write these numbers down as you hear them.

Dates and time of day

Dates may be written as:

- day/month/year in numbers e.g. 3/5/99
- day/month/year in numbers and words e.g. 3 May 1999 or 3rd May 1999
- month/day/year in numbers e.g. 5/3/99
- month/day/year in words and numbers e.g. May 3 1999

If you do not have all three pieces of information you may use numbers or numbers and words:

- day/month in numbers e.g. 3/5
- day/month in numbers and words e.g. 3 May or 3rd May
- month/day in numbers e.g. 5/3
- month/day in words and numbers e.g. May 3
- month/year in numbers e.g. 3 1999
- month/year in words and numbers e.g. March 1999

You may abbreviate the months, but use the conventional abbreviation such as Jan., Feb., Oct. etc.; these can be found in a dictionary. You must be consistent. Do not switch between day/month/year and month/day/year. Choose the way of writing dates which is used in the place where you are learning English, and do not deviate from it.

A decade can be written '1920s' or '1920's'. In speech a decade may be referred to as 'the twenties' or 'the sixties'.

A century can be written with a 'C' and a number (C20) or as an ordinal number (20th century).

The time of day can be written 'a.m.', 'AM' or 'A.M.' for morning and 'p.m.', 'PM' or 'P.M.' for any time after noon.

6 You will hear ten dates. Write the dates you hear.

Fractions, percentages, money and decimals

The British pound is written £.

7 You will hear ten numbers read. Write every fraction, percentage, decimal number and amount of money you hear. You should include any currency you hear.

The alphabet

Sometimes the pronunciation of the letters of the alphabet can be confusing. The Americans pronounce the last letter of the alphabet 'zee', the British, Australians and many other countries say 'zed'. Each is correct in its own context. Check with your teacher for the pronunciation used in the country where you are learning English.

8 Sit with your back to your partner and spell the words in your address. Then listen as your partner spells the words in her/his address.

Were any letters hard to understand? Ask your teacher for help. Practise spelling words to each other.

Spelling places and names

There are differences in the way letters are said in British and American English. The British will often say 'double' when a letter occurs twice. Thus the word 'letter' could be spelt:

L-E-double T-E-R   (British English) OR
L-E-T-T-E-R   (American English)

Both are correct.

Candidates need to be able to recognize various ways of spelling.

9 You will hear ten names. Write every name or place name that you hear.

The instructions

The instructions on the tape will tell you what to do. In some cases part of the instructions will also be printed on the page. You will usually be given 30 seconds to look at the instructions and read the questions through.

Tasks which involve graphs

These tasks may involve charts, graphs, maps, plans, pictures or any other information which is looked at rather than read. You should use the information you see to help you predict what you may hear.

Work with your partner or group. Look at the pie charts below:

What do you expect the question to be about?

What do you think the words *toxic, nuclear, industrial* and *chemical* refer to?

What are the distinguishing features of the different pie charts?

What vocabulary do you expect to hear? (You may like to refer to the section on Academic Writing Task 1.)

1. Listen and identify the pie chart being discussed.

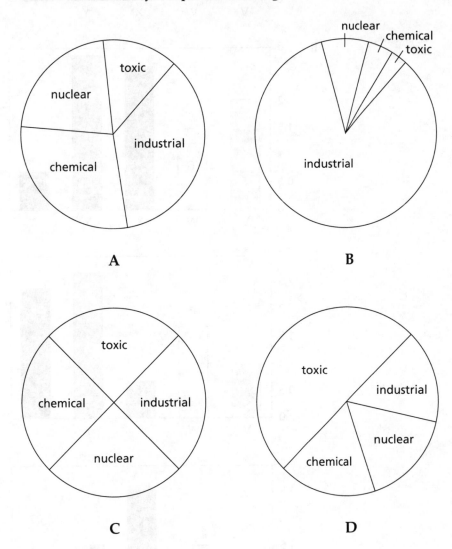

2. Listen and identify the graph being discussed.

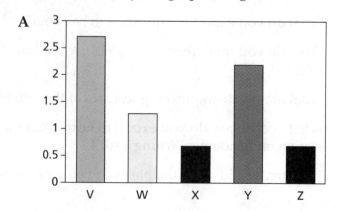

A

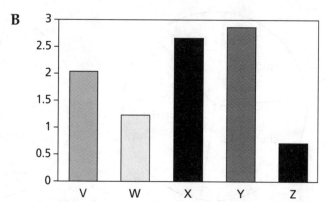

B

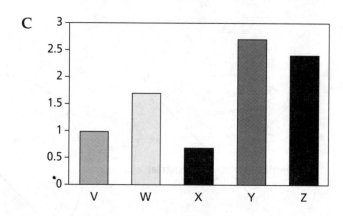

C

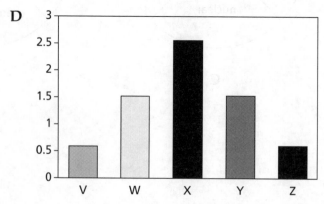

D

3. Listen and identify the graph being discussed.

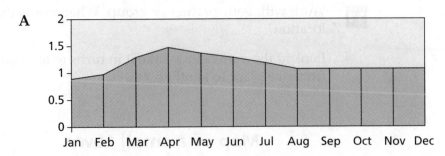

A

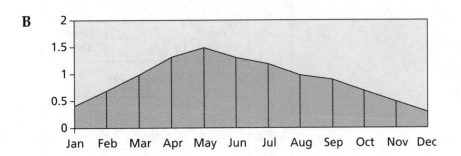

B

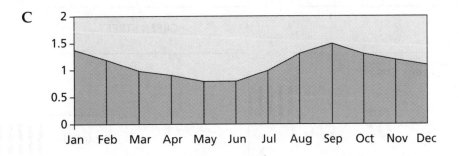

C

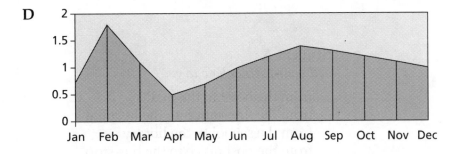

D

Maps

11 Work with your partner or group. What words do you use to explain location?

Look at the map below. Take it in turns to tell your partner how to go from one place to another.

Map of a small town

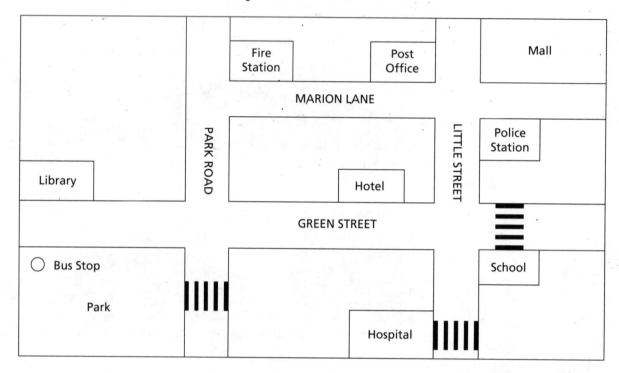

 Pedestrian Crossing

Student A
Tell your partner how to go:

> from the hotel to the mall
> from the fire station to the hospital
> from the school to the library
> from the post office to the bus stop.

Student B
Tell your partner how to go:

> from the school to the mall
> from the fire station to the hotel
> from the park to the police station
> from the post office to the mall.

PREPARE FOR IELTS: The IELTS Preparation Course
Unit 2 The Listening Test

12 Look at the people below. What vocabulary do you expect to hear to describe them?

Listen to the taped descriptions of the people in the illustrations below, A to H. Match the description to the figure.

A _6_ B _3_ C _1_ D _8_

E _5_ F _7_ G _4_ H _2_

Thinning / _Clean-shaven_

Loose

Casual / _formal_

Conservatively

Forms

You may be asked to complete a form while listening to a conversation. The form will show you what to listen for. It is important to remember that there are a lot of different ways to give or ask for the same information. Please listen for the meaning of what is said.

For instance, forms often begin with a line like this:

Name: _____

To get this information, a questioner could say:

What's your name, please?
Give me your name.
Name?
Let me have your name, please?
May I have your full name, please?
I need your name. Family name first, please, then one given name.
Family name, given name, middle initial, please.

Work with your partner. What questions could be asked to fill in this form? Write down at least four questions for each heading.

```
Name:        _____
Address:     _____
Occupation:  _____
Nationality: _____
Education:   _____
```

13 Listen to the dialogue and fill out the application form while you listen.

This activity may be photocopied

Calvi
Mario
Italian

```
1. Family name: ____George Row Look_____

2. Other names: ____St Green Street, Strathfield 2135____

3. Nationality: ____†____

4. First language: ____German____

5. Number of years you have studied English. Check ✓ the box:
   ☐ Less than 1  ☐ 1  ☐ 2  ☐ 3  ☐ 4  ☐ 5  ☐ 6  ☐ 7  ☑ more than 7

6. Level of education completed. Check ✓ the box:
   ☐ Secondary up to 16 years    ☐ Secondary 16–19 years
   ☐ Degree or diploma           ☑ Post-graduate

7. Date you wish to take the test: ____13/8____

8. Second choice of test date: ____30/8____
```

Listening for meaning

Accuracy

It is important that you listen accurately. Look at these sentences:

All teachers are university graduates.
Some teachers are university graduates.

What is the difference in meaning?

You should also listen for the forms of verbs. Look at these sentences:

The class may go on an excursion later in the term.
The class will go on an excursion later in the term.
The class could go on an excursion later in the term.
The class must go on an excursion later in the term.

What is the difference in meaning? Which is the strongest statement?

Tense is always important:

The school will be closed next week.
The school is closed now.
The school was closed in March.

Fortunately there is usually a word like 'now' to help clarify tense.

This activity may be photocopied

14 Listen to this passage and answer the questions below.

The speaker is explaining the process of a move to a new campus. As you listen, answer questions 1–7 by marking T for true and F for false. (This exercise tests the accuracy of your listening skills. T/F is not an IELTS listening test question type.)

Look at the statements before you listen.

1. All Agricultural Science students will stay where they are. T F

2. History students will move to the new campus. T F

3. Some history teachers will move immediately to the new campus. T F

4. Engineering staff have already made their move. T F

5. The Philosophy department will use the old engineering building. T F

6. Part of the Faculty of Law is in its new premises. T F

7. The former law premises may become an art gallery. T F

After you have corrected your work you may listen to the tape again. Identify the key words in each question.

Summary of listening strategies

Before you listen:

Read the question.

Check where you have to write your answer, and in what form (a name, a number, a tick or a cross, a phrase, circle the correct answer, ...).

Predict the content of what you will hear.

Anticipate the words and phrases you are most likely to hear.

'Translate' any pictures into words, to anticipate hearing them in the listening passage.

Predict possible answers to the questions, to prepare yourself to hear the answers.

Anticipate synonyms and ideas expressed in different words.

Concentrate!

While you listen:

Listen carefully to any taped **instructions** for each section.

Focus on more than one question at a time.

Do not stop on an answer you do not know: move on.

Listen for the specific information pin-pointed in your pre-listening preparation.

Don't worry if you do not understand every word when listening for the overall meaning or gist.

Write an answer for every question: marks are not deducted for wrong answers, and sometimes your guesses are accurate: your ears hear more than you think!

Do not accept the first answer that seems correct: subsequent information may change it.

At the end of each section, check your answers.

At the end of the test, transfer your answers *with care* **to the Listening Answer Sheet.**

Listening skills practice

Listening for distinguishing features / accuracy / predicting vocabulary

15 Look at the pictures below. What distinguishes one picture from another? Try to anticipate the vocabulary. Write some words you are likely to use about each picture. Work with your partner or group.

Listen and write A, B, C or D to indicate which picture is being discussed.

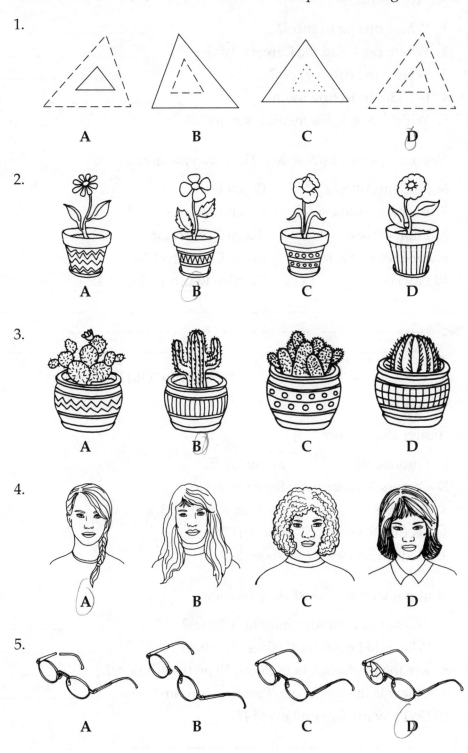

1.

    A   B   C   D

2.

    A   B   C   D

3.

    A   B   C   D

4.

    A   B   C   D

5.

    A   B   C   D

Listening for specific information

This activity may be photocopied

16 Pair practice: ask your partner the questions on your form, and give your partner the answers to their questions.

WHICH ROOM?

Student A

Ask your partner:

1. Where do I go to enrol? _____
2. Where can I find the Careers Adviser? _____
3. Where do I pay my fees? _____
4. Is C130 the lecture room? _____
5. Which room is the medical service? _____

Now your partner will ask you. These are your answers:

6. Student Adviser: Room D47.
7. Business Studies: Room C592
8. Photocopies: Room 2, 3rd floor.
9. Professor's Secretary: Room G94, Level 26.
10. Pay Fees: Cashier, Room 17, Level 4.

✂ -

WHICH ROOM?

Student B

Answer your partner:

1. Enrolments: Room Q775.
2. Careers Adviser: Room F9941.
3. Pay Fees: Cashier, Room K33.
4. Lecture Room: Room J17.
5. Medical Service: Room S40

Now, it is your turn to ask the questions:

6. Where can I find the Student Adviser? _____
7. Where do I enrol for Business Studies? _____
8. Are the photocopiers in Room 10 on the 4th floor? _____
9. Where is the Professor's Secretary's room? _____
10. Do I pay my fees on Level 14? _____

PREPARE FOR IELTS: The IELTS Preparation Course

Unit 2 The Listening Test

Swallow Life Insurance

Established 1876

Name of Applicant:	**(1)** George Rowlands
Address:	**(2)** 52 Green Street *Strathfield* Postcode 2135
Age:	*35*
Height:	**(3)** 1 m 73 cm
Weight:	**(4)** 80 kilos
Marital status: (circle the appropriate word)	**(5)** (Single) Married Divorced Widowed

Medical History

Serious illness: (please indicate dates, or write 'none' if no illnesses)	**(6)** None
Major surgical operations: (please indicate dates, or write 'none' if no operations)	**(7)** None
Any current medical conditions: (write 'none' if no current medical conditions)	**(8)** Hay fever
Are applicant's parents still living? (circle the appropriate information)	**(9)** Mother: (Yes) No Father: Yes (No)
If not, at what age did they die?	**(10)** Mother: _____ Cause of death: _____ Father: _67_ Cause of death: _Car accident_
Is the applicant currently a smoker?	**(11)** Yes (No)

This activity may
be photocopied

Cue cards for further practice

Using the cue cards, work in pairs to practise conversations on this model, asking and answering questions to complete further Insurance Application forms, role-playing the applicant and the interviewer. The 'Interviewer' has a blank application form to complete, and the 'Applicant' the cue card.

Applicant details:

Jennifer Evans, aged 27
320 Victoria Road, Flat G8, Hong Kong
162 cms; 56 kilos. Single
No serious illness or medical conditions
Operation to repair knee damaged
playing netball, four years ago
Both parents living
Smoker

Applicant details:

William Lee, aged 45
2217 Macomb Street NW
Washington DC 20008
6 feet 1 inch; 190 pounds. Married
Suffered malaria, aged 12
Has constant high blood pressure
Had operation to repair hand injured
in industrial accident in 1978
Father died aged 60, heart failure
Mother died aged 47, brain tumour
Smoker

Applicant details:

Elizabeth Nguyen, aged 36
552-6th Avenue SE
Calgary AB T2G 4S6
150 cms, 54 kilos. Married
Had pneumonia, 10 years ago
Gall bladder removed, two years ago
Takes medication since operation
Both parents deceased: father killed
at age 38; mother died 69, heart and
respiratory failure
Non-smoker

Applicant details:

Michael Kim, aged 42
15 Rushmore Hill Rd, Knockholt
Kent TN147NS
174 cm; 96 kilos. Married
Heart disease from childhood
Heart transplant, 1989
Medication daily for heart but fit
and healthy, gets lots of exercise
Both parents living
Non-smoker

Applicant details:

Marilyn Habib, aged 55
Farm Road, Northland, Wellington 6005
162 cms; 60 kilos. Divorced
Operation for broken hip, 1988
Allergic to penicillin and to cats
Vegetarian
Asthmatic; takes asthma medication
Father died aged 40, industrial accident
Mother still living
Non-smoker

Applicant details:

Scott Ivanisovic, aged 23
14 Philips Street, Shiftwich, 2678
180 cms; 102 kilos. Single
Appendix removed at age 12
Broken leg playing rugby 5 years ago
Dislocated shoulder playing
basketball last year
Allergies, takes daily medication
Both parents living
Non-smoker

Anticipating specific vocabulary items

18 Listening tasks are made easier if you anticipate the kinds of key words likely to be used in what you hear.

Look at the following example. Before you listen to the talk, can you add to the lists?

Can you add more words after you hear the talk? Which words are difficult for you?

Example 1 **Topic: Earthquakes**

Nouns	Verbs	Adjectives
disaster emergency destruction lives services	strike kill injure	severe emergency

Add extra vocabulary items

Difficulties (pronunciation / meaning / usage):

struck/stuck   Richter

This type of vocabulary prediction exercise can be practised without listening to a talk at all. For example, what terms can you add to the lists below?

Work in groups to produce a brief talk on global warming and share it with the class.

Example 2 **Topic: Global warming**

Nouns	Verbs	Adjectives
damage infrastructure flooding water disaster	damage predict cause	coastal beachfront predicted natural

Add extra vocabulary items

Difficulties (pronunciation / meaning / usage):

damage (noun/verb/adjective + ed)

This activity may
be photocopied

19 **Topic: Problems of developing countries**

Imagine you are going to hear a talk about the problems of developing countries. What words do you expect to hear?

Nouns	Verbs	Adjectives

Difficulties (pronunciation / meaning / usage):

Topic: Pollution

Imagine you are going to hear a talk on pollution. What words do you expect to hear?

Nouns	Verbs	Adjectives

Difficulties (pronunciation / meaning / usage):

This activity may
be photocopied

Predicting practice: master sheet
Use this master sheet to practise this listening skill.

Listening to recorded radio and television news is one opportunity for practice: listen to the news summary at the beginning of the news, and predict what you will hear before you listen to the rest of the news. Check your predictions against what you hear.

Nouns	Verbs	Adjectives

Difficulties (pronunciation / meaning / usage):

Nouns	Verbs	Adjectives

Difficulties (pronunciation / meaning / usage):

Predicting possible content details

20 How do you think these beginnings could continue? Work with your partner or group and write continuations to the sentences.

Listen to the suggestions written by other students to see how many ways these sentences could continue.

Note: these exercises are not an IELTS-type listening task; thus, there are no correct answers. They practise predicting as a listening skill.

Reservations (Dialogue)

A: Have you booked your _____?
B: Yes I have. I'm going to _____

A: Why did you choose that?
B: Oh, really I guess the main reason was _____

A: Was it very expensive?
B: No, not really. It cost _____
   What about you? Have you made up your mind?

A: I'm having a problem deciding between _____
B: The first one sounds good.

A: Yes, but the second one _____

Club Membership (Monologue)

'In this short talk I'd like to tell you about some of the future activities of the Club, but first I'd like to explain the application procedures, because I know most of you are keen to join.

To become a member of the Club, the first thing you must do is _____

Then, applications are accepted between _____

You must take your application to _____

In your application you must give us some details of _____

For example, you might like to describe _____

The cost of membership is _____

There are only a few rules of the Club. I guess the most important is that you must _____

If you have any problems with your application you should _____

Well, now that application procedures are explained, let me tell you about some of the exciting things we plan to do this year. The first activity we have planned is _____ '

21 Can you suggest what the rest of these radio news statements might tell the listener?

1. **Sydbourne Earthquake**

    i. An earthquake measuring 6.5 on the Richter scale _____

    ii. Emergency crews say that there is a shortage of _____

    iii. A witness said that it was the worst _____

    iv. The latest quake followed a _____

Now listen to the news broadcast and compare what you hear with what you have predicted.

2. **Storm lashes Sydney**

    i. Severe storms hit _____

    ii. In the car park, a Toyota Corolla was badly damaged by _____

    iii. Winds were recorded at speeds of _____

    iv. People were trapped in cars for up to an hour because _____

    v. In Lucas Heights, a tree fell on a _____

Now listen to the news broadcast and compare what you hear with what you have predicted.

Question types in the Listening test

A variety of questions are used, chosen from the following types:

- multiple choice
- short-answer questions
- sentence completion
- notes/summary/diagram/flow chart/table completion
- labelling a diagram which has numbered parts
- classification
- matching

(*The IELTS Handbook* 1998, p. 7)

The Listening module is recorded on a tape and is heard ONCE only.

Multiple choice tasks

Multiple choice tasks require the listener to activate many of their listening skills.

Use these strategies to choose the appropriate response.

- *Read* the questions in the time given.
- *Anticipate* the vocabulary and ideas you might hear.
- *Predict* what to listen for to decide the answer.
- *Do not eliminate* any answers until you have heard the text, no matter how unlikely they may seem.

This activity may be photocopied

22 Enrolment Day

You will hear part of an introductory talk by a Student Information Officer.

As you listen, answer questions 1 to 7. Circle the correct answer.

1. Overseas students will enrol on

   A   8th February
   B   16th February
   C   17th February
   D   18th February

2. Undergraduate students must enrol

   A   between 8.00 and 10.30 am
   B   between 9.30 am and 12.30 pm
   C   between 12.30 and 2.30 pm
   D   between 2.00 and 4.30 pm

3. The venue for enrolment is

   A   in the Mathematics Faculty
   B   on Level 158
   C   in Room C658
   D   in Room C6

4. At enrolment, all students

    A must show a letter of acceptance from their faculty
    B need not show their letter of acceptance
    C need not bring any identification
    D must prove their level of English proficiency

5. Students who have paid their fees

    A should go to the International Students' Office
    B are guaranteed a place at university
    C must get a bank cheque
    D should pay a further $10,000

6. The Student Card

    A is issued before enrolment
    B has the student's identification number
    C is issued by the Library
    D is not laminated

7. During university term, the Library will be open

    A from 9.00 am to 4.00 pm
    B from 9.00 am to 9.00 pm
    C from 8.30 am to 9.00 pm
    D from 4.00 pm to 9.30 pm

Short-answer tasks

Use these strategies to find the answers to question requiring short answers of a few words.

- *Read* the question accurately.
- *Anticipate* the sort of vocabulary you will hear.
- *Predict* what to listen for to decide the answer.
- *Do not try to answer from your own knowledge* before you have heard the tape.

This activity may be photocopied

23   Heathrow Airport

Listen to the information about London Heathrow Airport.
Write **NO MORE THAN THREE WORDS** for each answer.

1. Which terminal takes British Airways flights to Philadelphia? ____

2. How long does it take to travel by coach between terminals? ____

3. Where do you go if you do not have a boarding pass for a connecting flight? ____

4. How many passengers may a taxi carry? ____

5. How long is the journey on the Underground? ____

Use these strategies
to complete the
sentences.

Sentence completion tasks

- *Read* each partial sentence.
- *Anticipate* possible completions.
- *Anticipate* grammatical form as well as vocabulary.
- *Be prepared* for synonyms.
- *Be prepared* for ideas, not just words.

 24 Student Counsellor's Talk

This activity may
be photocopied

Complete the sentences below. Write **NO MORE THAN THREE WORDS** for each answer.

Example:

The counsellor's talk is about ___*students' problems*___ .

1. When they arrive, students initially feel _____

2. The first cause of student unhappiness mentioned is _____

3. The second cause of depression mentioned is _____

4. One cause of academic problems is _____

5. The counsellor advises students to be _____

Diagram completion tasks

Use these strategies to complete a diagram.

- *Examine the diagram* closely in the time given.
- *Predict* what the parts/sections/places might be called.
- *Anticipate* how locations/features might be described.
- *Listen* carefully to instructions.

25 **Library Tour**

This activity may be photocopied

Listen to the guided tour commentary and label the places marked. Choose from the box below. Write the appropriate letters A to J on the diagram.

A	Information Desk	**F**	Circulation Desk
B	Catalogues	**G**	Newspapers
C	Reference Section	**H**	Returns area
D	Current magazines	**I**	Restrooms
E	Photocopying Room	**J**	Conference Room

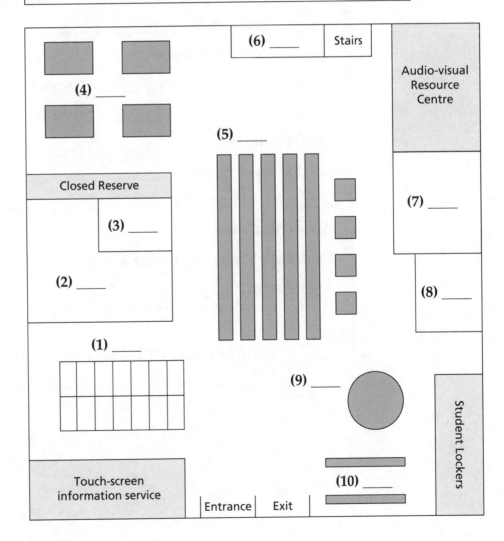

Table completion tasks

- *Read the table carefully* and think of how the words will sound when you hear them.
- Although you must *try to predict*, don't cling too tightly to your predictions.

 26 The Video Shop

This activity may
be photocopied

Complete the following application form. Write **NO MORE THAN THREE WORDS OR ONE NUMBER** for each answer.

STARLIGHT VIDEO SHOP

Membership Application

Name: (Mr) Mrs   Ms   Miss

(1) _____ (2) _____
        First name   Family name

Address: (3) _____ Apartment (4) _____

Houston, (5) _____ 77042

Contact telephone numbers:

(6) _____ (Home)

(7) _____ (Work)

Date of birth: (8) _____

I.D. documents: type: (9) _____

no.: (10) _____

Password: *Horace*

Date of application: September 9, 1998

Authorised by: _____

Starlight Video - all you need in entertainment

Labelling a diagram which has numbered parts

Use these strategies to label a diagram.

- *Look carefully at the diagram* in the time given.
- *Think about what you know* about the object in the diagram.
- *Anticipate the vocabulary* and ideas you might hear.
- *Predict* what to listen for to decide the answer.
- *Ask yourself* if there is a process or sequence of events illustrated.

27 | **The Bicycle Pump and Tyre Valve**

This activity may be photocopied

Listen to the tape and label the parts of the bicycle pump and tyre valve. Write **NO MORE THAN TWO WORDS** for each answer.

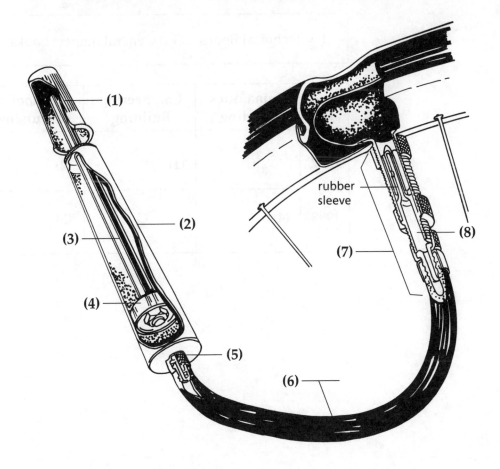

Classification tasks

Use these strategies to use a key in the task.

• *Familiarize yourself with the key* so it is easy for you to use it. The items in the key may bear a direct relationship to the words they represent, e.g. it may be the first letter of the word.

28   Book Sales

This activity may be photocopied

You will hear a talk about book sales in the University Book Stores. As you listen, answer questions 1 to 6 by completing the table showing the type of books sold in greatest numbers at the different University Book Stores.

T = Technical Books   G = General interest books   N = Novels

	Humanities Building	Engineering Building	School of Nursing	Sports Centre
1997	G	(1)	(2)	(3)
1998	(4)	G	(5)	(6)

Matching tasks

Use these strategies for matching tasks.

- *Look carefully at the graphics* in the time given.
- *Think about what you know* about the object in the diagram.
- *Anticipate* the vocabulary and ideas you might hear.
- *Identify the differences* between the pictures.

29

This activity may be photocopied

Listen and write A, B, C or D to indicate the illustration being discussed.

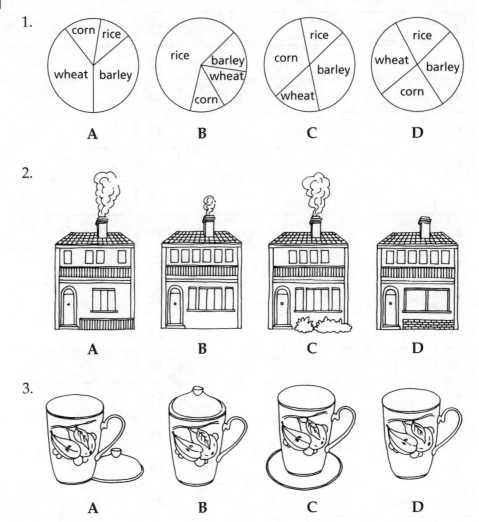

1.

A   B   C   D

2.

A   B   C   D

3.

A   B   C   D

Listening activities answer sheet

You may photocopy this page.
In the IELTS test, candidates will transfer their answers to an Answer Sheet similiar to this.

1		21	
2		22	
3		23	
4		24	
5		25	
6		26	
7		27	
8		28	
9		29	
10		30	
11		31	
12		32	
13		33	
14		34	
15		35	
16		36	
17		37	
18		38	
19		39	
20		40	

Unit 3
The Reading Test

ACADEMIC AND GENERAL TRAINING READING MODULES

Introduction to the Reading test

1 Read the information below on the IELTS Reading test. Make a note of the time you take.

Note the time you started reading.

Introduction to the IELTS Test

About the IELTS test
English has become an international language, and is used by more and more people around the world as a medium of post-school study. To help universities and colleges select students with sufficient English skills to succeed in their courses, the IELTS test was introduced in 1989 to assess candidates' readiness to study or train in English, and is now used world-wide.

Depending on the course of study that students plan to take, students must choose to sit either the Academic IELTS test or the General Training IELTS test. This choice must be made when applying to sit the test. The Academic IELTS test is necessary for students who plan to study at university (undergraduate or postgraduate courses) and will test the student's ability both to understand and to use complex academic language. The General Training IELTS test is required by other institutions, such as colleges and high schools, for courses that require less complex language skills, and is also used as a general test of English proficiency.

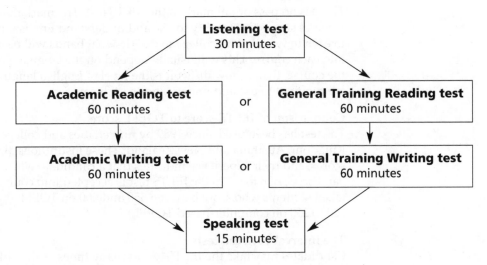

The Speaking test may take place a day or two later at some test centres.

The Listening test or module lasts for about 30 minutes. It consists of four sections, played on cassette tape, in order of increasing difficulty. Each section might be a conversation or a monologue. The test is played once only, and the questions for each section must be answered while listening, although time is given for candidates to check their answers.

The Reading module lasts for 60 minutes. Candidates take either an Academic Reading module, or a General Training Reading module. Both modules consist of three sections, and in both modules different question types are used to assess comprehension. In both tests the sections are in order of increasing difficulty.

The Writing module also lasts for 60 minutes. Again, candidates take either an Academic module, or a General Training module. Candidates must perform two writing tasks, which require different styles of writing. There is no choice of question topics.

The Speaking module consists of a one-to-one interview with a specially trained examiner. The examiner will lead the candidate through a series of questions and a question-asking task, in order to assess the candidate's oral ability. This interview lasts for 10–15 minutes.

The Marking scale
Each module is marked on a scale from 1 up to 9. These band scores are given according to highly detailed marking guidelines. These marking guidelines are not made public, but correspond roughly to the following band descriptions:

1 Non User
2 Intermittent User
3 Extremely Limited User
4 Limited User
5 Modest User
6 Competent User
7 Good User
8 Very Good User
9 Expert User

The test results form will show the mark for each module as well as an average (overall) band score.

What do the band scores mean?
There is no pass or fail mark in the IELTS test. The mark that a candidate receives shows their ability to use and understand English. However, it is up to each university and college to decide what bands will be acceptable for entry into each course. This will usually depend on the language requirements for the course, that is, how difficult is the level of English language that students are required to use and understand in each course.

Comparison of IELTS score to TOEFL score
The test has been used since 1989 by universities and colleges in the United Kingdom, Australia and New Zealand. These institutions also accept TOEFL scores, and their experience indicates that a candidate who achieves a global band score of 6 to 6.5 in the IELTS test is accepted into courses which have taken students who score between 550 and 600 on TOEFL (approximately 220 to 250 on computer-based TOEFL).

The interval between tests
Candidates may take the IELTS test as many times as they like, but after sitting an IELTS test, they must wait for THREE MONTHS before they can take it again. This is an official rule, but in any case it is unlikely that a student's score will improve in less than three months.

The Reading Test

This information on the reading test is taken from *The IELTS Handbook, 1998* pp. 8 and 10

Academic Reading

The Academic Reading Module takes 60 minutes. There are 40 questions. There are three reading passages with a total of 1,500 to 2,500 words.

Texts are taken from magazines, journals, books and newspapers. Texts have been written for a non-specialist audience, and all the topics are of general interest. They deal with issues which are appropriate and accessible to candidates entering postgraduate and undergraduate courses.

At least one text contains detailed logical argument. One text may contain non-verbal materials such as diagrams, graphs or illustrations.

If texts contain technical terms a simple glossary is provided.

Texts and tasks become increasingly difficult through the paper.

Some of the questions may appear before a passage, some may come after, depending on the nature of the questions.

A variety of questions are used, chosen from the following types:
- multiple choice
- short-answer questions
- sentence completion
- notes/summary/diagram/flow chart/table completion
- choosing from a 'heading bank' for identified paragraphs/sections of the text
- identification of the writer's views/attitudes/claims - yes, no, not given
- classification
- matching lists
- matching phrases

Instructions are clear and easy to follow. Examples of any unfamiliar question types are given.

Texts and questions appear on a Question Paper which candidates can write on but not remove from the test room.

All answers must be entered on an Answer Sheet. (At the end of this unit there is a photocopiable Answer Sheet to use for practice.)

General Training Reading

The General Training Reading Module takes 60 minutes. There are 40 questions. There are three sections of increasing difficulty with a total of 1,500 to 2,500 words.

Texts are taken from notices, advertisements, official documents, booklets, newspapers, instruction manuals, leaflets, timetables, books and magazines.

The first section, *social survival*, contains texts relevant to basic linguistic survival in English with tasks mainly about retrieving and providing general factual information.

Training survival, the second section, focuses on the training context, for example on the training programme itself or on welfare needs. This section involves a text or texts of more complex language with some precise or elaborated expression.

The third section, *general reading*, involves reading more extended prose with a more complex structure but with the emphasis on descriptive and instructive rather than argumentative texts.

Some of the questions may appear before a passage, some may come after, depending on the nature of the questions.

A variety of questions are used, chosen from the following types:
- multiple choice
- short-answer questions
- sentence completion
- notes/summary/diagram/flow chart/table completion
- choosing from a 'heading bank' for identified paragraphs/sections of the text
- identification of the writer's views/attitudes/claims - yes, no, not given/true, false, not given
- classification
- matching lists
- matching phrases

Your success in tests of this nature depends partly on the speed of your reading. For this reason, you will find reminders on many passages to note the time you started reading and the time you finished reading.

Instructions are clear and easy to follow. Examples of any unfamiliar question types are given.

Texts and questions appear on a Question Paper which candidates can write on but not remove from the exam room.

All answers must be entered on an Answer Sheet. (At the end of this unit there is a photocopiable Answer Sheet to use for practice.)

Note the time you finished reading and the time elapsed.

Reading skills to increase speed and efficiency

Using diagrams and tables

2 Look at the diagram on page 39 and answer these questions.

a) Can you take both Academic and General Training modules?
b) Which tests are common to both modules?

Using titles and headings

Look at page 40.

c) How many bands are in the scale?
d) What is the top band?

Look at pages 41 and 42.

e) Which test description is more important to you? Why?
f) How could you quickly choose the passage you want to read?

Skimming for general information

Using the whole passage, answer these questions.

g) What are the four parts of the test?
h) Which parts of the test are different in the Academic and General Training modules?
i) After a candidate does the test, when may she/he do it again?

Scanning for particular information

Look at the detailed descriptions of the Reading modules on pages 41 and 42.

j) Where do the texts for the Academic Reading module come from?

k) Where do the texts for the General Training Reading module come from?

l) What are the differences between the question types for the Academic Reading module and the General Training Reading module?

m) What information is the same for both modules?

Pre-reading strategies

Discuss this outline with your teacher.

Before you read, ask: **What do I know about the topic?**

What am I reading?   (What kind of text is it?)
Why am I reading?   (What is my purpose?)
How should I read?   (Fast, slow, skimming?)

Surveying the text means:

Reading the title and headings
Looking for captions of diagrams, tables, graphs and illustrations
Skimming over the text for the general idea (especially the introduction)
Ignoring unknown words
Reading quickly for 1 to 2 minutes

Through **surveying** (overviewing) you will:

Know the **topic**
Know the writer's **purpose** ⟶ e.g. describing a process
writing a report
discussing problems
proposing solutions

Identify the **text organization**

find the **topic sentence** in each paragraph
(often summarizes the main idea)
(may be 1st or 2nd sentence in paragraph)
find other sentences which **support/develop** an idea

Recognizing text organization

One quick way to overview a passage is to identify the **topic sentence**. A topic sentence gets its name because it effectively summarizes the content of a paragraph.

3 Look at the topic sentence in this paragraph. It has been printed in bold.

A Walk in the Woods

One hundred and fifty years ago Vancouver was covered by a dense, green blanket of old growth temperate rainforest. Centuries-old western red cedar, Douglas-fir, Sitka spruce and Western hemlock formed a virtually unbroken evergreen canopy from the Fraser River to Point Grey, around Burrard Inlet to the North Shore mountains. It was this magnificent forest that attracted the city's first settlers in 1862, loggers who saw their fortune in the great stands of timber.

How do the other sentences support and add to the information in the topic sentence?

Identify the topic sentences in the paragraphs below.

Through the end of the 19th century, Vancouver was the centre of British Columbia's logging and sawmilling industry. Its forests provided some of the finest straight masts and spars the world's shipyards had ever seen. Framing timbers, 70 feet long and 20 inches square with scarcely a knot or blemish, fed hungry markets in the United States, Europe and the Orient. China's Imperial Palace was constructed with beams shipped from Vancouver to Peking in 1879.

Today, Greater Vancouver is home to 1.6 million people. Although temperate rainforest has given way to high-rises and highways, manicured lawns and suburban sprawl, vestiges of the region's original ecology remain. Though logged to various degrees around the turn of the century, the North Shore mountains, Stanley Park and Pacific Spirit Park are all examples of the temperate rainforest ecosystem that once dominated British Columbia's south coast.

How do the other sentences support or develop the ideas in the two paragraphs above?

Look at the topic sentence in this paragraph. It has been printed in bold.

For decades the civil engineers have been 'going to survey camp', a once-a-year ten-day excursion for final year students. For fifty years or more the destination has been a site in hilly and beautiful bushland at Yarramundi in Sydney's west. This facility comprises residential huts as well as canteen facilities cheered by the omnipresent call of bellbirds. Organiser Associate Professor Rob Wheen said, 'This continues to be one of the really worthwhile things that we do. Quite apart from its social value, students are required to carry out surveys and design work in a very challenging environment.'

How do the other sentences in the passage above support or develop the idea expressed in the topic sentence?

Identify the topic sentence in the paragraph below.

Obstructions in the vicinity of an airport, whether they be natural features or man-made structures, may seriously limit the scope of its operations. Ideally a new airport will be located in an area where airspace is relatively free of obstacles that might prove hazardous to aircraft. Existing airports were no doubt sited with the same requirements in mind, but as airports have grown so too have their aerospace protection requirements. High terrain or high-rise buildings once considered remote from an airport may now be the critical obstructions in the design of instrument flight procedures and may impose limits on the range of weather conditions in which aircraft take-off and landing can now take place. New structures may further restrict available flight paths or the length of a runway that can be used for take-off and landing. The impacts of any one obstacle may be relatively minor but together a number of obstacles may seriously limit runway utilisation, cause airspace congestion and reduce the effective handling capacity of the airport.

Note again how the other sentences support or develop the topic sentence.

 Now quickly read the following passage. Identify the topic sentences as you read.

Note the time you started reading.

Bird Hazard

A collision between an aircraft and one or more birds is termed a birdstrike. Pilots sometimes record a birdstrike while at cruising altitudes, but most of them happen when an aircraft is relatively close to the ground, usually in proximity to an airport and during the circling, descent to land or take-off phases of a flight.

Birdstrikes may cause significant damage to an aircraft and/or, if the birds are ingested into a jet engine, a significant and sudden loss of power. If this were to happen during take-off or initial climb of a fully loaded passenger aircraft the results could be catastrophic – loss of the aircraft and the lives of those on board. Any bird is a potential hazard to aircraft and this is especially true as bird numbers and bird size increase.

Unfortunately airports themselves can be attractive to birds – rodents, insects and other small animals are a food source often found in flat grassed areas such as the runway strips. Even so, this problem can be reduced by careful habitat management or bird harassment techniques practised by airport maintenance and safety personnel.

Further problems may arise because the airport is located on bird migration routes. These may have existed prior to the airport site selection—but may not have been taken into account because the problem was not understood at the time—or have only been recently established because the birds have found an attractive new food source. Care needs to be taken by local authorities in deciding the location of rubbish tips, or when permitting other land uses that may be attractive to birds in this way. Of course these effects cannot always be anticipated with certainty since birds such as gulls have been recorded as travelling 50 kilometres or more from their roosting area to an attractive food source.

Agricultural uses may be thought desirable because they are compatible with high levels of noise exposure, but they can have an adverse effect on aircraft operations if birds are attracted during seeding or crop cultivation. Birds may also be attracted to pig farms where garbage is used as fodder. Even tree plantings can present a hazard if the species provides an attractive food source or nesting habitat.

Local authority planning schemes often apply strict controls on developments such as abattoirs, cattle feed lots, grain handling, piggeries, canals and marina developments, fish farms, and suchlike. In most cases these uses will not be permitted without a full environmental study. That study should be required to deal with the question of likely bird hazards if the proposed location is in proximity to an airport.

In some instances it may be necessary to consider ways of managing a particular land use in order to reduce its attractiveness to birds, for example the adoption of land fill measures at garbage tips, or enclosed rather than open air activity. Specialist ornithological opinion may be necessary. In such cases it may not be possible to implement immediate changes in land use, but this should not inhibit the adoption of long-term measures which are designed to achieve this.

Note the time you finished reading and the time elapsed.

Look back at the topic sentences in the passage above. How much can you learn from the passage just by using the topic sentences?

Read the passage again. Discuss the main ideas with your partner.

Vocabulary strategies

5 Read the passage **Theatre in the West End of London** below. Identify the words which you find difficult after the first reading. Try to guess their meanings.

Do not spend too much time worrying over one word. Try to get the general idea of the passage.

Does the context help?
Are they similar to words you already know?
What part of speech are they?

Note the time you started reading.

Theatre in the West End of London

London's West End has been the home of famous theatres from the time of William Shakespeare, arguably the father of English theatre. Shakespeare was involved with founding The Theatre in 1576, but is more famous for The Globe, which was built in 1597, and was the scene of many of his plays.

These early theatres were not designed to be comfortable, and patrons braved the fickle English weather in unroofed, circular theatres, the cheapest places going to the groundlings who watched from standing room in the pit of the theatre. The plays were superb entertainment, witnessed by their continued success today, and dealt with contemporary themes which are still relevant more than four hundred years after The Theatre was built.

The actors were all men, the women's parts being taken by boys. This tradition continued, and for many years acting was considered to be an unsuitable profession for a woman. One of the principal forces to change this was Mrs Sarah Siddons (1755–1831), who brought respectability to the stage. By Mrs Siddons' time the design of the theatre had been changed and the auditorium was horseshoe-shaped, the stage flanked by richly decorated tiered boxes.

Opulent design is still to be seen in some of the London theatres of today. Thick velvet curtains, ornate stonework and gilt decoration endure in some of the older theatres like The Drury Lane Theatre Royal, which opened in 1812, the fourth theatre of the name to occupy the same site. For sheer sumptuousness, however, it is hard to surpass the interior of the Theatre Royal in Haymarket, which is designed in the style of Louis XIV of France, with heavily carved embellishments and a great deal of gilt.

Note the time you finished reading and the time elapsed.

Checking your understanding

You will read more quickly and easily if you use the reading skills you have already practised, namely, scanning, using headings and skimming. Other reading skills you can use to check your understanding are summarizing the main points and paraphrasing.

A summary shows that the reader has understood the main points of a longer piece of text. When we paraphrase we express ideas in different words. This demonstrates an understanding of the details.

6 Read the article again on **Theatre in the West End of London.** Try to understand as much as you can as quickly as possible.

Talk to your partner. What are the important points in each paragraph? Be brief. You should look back at the article.

Example: 'London's West End has been the home of famous theatres from the time of William Shakespeare, arguably the father of English theatre. Shakespeare was involved with founding The Theatre in 1576, but is more famous for The Globe, which was built in 1597, and was the scene of many of his plays.'

Summary: 'There have been many famous theatres in the West End of London since the end of the 16th century.'

7 Read **Cultivating a Passion for Learning: The Voluntary Member's Story**.

What are the main, or most important points in each paragraph?

Note the time you started reading.

Cultivating a Passion for Learning: The Voluntary Member's Story

Adults Learning, Feb. 1998
Adults Learning Publications Department, Leicester, UK

Note: The WEA (Workers' Educational Association) referred to in the passage is the UK organization devoted to the education of adults. It is run by professional staff with the help of volunteers.

Just over a year ago I was a member of a Workers' Educational Association (WEA) working group, a mix of professional and voluntary workers, which was looking at training across the Association.

Active WEA voluntary members are a diverse group who emanate from all sections of the community. The majority of active voluntary members work only at branch level; others also work at district and national levels.

At present, WEA voluntary members are essential and invaluable at branch level, but their value at other levels often depends largely on their professional and other experience outside WEA. Many lack the confidence and skills to become involved at district and national levels. Many do not wish to do so. Sadly, many make tea when, with appropriate training, they could do much more in the WEA and outside.

The WEA has set about involving more people. Now all voluntary members who wish to deliver the programme in districts must complete a training programme of two days and a residential weekend. We are working on systems of recognition and possibly accreditation, and are developing support systems for the trained discussion leaders. The group which has completed the 'training the trainers' sessions has met again to discuss these matters. Some have already led district sessions after appropriate consultation with their district secretary who is an essential support if the initiative is to succeed. We also have several members with appropriate professional and voluntary experience to assist in any further training which might be needed.

We call the programme which has developed from the work, 'Cultivating a passion for learning' because an important part of active voluntary work in the WEA is enthusing students and bringing them into classes.

Note the time you finished reading and the time elapsed.

Discuss the important points you chose with your partner. Why did you say they were important?

One good way of recognizing and remembering the most important points is to write a title for each paragraph. Work with your partner to choose a title.

8 Read this first part of the article **The Bamboo Organ.** Try to understand as much as you can as quickly as possible.

Note the time you started reading.

The Bamboo Organ

A Famous Musical Instrument in the Philippines

Organs have existed in one form or another for over 2,000 years. Techniques for building them have varied, but common to all organs are the rows of pipes that are part of the sound-producing mechanism. These are generally made of wood and metal. The organ we wish to tell you about, however, has pipes primarily made of bamboo. A total of 832 of its 953 sound-producing pipes are bamboo. The others are metal. In addition, there are some pipes that are only decorative.

How does the bamboo organ work? The principle is the same as for other pipe organs. Two types of pipes are used, and wind is pumped into them to produce musical sounds. Flue pipes—with half-circle holes close to their points of connection with the console—produce sound in much the same manner as a flute. Reed pipes—with a vibrating element inside—produce sound in a manner similar to a clarinet or a saxophone. The fact that most pipes are made of bamboo gives this organ special acoustical characteristics.

Building the Organ

Construction of this bamboo organ was begun in 1816 by a Spanish missionary, Diego Cera. Why was bamboo used? Considering the relative poverty of the area, perhaps the need to use inexpensive materials was a factor. Moreover, the maker of the organ no doubt desired to use appropriate local materials.

In 1816, bamboos were cut and buried under the sand of the seashore for about a year. Those that survived this exposure to insects and the elements were considered of durable quality and used in building the organ. Over the next several years, the various parts of the organ were put together. When the bulk of it was finished in 1821, it was proclaimed 'the finest and the first of its kind in the country'.

Note the time you finished reading and the time elapsed.

Identify the important points in the article. Talk to your partner. You might consider these questions:

Paragraph 1: What was the organ made of?
Paragraph 2: How does it work?
Paragraph 3: Why was bamboo used?
Paragraph 4: How was the bamboo tested for durability?

Be brief. You should look back at the article.

Work with your partner and write <u>brief</u> notes in your own words about the detail of what you have read.

9 Read the next section of **The Bamboo Organ.** Look for the important points in each section. Make notes on a sheet of paper.

The Bamboo Organ (2)

Note the time you started reading.

Surviving Adversity

Life for the bamboo organ has not been easy. The year 1829 saw earthquakes in the town of Las Piñas where the organ is located. The roof of the building that housed it was destroyed, and likely the organ was exposed to the elements for a while. In 1863 an exceptionally strong earthquake caused more damage to the organ. Some pipes were replaced, but insects ravaged these over a period of time. In 1880 another catastrophic earthquake badly damaged the building housing the organ, and a typhoon struck before the building was completely repaired. By then various pieces of the organ were scattered about.

Some repairs were attempted over the years, but one such attempt resulted in permanent damage. A repairman sawed off portions of the bamboo pipes in order to apply some tuning valves. This permanently changed the instrument's pitch. And, despite the repair efforts, the organ continued to deteriorate.

The organ also endured war. Las Piñas was a scene of skirmishes between Filipinos and Spaniards during the late 1890's, and between Filipinos and Americans during the Philippine–American War. Nevertheless, despite its deterioration, records from 1911 to 1913 indicate that visitors came to see the organ.

The years 1941 to 1945 brought the second world war to the Philippines. During the Japanese occupation, the organ received attention from the Marquess Y. Tokugawa, a relative of Emperor Hirohito. He arranged for partial repairs, but after that very little was done to the instrument for many years.

Then, in the 1970's, a clamor arose for its restoration. Of the hundreds of bamboo pipes, 45 were missing, and 304 were not working. A bird's nest was found inside one. Could anything be done to get the organ back to performance standard?

Restoration

The restoration project was started in March 1973, a reputable foreign firm being entrusted with the work. The pipes were shipped to Japan, and the rest of the organ was shipped to Germany. There, a special room was built to simulate the climate of the Philippines. In this room the restoration work proceeded.

The goal was to keep things as close as possible to the original design. Finally, the repairs were finished. Pipes repaired in Japan were flown to Germany. The complete organ was reassembled and tested. Then, on February 18, 1975, it delighted the ears of a German audience in a one-hour concert.

Soon afterward the organ was packed into a dozen crates, and all 12,400 pounds of it was shipped back to the Philippines through the courtesy of a Belgian airline. It received a grand welcome in Las Piñas, the town where it would be housed. Thirty thousand watched a parade complete with floats depicting episodes from the history of the instrument.

By May 9, 1975, the bamboo organ was ready for its inaugural concert. A German organist was featured along with Filipino musicians as the bamboo organ was reintroduced to the Philippines.

If you ever have the opportunity to hear the bamboo organ in Las Piñas, you will no doubt enjoy this special Philippine musical instrument.

Note the time you finished reading and the time elapsed.

Discuss the points you chose with your partner. Why did you say they were important?

Understanding relationships of meaning

A passage of English which can be regarded as a unit is referred to as text. We recognize a text because it has a central theme which unites it.

People read more effectively if they understand how a piece of writing holds together. This cohesion can be achieved by relationships of meaning, linking words and topic sentences.

10 Read the following passages and identify the ways new ideas and information are added. Look for examples where:

  A. supporting evidence is given for an idea which is already introduced
  B. information is added by reference to time or place
  C. a general rule is given, followed by particular examples
  D. the writer compares or contrasts information.

Identify the way in which new information is added in passages 1–6 according to **A–D**. Some passages have information added in more than one way.

1. Dog lovers may well be confused by the many varieties of dogs which one might see at any dog show, but they can be sure of finding an animal which will suit their needs. From the extremely small chihuahua, which is about the size of a rat, to the enormous Great Dane, which is like a small pony, there is bound to be a dog the right size. If the owner would like to run marathons, the long-legged Afghan hound would be a suitable companion, while the slower walkers may prefer a beagle or a dachshund. Some dogs are extremely noisy and aggressive and make excellent guard dogs, while others are so friendly they may help the robbers remove the family silver.

2. In the lead-up to World War II Hitler's troops invaded the Sudetenland, then Poland, but the war did not begin until they invaded Belgium. The reasons for the slow response by the allies were complex, but included the war weariness of Europe, where the scars of the 1914–18 conflict were still well remembered. People did not want to fight again: indeed they did not want to believe that they would ever need to fight, and the general feeling was to deny what was before them.

3. The constable was a good witness who read the information directly from his notebook. At 11 am he saw the suspect enter the museum through the front door. He was empty-handed, and apparently not challenged by the guards on duty. At 11.15 the suspect left, carrying a small brown leather bag. At 11.20 the constable arrested the suspect.

4. Where once it was necessary to travel to school, or university, there are now many ways to study from the comfort of one's home. In some ways this is a very good thing: people can get information quickly and easily over the Internet, and the reading lists provided ensure that they will read what is required to achieve a basic understanding of the topic they are studying. Avoiding the library is not necessarily a good thing, however, for the opportunity to browse through a section of the subject you are studying may well reveal aspects of the topic which have been omitted from your reading list.

    Home students can study where and when they will, but this is another mixed blessing: studying at home usually means studying alone, and the dialogue which helps many people learn is missing. As the home student often does a full day's work before opening their books, they may be tired and less likely to concentrate on their studies. The biggest problem for the student who is studying at long distance may well be the self-discipline required to start work, alone and unaided, on a regular basis.

5. A business plan should be written with the customer clearly in mind. If this is not done, the whole point of the exercise is lost. Imagine a teacher who gave a lesson in mathematics to the geology class: this is a fair analogy with the sort of results achieved by not identifying the customer who will buy or use the product.

6. Fires can be minimized in the home if people follow some simple rules.
   • Never let children play with matches.
   • Always keep a fire extinguisher near the kitchen.
   • Never throw water onto an oil fire.
   • Keep the area around the home free of dry litter.
   • Keep the gutters of the roof free of litter.

Linking words

Some words and phrases are used to link ideas. These linking words may be used in many different positions. Look at these examples:

Within sentences
Young children enjoy playing active games <u>such as</u> chasing, hide and seek, and tag.

Between paragraphs
When they get a little older, boys and girls seem to enjoy different games. The boys continue to enjoy rough games, while the girls play more quietly. That is what we used to believe.

This judgement, <u>however</u>, may not be really true. Nowadays there seem to be many noisy little girls. They are just as boisterous as their brothers, and this seems to continue until they enter high school.

Between clauses
Some of the high school girls will become more dignified, <u>although</u> the boys are slower to mature and to settle into the ways of older children.

Indeed, children in the lower classes of high school are very active, regardless of gender. Their games are noisy, <u>and</u> are usually well organized. Both boys and girls enjoy team games.

Between words
So, be they girls <u>or</u> boys, we can expect noise and activity from children.

Between sentences
This is exactly as it should be. Can anyone imagine a silent school playground? <u>Or</u> a quiet football game?

No linking words
So we can conclude
• boys are no noisier than girls
• children enjoy active games.

The last example uses punctuation to hold the ideas together.
It is similar to the earlier example about preventing fires.

11 Read the paragraphs below and take note of the underlined words used to link the ideas.

People sometimes debate <u>whether</u> it is better to live in a hot climate or a cold climate. Those who prefer a hot climate will point out that warm weather leads to a more relaxed lifestyle, <u>while</u> those who like colder weather will say that the cold is bracing, and helps people to be active and productive. They will argue, <u>moreover</u>, that people have learned to be very ingenious because of the cold.

This will not please the heat lovers, who may counter that a warm climate is <u>not only</u> pleasant <u>but</u> is far kinder to the poor. Warmth means people can survive more easily <u>because</u> they do not need to worry about keeping warm. This may <u>indeed</u> be true, the cool climate people will respond, <u>but</u> many diseases, <u>such as</u> malaria, flourish in warm climates.

The argument will probably never end, <u>because</u> different people like to live in different climates.

What do the underlined words in the passage tell you to expect? Arrange them in the table below. Some columns may be left empty, and some may contain more than one word. Some words may appear in more than one column.

adding an idea	giving an alternative idea	explaining	giving an example	ending, summarizing	giving a result	repeating for emphasis
			such as			

Scanning and using headings

When you scan you are looking for a particular piece of information.

12 Look at the Local Bus Guide for the Lewisham, Greenwich, Catford and New Cross areas of London, UK.

The bold numbers refer to the bus services which will get you to a particular place. For instance, if you want to go to the Brockley Police Station you may catch the 122, 171, 172, L1 or N86.

LOCAL BUS GUIDE

CITIZENS' ADVICE BUREAUX
Catford *120 Rushey Green* **36, 36B, 47, 54, 75, 124, 124S, 138, 160, 160S, 172, 180, 181, 185, 202, 208, 284**
Eltham *Eltham Library, High Street* **21, 124, 124S, 126, 160, 160S, 286, 386, 396**
New Cross *2 Lewisham Way* **21, 36, 36B, 53, 53X, 171, 172, 177, 184, 225**
Sydenham *299 Kirkdale* **122, 176, 202, 312**

LIBRARIES
Blackheath *Old Dover Road* **386 or short walk from 53, 53X, 54, 89, 108, 178, 286**
Blackheath Village *3-4 Blackheath Grove* **54, 89, 108, 202**
Catford *Laurence House, Catford Road* **36, 36B, 47, 54, 75, 124, 124S, 138, 160, 160S, 172, 180, 181, 185, 202, 208, 284**
Crofton Park *Brockley Road* **122, 171, 172, P4**
Downham *Moorside Road* **36, 36B, 124, 124S, 172, 284 or short walk from 138**
Forest Hill *Dartmouth Road* **122, 176, 312**
Greenwich *203-207 Woolwich Road* **108, 177, 180, 286, 386**
Grove Park *Somertrees Avenue* **short walk from 286**
Kidbrooke *Brook Lane* **178 or short walk from 286**
Lewisham and Central Reference *366 Lewisham High Street* **36, 36B, 47, 54, 75, 160S, 180, 185, 208**
Manor House *Old Road* **21, 122, 178, 261**
New Cross *116/118 New Cross Road* **21, 36, 36B, 53, 171, 172, 177, 184**
St Catherine's *Kitto Road, Nunhead* **P12**
Stanstead Road *300 Stanstead Road, Catford* **172, 185**
Sydenham *Sydenham Road* **194, 202**
Torridon Road *Hither Green* **124, 124S, 180, 181, 284**
Wavelengths *Giffin Street* **47, 53, 75, 177, 188, 199**
West Greenwich *Greenwich High Road* **177, 180**

POLICE STATIONS
Brockley *4 Howson Road* **122, 171, 172, L1, N86**
Catford *333 Bromley Road* **36, 36B, 54, 172, 181, 208, N47, N70, N85**
Deptford *116 Amersham Vale* **short walk from 47, 75, 188, 199, 225, N47, N70**
Greenwich *31 Royal Hill* **177, 180, 199, N77**
Lee Road *418 Lee High Road* **21, 122, 178, 202, 261, N62, N72, N82**
Lewisham *2 Ladywell Road* **36, 36B, 47, 54, 75, 122, 160S, 180, 181, 185, 208, 284, L1, P4, N47, N70, N85**
Penge *175 High Street* **75, 176, 194, 227, 312, N3, N86**
Shooters Hill *Shooters Hill* **89, 122, 178, N72, N82**
Sydenham *179 Dartmouth Road* **122, 176, 312, N86**
Westcombe Park *11 Combedale Road* **108, 177, 180, 286, N77**

MAIN POST OFFICES
Bellingham *12 Randlesdown Road* **36, 36B, 54, 138, 172, 181, 208**
Blackheath Village *Blackheath Grove* **54, 89, 108, 202**
Catford *187/189 Rushey Green* **36, 36B, 47, 54, 75, 124, 124S, 138, 160, 160S, 180, 172, 181, 185, 202, 208, 284**
Downham *488 Bromley Road* **36, 36B, 172, 208**
Downham Way *457 Downham Way* **36, 36B, 124, 124S, 172, 284**
Forest Hill *24 Dartmouth Road* **78, 115, 122, 176, 185, 312**
Greenwich *261/267 Greenwich High Road* **177, 180, 199**
Lee Green *151/157 Lee Road* **21, 122, 178, 202, 261**
Lewisham *107 High Street* **21, 36, 36B, 47, 54, 75, 89, 108, 122, 160S, 178, 180, 181, 184, 185, 199, 208, 225, 261, 284, 380, L1, P4**
New Cross *480 New Cross Road* **47, 53, 53X, 75, 177**
New Cross Gate *199/205 New Cross Road* **21, 36, 36B, 53, 171, 172, 177, P3**
Sydenham *44 Sydenham Road* **75, 194, 202**

---

1. What are the four headings?

2. As quickly as possible, write the bus services you will take to go to:

   a) Blackheath Village Library
   b) St Catherine's Library
   c) Sydenham Post Office
   d) Sydenham Citizens' Advice Bureau
   e) Greenwich Police Station
   f) Lee Green Post Office

   How was this information organized? Did this make it quicker for you?

3. As quickly as possible, write the street address of:

   a) Catford Citizens' Advice Bureau
   b) Manor House Library
   c) Penge Police Station
   d) Downham Post Office

4. Work in pairs and ask each other questions such as: 'Which bus can you take to Kidbrooke Library?' Try to ask (and answer) quickly.

More scanning exercises

13 How much will it cost to clean these items in the laundry or dry cleaning?

Item	Laundry	Dry cleaning		Laundry	Dry Cleaning
1 x Sport shirt	_____	_____	1 x Swimsuit	_____	_____
1 x Slip	_____	_____	1 x Tie	_____	_____
1 x Vest	_____	_____	1 x Blouse	_____	_____

LAUNDRY

Shirt Starch: _____ None _____ Light _____ Medium _____ Heavy _____

Guest Count	Laundry Count		Charge	Amount
		Handkerchiefs	1.50	
		Shirt	4.50	
		Sport Shirt	4.00	
		Shorts	5.75	
		Sweatshirt	4.50	
		Sweatpants	4.50	
		Trousers/Slacks	7.00	
		Socks	2.00	
		Undershorts	2.50	
		Undershirts	2.50	
		T-shirts	3.50	
		Swimsuits	3.50	
		Brassieres	2.50	
		Panties	2.50	
		Pantyhose	2.50	
		Slips	2.50	
		Pajamas	5.00	
		Nightgowns	4.50	
		Robes	5.50	
		Blouse	6.75	
		Children's pieces	3.00	

DRY CLEANING

Guest Count	Laundry Count		Clean/Press	Amount
		Shirt	7.00	
		Sport Shirt	6.75	
		Suit (2pc)	12.00	
		Jacket/Sports coat	7.00	
		Sweater	7.00	
		Tie	3.75	
		Trousers/Slacks	7.00	
		Vest	3.50	
		Tux/Tails	15.00	
		Overcoat	12.50	
		Blouse	7.00	
		Dress	12.00	
		Dress - Formal	15.00	
		Jumpsuit	12.00	
		Skirt	7.00	

Laundry and Valet services are available daily. Garments received by 10:00 am will be returned the same day by 6:30 pm. Care labels will be followed. Please call extension 5226 for more details regarding leather, suede or fancy items. Damaged or lost article claims are limited to ten times the cleaning charge.

FULLERS

Four Star Sophisticated Dining
featuring regionally inspired cuisine.
Serves Lunch & Dinner.

PIKE ST CAFE

Casual Dining
featuring northwest specialties.
Serves Breakfast, Lunch & Dinner.

SCHOONERS

Sports Pub
Large Screen TV, Pool Table & Dancing.

Telephone Numbers

Emergency	3333
Hotel	(206) 621-9000
Hotel Fax	(206) 621-8441
Front Desk	5235
Luggage Service	5208
Parking	5236
Lobby Concierge	5207
Club/Towers Desk	5569
Wake-up Service	0

ANDIAMO PRESTO

Italian - Mediterranean Bistro & Deli
specializing in pizza, salads, pasta & panini sandwiches.
Serves Breakfast, Lunch & Dinner.

Fresh Oysters shucked to order.
Cocktails, Hors d'oeuvres, Live Entertainment.

Room Service is available 24 hours a day - See our in-room menu.

Room
916

Check-out time is 12 noon

1. Where do you go to if you want to:

   eat oysters?
   watch TV?
   eat Italian food?

2. What time is check-out?

3. What number do you call in an emergency?

Skimming for general information 2

When you are skimming you are reading for general information. You need only understand the gist, or main idea, of the passage. It is very useful to skim a passage to find out what it's about.

 Read the passage below as quickly as you can and complete the exercises that follow.

Note the time you started reading.

General Information about New Zealand

Airport transfers
New Zealand has three major international airports: Auckland, Wellington and Christchurch; and four secondary international airports receiving services from Australia (Queenstown winter only). Shuttle buses and taxis meet all flights. City transfer details from each of these airports follow:

- Auckland (21 km): taxis NZ$35, shuttle NZ$15 single and NZ$5 each additional person, bus fare NZ$10 per person;
- Wellington (8 km): taxi NZ$15, shuttle NZ$8, bus fare NZ$4;
- Christchurch (11km): taxi NZ$18, shuttle NZ$10, bus fare NZ$3;
- Hamilton (15 km): taxi NZ$20, shuttle NZ$8;
- Palmerston North (6 km): taxi NZ$12, shuttle NZ$6;
- Dunedin (30 km): taxi NZ$35, shuttle NZ$10;
- Queenstown (7 km): taxi NZ$12, shuttle NZ$5.

Climate
New Zealand enjoys a range of temperatures approximate to those experienced by Australia's eastern seaboard. Free from the influence of any close land mass, yearly temperature variations are small – approximately 10ºC variation between winter and summer.

The north of the country tends to be sub-tropical and the south, temperate. Mountain ranges extend down much of the length of New Zealand, with the regions lying west of the ranges experiencing much higher rainfalls than those to the east. The drier eastern regions average over 2000 hours of sunshine a year and contain the main wine-growing areas and summer resorts.

Snow is largely confined to the alpine areas of the central North Island and the Southern Alps, though it can fall to low levels in the deep south for a day or so at a time.

Banking/currency
No restrictions apply on the amount of foreign currency that can be taken in or out of New Zealand. All major credit cards may be used for the purchase of goods and services, and travellers' cheques are accepted at hotels, banks and some stores.

Banks are open from 9.30 am to 4.30 pm, Monday to Friday, except public holidays.

Provided they are encoded with a PIN number, international credit cards may be used to withdraw cash from automatic teller machines (ATMs), widely available in the main shopping centres and suburban malls. Check with your bank before leaving home to determine whether this facility is available to you.

Note the time you finished reading and the time elapsed.

1. What country is the passage about?

2. How can you get from the airports to the towns?

3. Which phrase below describes the climate?

> hot and dry   wet and very windy   very cold
> different in different parts

4. In this passage, what was the author doing?
   (There may be more than one answer.)

> informing   describing   discussing a problem
> suggesting a solution reporting   trying to persuade

> You should not worry about detail at the first reading.
> You will be able to find details much more quickly at the
> second reading.
>
> Make a habit of skimming anything you read. Think about
> the subject and the author's intentions.

More scanning exercises

16 Scan the passage **General Information About New Zealand** and
answer these questions as you read.

1. How far is Hamilton from the nearest airport?

2. Where does the sun shine 2000 hours per year?

3. When are the banks open?

   What advice would you give to a student who is trying to read
   quickly and accurately?

Question types in the Reading test

The IELTS test has different question types to test different facets of understanding. The purpose of the next sections is to familiarize the student with the types of question they may be asked, and to suggest ways to approach them.

All these questions have one thing in common: they are designed to see if the passage has been understood.

English is an international language, so passages of writing have been chosen from some of the places where English is used. The passages have been changed as little as possible to expose students to the varied vocabulary and structures of English in daily use. There may be a great deal of new vocabulary which should help the student with future reading.

It is very important that students discuss their answers to these questions.

There are examples of the different question types in both modules, Academic Reading and General Training Reading.

- Read the questions carefully.
- Think about anything you know about the topic.
- Consider the purpose of the text while you read.
- Approach the questions in any way you like: skim, scan, paraphrase.
- Read the passage before the questions or the questions before the passage, whichever you find easier.
- Don't worry about unknown vocabulary: look at the context.
- Be careful to answer using the information that is in the passage.

Use whichever method of understanding a passage is most comfortable for you.
You cannot read too much! Please read everything you can; the newspaper, magazines, anything.

Before you read, ask yourself:
what do I know about this topic?

While you read, ask yourself:
what does this mean?
what is the author trying to tell me?

After you have read, ask yourself:
what were the main points?
could I explain what I have read to someone else?

Question types in the Academic Reading module

Multiple choice questions

Multiple choice questions have one correct answer and two or three incorrect answers called 'distractors'. As their name implies, distractors are intended to mislead the reader, and may seem partly but are not completely correct.

 Read the passage below and answer the multiple choice questions which follow.

Note the time you started reading.

The Efficient Reader

Experts on reading skills will disagree on the best ways for a student to improve their reading speed. The problem seems to be that the purpose for reading varies from situation to situation, and any advice for students needs to take into account their particular context.

As well as the impact of the purpose for reading, a reader may encounter certain linguistic features in a text that provide valuable shortcuts in absorbing the text's information. With newspapers, for example, an experienced reader will focus on pictures, headlines, and boxes which contain reports. This technique is termed 'skimming' and is used by a reader who already knows what they want to read, and has predicted the text's contents.

Texts may be classified by type or genre, and some may be more familiar than others. Text types include:
- letters and postcards
- magazine advertisements
- newspaper reports
- newspaper 'human interest' stories
- comics
- official reports, procedures, rules
- poems and novels
- puzzles and rules for games
- timetables
- exam directions
- visual information such as graphs, maps and diagrams
- form guides for sporting events.

Most experts agree that an efficient reader will find the information he or she needs, and ignore irrelevant information. This assumes that the reader already knows what is relevant and what is not. This knowledge depends very much on the reader's age, level of maturity, familiarity with his/her culture, and prior reading experience.

The type of text will also require more or less attention to details. Newspaper articles often put the topic or 'gist' of the story at the beginning, while the remainder of the report fills in the details. On the other hand, poems require that every phrase or word is considered for its connotative meaning. Academic texts often require the reader to follow a detailed analysis or argument.

Methods of reading include:
- skimming to get the gist

- scanning to find particular pieces of information such as names, dates, statistics
- extensive reading to gain an overall understanding of the text's purpose, or for pleasure
- intensive reading for short units of text, where accurate knowledge is required, or where the ideas are complicated.

No one can say conclusively whether faster readers are better than slower readers. Research suggests that good readers read slowly and retain in their memory a great deal of the text's meaning. Again the answer lies in the social pressures acting upon the reader. In other words, the speed of reading depends on the task requirements. Clearly reading a Sunday newspaper is a leisurely activity, while reading a number of journal articles to prepare for an essay due in a few days is not. The amount of reading demanded by university courses is very high, and many students think they must read everything on a reading list. However, they should select the relevant material based on the requirements of an assignment.

What then are the skills needed for effective reading in an academic context?

Readers should identify firstly the purpose of a text and use that knowledge to anticipate its contents. For example, most people can predict that a letter from a close friend will contain personal information. An academic research report, however, will probably contain a description of research methods, results and conclusions. There are several reading skills needed to deal successfully with such texts. For academic texts, a student under time pressure should look for and distinguish main ideas from supporting details. He/she should also be able to see connections between ideas, on a sentence and a paragraph level. The learner should also apply his/her own knowledge to interpret the text. For visual information like graphs, the reader should interpret the symbols used to encode the information; in other words, the reader should 'translate' visual symbols into words and sentences.

The best advice is: practise with texts you are most likely to encounter at university.

Note the time you finished reading and the time elapsed.

Circle the letter of the correct answer.

1. The passage's main purpose is to:
    A   give advice on reading quickly
    B   present research ideas on what makes a good teacher
    C   prove that reading carefully depends on text type and purpose
    D   show that text types determine reading methods.

2. The passage points out that:
    A   rapid reading is essential for successful tertiary study
    B   students who read more slowly are more successful at tertiary study
    C   reading speed is determined by the purpose for which one reads
    D   students who read intensively are more successful.

3. The efficient reader:
    A   knows a wide range of text types
    B   reads quickly
    C   reads slowly
    D   finds relevant information.

This activity may be photocopied

4. The efficient reader:
   (A) relates his/her own knowledge to the text
   B reads intensively a wide range of texts
   C reads newspapers as well as academic journals
   D reads slowly.

5. The efficient reader:
   (A) uses the way a text is constructed to assist comprehension
   B can understand a text from headings and sub-headings
   C takes notes using all the headings and sub-headings
   D checks all unknown vocabulary in a dictionary.

6. The most conclusive advice for improving reading is:
   A practise reading a wide range of texts
   (B) decide what you need to read and practise
   C decide what material on a reading list is relevant
   D read intensively as well as extensively.

Short-answer questions

18 Answer the questions that follow the passage below.

Note the time you started reading.

In April 1973 a Boeing 747 aircraft suffered a multiple birdstrike during take-off from the main runway at Sydney Airport. Subsequent examination showed 16 separate birdstrikes on the wings and underparts of the aircraft and in all four engines. The bird species involved was the Silver Gull.

Number 3 engine had to be shut down because of extreme vibration. This was caused by the failure of a fan blade which pierced the engine housing, struck the runway and rebounded causing further external skin damage to the aircraft. Number 4 engine suffered initial loss of power and overheating but subsequently recovered.

An eyewitness who observed the incident from the public viewing area of the International Terminal described the subsequent climb as 'agonisingly slow' and from that vantage point the aircraft appeared to fly out to sea between the heads of Botany Bay. It was a very hot day in Sydney and the aircraft—destination London—had departed at or near to maximum weight.

The aircraft dumped 62,000 kilograms of fuel at sea and returned to land on three engines without further incident. Two engines were so badly damaged they had to be replaced.

The incident illustrates what can happen even if large aircraft suffer birdstrikes and relatively few birds are involved.

Note the time you finished reading and the time elapsed.

Answer the questions using **NO MORE THAN THREE WORDS.**

1. What words give a name to the incident? _Multiple birdstrike_

2. Where did the incident occur? _Sydney Airport_

3. What caused the vibration which forced Number 3 engine to be closed down? *failed fan blade*

4. What did the pilot do before he returned to land? *dumped fuel*

Sometimes these questions say 'USING NO MORE THAN THREE WORDS taken from the passage'. The instruction for this passage said: 'Answer the questions using NO MORE THAN THREE WORDS'.

What is the difference between these two instructions?

Was it easy to use one to three words? Did it force you to read carefully to understand?

Sentence completion

Answer the questions that follow the passage **Medicare Benefits Weathy Most**.

Note the time you started reading.

Medicare Benefits Wealthy Most

National Bureau of Economic Research Digest (USA) Sept. 1997

> *'Wealthy enrollees pay more into Medicare than poorer people do (in the form of general federal tax revenues and payroll taxes). However, they reap greater benefits over their lifetimes because they live longer and use more medical services.'*

Note: In the United States people pay part of their income into a medical benefits fund called Medicare. They can access Medicare when they are 65 years old.

Hear the phrase 'Medicare beneficiary' and you might picture someone counting pennies in a modest house or apartment. Think again. According to a study recently published by the National Bureau of Economic Research, those who benefit the most from Medicare are the wealthiest older Americans, not the poorest ones.

In **The Incidence of Medicare** (NBER Working Paper No. 6013), Jonathon Skinner and Mark McClellan find that while all current Medicare enrollees are getting much more out of Medicare in benefits than what they paid into the program in taxes, the windfall is greatest for the wealthy. Wealthy enrollees pay more into Medicare than poorer people do (in the form of general federal tax revenues and payroll taxes). However, they reap greater benefits over their lifetimes because they live longer and use more medical services, the paper finds.

Skinner and McClellan begin by calculating how much Medicare spends, over a lifetime, for each of a random sample of approximately 1.4 million elderly Medicare beneficiaries, for both Part A (hospital) and Part B (outpatient and physician) benefits. Using zip-code level income data from the 1990 U.S. Census, they sort the beneficiaries into ten income brackets to figure how income level correlates with length of life and lifetime Medicare expenditures. They use a different data source (The Panel Study of Income Dynamics at the University of Michigan) to track accumulated Medicare tax payments since 1966 (the birth of the program), again for each of these ten income brackets.

Not surprisingly, they find that all those currently on Medicare are expected to receive over their lifetimes much more from the system than they paid into it.

> **Remember to scan for suitable words if you have to use words from the passage.**

What is surprising is that these net gains are greatest for the upper income brackets. For example, the second-highest income decile has a lifetime net gain of $18,900, while the third-lowest decile has a lifetime net gain of $15,500. In other words, the Medicare program effectively transfers money from low to high income groups.

One proposal for Medicare reform is to provide vouchers to each Medicare enrollee; the vouchers could then be used to purchase a minimal level of health insurance. Those willing to pay more could buy supplemental insurance coverage out-of-pocket. McClellan and Skinner estimate that such a plan would still result in high income elderly consuming more health care, but (unlike under the current Medicare system) these high income people would bear more of the extra cost.

Note the time you finished reading and the time elapsed.

Complete the sentences below with words taken from the passage. Use **NO MORE THAN THREE WORDS** for each answer.

1. An old person, whether rich or poor, can be a _medicare beneficiary_

2. Medicare pays most to people in _upper income brackets_

3. Under the voucher system rich people would pay more for _supplemental insurance coverage_

Look again at the question. Note the words used: 'Complete the sentences below with words <u>taken from the passage</u>'.

One approach to these questions might be to skim and scan the passage quickly to recognize which paragraphs contain answers to the questions.

4. Which paragraphs do NOT contain answers to the questions?   *2/3*

To paraphrase is to re-word a passage so it is easier to understand.

Work with a partner or small group. Paraphrase the paragraphs which did NOT contain the answers to Questions 1, 2 and 3 above. You may do this orally.

Notes/summary/diagram/flow chart/table completion

This type of question tests your ability to understand the overall meaning of a passage, and to extract particular information from it.

20 Answer the questions that follow the passage **Japanese Schools, Foreign Students.**

Note the time you started reading.

Japanese Schools, Foreign Students

Many foreign families living in Japan consider sending their children to Japanese schools. Those who do are often richly rewarded.

The families who send their children to Japanese public schools are likely to be long-time residents who have already made a commitment to living in Japan. Sojourners, people who plan to move on after a limited stay in the country, are far less likely to use the Japanese public schools, and tend to send their children to the international schools which teach in English and often advertise that aspects of their curriculum will prepare students to move on to other international schools. Bi-cultural families will often choose the Japanese system, once again demonstrating an expectation that Japan will be their home for many years.

The problems perceived by the sojourners are real: the first, the language barrier, will be a serious impediment. People who expect to move on are unlikely to make the serious effort of learning another language and writing system, but without language the parent of a school child is handicapped every time a note is sent home or a school function occurs. However, if the stay in Japan is likely to be short, or its duration dictated from outside the family, it might well be foolish to settle a student into the Japanese system.

There are, however, great advantages for those foreigners who do choose to school their children in local schools. The Japanese system offers six years of elementary school from the age of six, three years of junior high school and then three years of senior high school followed by four years of university. The whole system is free to Japanese people and to those foreigners who hold an alien registration card. Most Japanese children attend nursery school or kindergarten before entering elementary school, although nursery school is only available to families where both parents are working. The best surprise for most foreigners is the discovery that the Japanese system is far less rigid and pressurized than they had imagined. One mother felt it was more creative and 'hands on' than her own early education in the United States had been.

For those who feel that schools are as much about socialization as they are about skills, Japanese education is an obvious stepping stone for their children's acceptance of and into the Japanese community. If the children are already playing with Japanese children and progress into kindergarten with them the idea of continuing in the system seems sensible. After all, these foreign children will not lose their own language, which will very probably be spoken at home.

Another positive aspect is the quality of both the teaching and the facilities. There are set text books which specify wide-ranging topics, and the Ministry of Education insists that all schools must have dedicated classrooms specially equipped for science, music, art and cookery. There must also be a gymnasium and a swimming pool. These rules apply to all schools from elementary level upward.

There are disadvantages: the classes are large, maximum size 40 pupils in elementary school and 45 in junior high. Language can be a barrier, although some schools provide extra Japanese classes for foreign students, and Minato-ku, the foreign embassy area, offers not only lessons but, if necessary, a personal interpreter during lessons.

Foreign families have been generally pleased with elementary education in Japan, but less pleased with the higher levels of the system. Some of their discontent can be traced to the juku, or private cram schools which force-feed students to help them gain access to a more desirable senior high school. The sheer amount of time consumed in attending school and juku means the students' lives are far more focused than their western counterparts.

Note the time you finished reading and the time elapsed.

Complete the summary on the next page. Choose your answers from the box below the summary.

NB There are more words or phrases than you will need to fill the gaps. You may use any word or phrase more than once.

Foreign families living in Japan have to decide whether to send their children to ____(1)____ schools or to make other arrangements. Those who choose to use Japanese schools are demonstrating a ____(2)____ to the Japanese way of life.

Many foreign families are concerned about their ____(3)____ to use the language and the possibility that they will only stay in Japan for a ____(4)____ time. Those who do use the Japanese system are pleased by the free education, standard of ____(5)____, the facilities, and the ____(6)____ of the elementary schools. They also see advantages for their children in becoming part of Japanese ____(7)____

There are some problems, largely to do with class ____(8)____ and language. Although ____(9)____ happy with Japanese elementary education, the foreign parents are less pleased with the Japanese education system as it applies to ____(10)____ school students.

generally	size	younger	connection	rigidity
inability	creativity	limited	teaching	university
society	sometimes	secondary	boarding	
elementary	commitment	Japanese	older	

One approach might be to read the passage quickly to get an overall idea of meaning. (Don't worry about unknown words.) Read the question, and consider the purpose of the text. Read the passage again and answer the question.

What help does the instruction 'Choose your answers from the box below the summary' give you?

The test is checking for overall comprehension, so you cannot simply scan the passage for words to go in the gaps. You must understand what you have read. How can this be achieved?

Think about the writer's purpose. What was the writer trying to do?

describe	discuss	evaluate	explain
offer solutions	make arguments		

Practise your vocabulary skills. Identify the words which you find difficult.

Try to guess their meanings:
     Are they similar to words you already know?
     Does the context help?

Choosing from a 'heading bank' for identified paragraphs/sections of the text

To answer a question using a list of headings, or heading bank, the student must:

- understand the detail and gist of the article
- understand how the article progresses.

How can this be achieved quickly? Choose whichever approach below suits you best:

- read the article and then the headings. Some of the headings will fit to the paragraphs or sections quite quickly. Make a note of these headings and pencil them in. Then, read the passage. As you read the passage, think about what each section means, and match it to a heading.

or

- read the headings first and then read the article with the headings in mind.

21 The reading passage **Top Marks for Singapore Schools** has 8 sections **A-H**. Choose the most suitable headings for sections **A-H** from the list of headings that follow the passage. Write the appropriate numbers **(i-xi)**.

NB There are more headings than paragraphs so you will not use all of them.
You may use any of the headings more than once.

Note the time you started reading.

Top Marks for Singapore Schools

by Andy Green, Reader in the Institute of Education, London
Published in Times Educational Supplement Reprinted in The Singapore Bulletin, Volume 25 August 1997
© Times Supplements Limited 1997

A. Education in Singapore is booming, and the world is taking notice. In the Third International Maths and Science Study, Singaporean 13-year-olds scored highest in both subjects out of 41 countries. In the equivalent 1988 science study, they came 14th: now they have topped Japan and South Korea, both traditional high achievers, and left England trailing (10th in science and 25th in maths). Some doubt the validity of comparisons based on international standardised testing, but this is not the only evidence of high average standards in Singapore. Research for last year's Government Skills Audit revealed that Singapore had caught up with Britain in the proportion of adults qualified to the equivalent of our level three or higher (two A-levels or equivalent vocational qualifications) and overtaken us in the output of level three qualifications among its young people.

B. This is a remarkable feat for a country where 35 years ago most people had only primary schooling. The Singapore Government is not yet satisfied—it wants to stimulate creative thinking and creativity—but international observers are clearly well impressed already. Last year, the World Competitiveness Yearbook, one of whose criteria is levels of education and training, placed Singapore second to the United States in overall competitiveness, and numerous articles in international journals have been extolling the achievements of Singapore in education and economic performance. So what are we going to learn from all this?

C. Policy-makers in Britain will no doubt be casting around frantically for the magic ingredient in Singapore which produces such results. As is their wont, they will often select the evidence out of context to support their own priorities. Supporters of whole-class teaching will probably put the whole thing down to the use of this method in Singaporean schools. Advocates of selection will point out that Singapore uses streaming—ignoring the fact that this is largely within comprehensive schools and is a response to multilingualism.

Others, wishing to dismiss the comparison as irrelevant to Britain, will ascribe Singaporean achievement to something called 'Asian values', as if these were uniform and unchanging, and ignoring the fact that educational development has varied markedly in Asia. They will have learned nothing about how education works in Singapore and even less about what the lessons might be for Britain.

D. International studies show that there is no single factor associated with educational success at the national level. None of the traditional indicators— class size, educational expenditure, selection and grouping policies, teaching styles or time spent on learning particular subjects—correlates systematically with outcomes over a range of countries. Rather, the outcomes of the educational process in different countries are the result of a host of factors, some relating to the internal features of education systems, and others to the social contexts.

E. Countries which do relatively well in school education, such as France, Germany, Japan, South Korea, and Sweden, have certain things in common. As nations, they emphasise educational achievement. They tend to have a 'learning culture', in which parents and teachers have high expectations of their children's educational achievements, where the education systems are designed to provide opportunities and motivation for all learners, and where the labour market, and society in general, rewards those who do well in education.

They have learned how to institutionalise high expectations for all through norm-reinforcing procedures and practices such as national curricula and guidelines on teaching and assessment methods, professionally-produced learning materials, interactive whole-class teaching, and so on.

F. Singapore has both the school and societal ingredients for success. Schools are well managed and put a strong emphasis on achievement for all. Government educational planning is concerted, coherent and closely tied in with manpower planning and long-term economic and social development strategies. Targets are set—for 25 per cent to achieve university degrees and 40 per cent polytechnic diplomas by 2000—and these are well financed and usually met. The four polytechnics, for instance, are state-of-the-art, with fully integrated, robotic manufacturing facilities, and computerised lecture theatres with students answering tests on their desktop PCs and lecturers receiving computer-analysed class results on their consoles.

There are still some English legacies around, like the A-levels taken only by the university-bound top 25 per cent of students. However, these have been modified to ensure breadth. Subject combinations are recommended and most students in junior colleges take—and pass—four or five subjects, including the General Paper.

G. The key success factors, however, are probably societal. Singapore is a small country with few natural resources and a tiny home market and has little to rely on except its strategic location and its skills. Nation-building in Singapore has been a matter of survival, pursued with relentless and cool-headed determination by an able and cohesive Government and civil service, and education has been at the heart of this.

This has not only meant developing the skills needed by a fast-expanding company, it has also meant forming a cohesive, motivated citizenry out of an extremely multi-ethnic and multilingual population. In both these objectives, Singapore has been very successful. It is one of the fastest-growing economies and is ranked fourth in the world in gross domestic product per capita.

H. Policy-makers cannot hope to take policies from Singapore and make them work in Britain. However, two things can be learned. One is that, in certain environments at least, concerted and long-term planning can pay dividends. The other is that education is about more than improving economic competitiveness. Forming skills and forming citizens can go hand-in-hand.

Note the time you finished reading and the time elapsed.

List of Headings

(i) Possible reasons for educational success in Singapore
(ii) How Singapore compares with England in education
(iii) What other countries can learn
(iv) Some factors which may influence educational outcomes
(v) Attitudes of other countries to Singaporean education
(vi) Comparisons between Singapore and America in competitiveness
(vii) Singapore's educational policies and facilities
(viii) The 'Asian values' factor
(ix) The effect of Singapore's characteristics as a nation
(x) Achievements of the Singaporean education system
(xi) Characteristics of successful education systems

Section	Answer
Section A	
Section B	
Example Section C	**(i)**
Section D	
Section E	
Section F	
Section G	
Section H	

Work with another student. Look at the reading **The West and American Unity** on page 82 and make up headings for the paragraphs. Your heading should indicate to the reader what the paragraph is about.

Compare your headings with those written by other students.

Identification of the writer's views, attitudes, or claims: Yes, No, Not Given

23 Answer the questions that follow the passage **Cleaner Industrial Production: Why?**.

Note the time you started reading.

Cleaner Industrial Production: Why?

Industry continues to pose a potential threat to the environment, both globally and locally. It accounts for approximately one-third of the world's greenhouse gas emissions and a large percentage of the hazardous waste generated.

For the past two decades, industry in most developed countries has relied on end-of-pipe pollution abatement as the main pollution control technique. Although end-of-pipe treatment is effective, it has proved to be expensive. Nowadays the more progressive countries are calling for cleaner industrial production, a preventive approach that attempts to minimize waste. This holistic approach demands that the industrial pollutants be treated not at the end-of-pipe stage, but rather that they be prevented altogether, throughout the production process. Cleaner production techniques range from inside-the-factory changes in management, to shop-floor operations and processes, equipment and sometimes alterations in the products themselves. Cleaner production means adapting industrial processes to use raw materials and energy more efficiently, to eliminate toxic raw materials and to generally reduce emissions and wastes.

Enterprises everywhere are reaping environmental financial benefits from cleaner industrial production. Many developing countries and economies in transition are unaware of the benefits of preventive measures: not only do they reduce wastes and the consumption of energy and water but they also offer the prospect of utilizing or recycling by-products. In some cases, these countries do not have information about cleaner production and in other cases, they fail to appreciate the environmental and financial benefits of cleaner production activities.

Note the time you finished reading and the time elapsed.

Do the following statements agree with the views of the writer in the reading passage about cleaner industrial production?

The information upon which you base your answers must be in the passage.

Indicate
YES	if the statement agrees with the writer
NO	if the statement does not agree with the writer
NOT GIVEN	if there is no information about this in the passage

1. End-of-pipe treatment is an ineffective way to control pollution.

2. Cleaner industrial production is the best way to control industrial pollution.

3. Cleaner production if fully implemented will involve management changes.

4. Some countries do not realize the financial advantages of clean production.

5. All industries have an obligation to control pollution.

Discuss your answers to questions 1 to 5 with other members of the class.

Classification

A classification question requires the student to arrange information in categories.

To answer successfully, a student must skim and scan for information and understand the gist of a passage.

24 Answer the questions that follow the passage **Small Change, Big Deal.**

Note the time you started reading.

Small Change, Big Deal

by Jay Teitel

(Article from *EnRoute*, the In flight magazine of Air Canada)

Glossary: *panhandling means begging*
a busker is a wandering musician who seeks money from passers by

CHANGE HAS CHANGED in Canada over the past 11 years, with the introduction of the photogenic 'loonie' (one dollar coin) in 1987, and the equally striking 'twonie' (two dollar coin) a few years ago. The fact is, change isn't change anymore in this country, not in the North American sense: it's now change in the European/Asian sense, which is something else altogether. Indeed, in the global coin picture we're still beginners. At least a dozen countries outside this continent have coins worth $5 and up; the current leader is the Japanese 500 yen coin. Regardless, when countries move to higher denomination coins, they usually do it for two reasons: to satisfy demands from major coin users, i.e. transit authorities with coin-in-slot payment systems, the vending industry (try paying for a $3 tuna sandwich with quarters); and to save money (the twonie will save the taxpayer $250 million over the next 20 years). What they often fail to anticipate is the revolutionary effect the new change can have at the grassroots level of our monetary culture.

Any Canadian knows that change warps a pocket. In the past, it was easy to shell out a dollar or two – doing so made our pockets and purses lighter. Nowadays, a few coins equals a lot of money. At the same time, what once cost 75 cents in a vending machine now costs a dollar, and what once cost $1.50 has gone up to $2. Caroline Manton, Executive Director of CAMA, the Canadian Automatic Merchandising Association, admits that vending machine prices have risen, but maintains that the rises have coincided with an increase in the size of the product. While it's true that some soft drinks did increase in can size from 280 ml to 355 ml around the time of the loonie's introduction, and the standard potato chip bag swelled by about 20 per cent, the advantages are largely mythical.

And then there is the 'Panhandling Windfall'. A busker who's been playing classical guitar at a Toronto subway stop near my house for the past six years claims that in the 30-day period following the introduction of the twonie in February 1996, he tripled his daily take. It's not surprising. Two years ago, dropping a two dollar bill into a guitar case would have been regarded as the height of philanthropy; today dropping a twonie can seem almost stingy. One photographer friend of mine recently estimated that he'd given the same homeless person more than $400 in a single year without realizing it. Meanwhile, the 'squeegee kids' swarming the intersections of Canada's larger cities regularly take in $100 over a four-hour period providing unsolicited car windshield-washing.

But what about the advantages of large denomination coins to the non-panhandling citizen? If you're a waiter, you don't have to ask. Because most tips that are left in Canadian restaurants are rendered in change, the natural instinct is to leave a bigger pile of coins to make up for the fact that no paper is included – a naked loonie just isn't as impressive as a dollar bill.

Note the time you finished reading and the time elapsed.

Look at the list of people below who use Canadian currency. Use the information in the passage to answer the questions.

Write:

   A if the person has received a benefit
   B if the person has been disadvantaged
   C if the person has not been mentioned by the writer

> Be very careful to answer using <u>the information which is in the passage.</u>

1. owners of vending machines
2. people who operate automatic turnstiles
3. people who give money to the homeless
4. beggars
5. people who clean windshields on the streets
6. children who receive pocket money
7. food servers in restaurants
8. coin collectors
9. people who work in banks

Matching

25 Answer the questions that follow the passage **Personal Communication in the Age of the Internet.**

Note the time you started reading.

Personal Communication in the Age of the Internet

Some people are concerned about the influence the computer has, and will have, on our daily communications. Dire pictures have been drawn of pale, overweight adolescents gazing myopically at the screen and gnawing at cold potato chips, while the rest of the world plays in the sunshine outside.

The pessimists see these young people retreating into isolation, unable to communicate with people, their total lack of social skills the direct result of their mastery of the computer, which they use for games, but not for communication.

There is another, very different picture. Although there will undoubtedly be some people who cannot bear to leave the screen, the vast majority of people will use the computer as a means of communication with others. People can e-mail friends in faraway countries, and the reply can be swift and, usually, succinct. In fact the very nature of communication by e-mail is somewhat casual: Writer A sends a message of, say, four paragraphs. Writer B responds paragraph by paragraph, picking out the points which seem to be important, and transmits. Writer A can quickly ensure that Writer B has understood the message. Swift, accurate communication has occurred, with a great saving of paper. There is no checking back into old letters to see what was said in the first place, and there is little time to forget.

If e-mail communication is quick, convenient, and casual, the chat line is quicker and wilder. This is conducted in real time, which means that people can contact each other and type messages, frequently misspelt in their hurry, exchanging views around the world. The language used is brief and to the point, communication of the idea being the supreme goal. There was a time when jokes travelled around the world when international telephone operators shared them during the long, boring night shifts. Those old jokes took about twelve hours to become current elsewhere. Today a joke can be in cyberspace as soon as it has been invented.

The benefits of communication through cyberspace are immense, and for some people it will break their isolation, not increase it. Consider a frail older person who finds the idea of an international flight daunting, but who has friends in another country. This person can quickly establish contact through the e-mail, and can be fully aware of her friends' daily doings. This can be made easier as screens are enlarged and keyboards modified, but the breaking down of isolation of the old and disabled is well worth the effort to improve the machinery. We should also think of the immense value of e-mail and Internet communication to people living in remote or isolated areas.

There is a negative side to all of this. While most people use their computers honestly, there are some who use the innate anonymity of cyberspace cruelly. These people may represent themselves as something they are not; it can be as innocent as pretending to be one's own sister, or as vicious as gaining the confidence of a correspondent with a view to robbing them. Confidence tricksters use computers too.

Communication through the Internet is here to stay. If we are to thrive as a society we must make sure that this tool is available to as many people as possible, so that we do not develop pockets of our community who are cut off from knowledge of the Net.

Note the time you finished reading and the time elapsed.

Use the material in the passage.

Match the social effect (1–7) with the cause (A–E). There may be more than one cause for a social effect.

SOCIAL EFFECT	CAUSE
B 1. adolescents become isolated	A. anonymity of cyberspace
B 2. young people lack social skills	B. use of computers for games
D 3. people contact each other quickly and accurately	C. keyboards are modified, screens enlarged
C 4. swift transmission of ideas, information	D. use of e-mail
CD 5. isolation is broken for old people	E. use of chat line
DE 6. isolation of people in remote areas is reduced	
A 7. computer users may be misled	

What do you consider to be the best way to approach this sort of question?

Read the questions
Skim the article
Re-read the questions
Scan the article for the answers

or

Skim the article
Read the questions
Scan the article for the answers

Be prepared to justify your answer.

Question types in the General Training Reading module

Multiple choice questions

To answer multiple choice questions well you must read accurately and understand the passage thoroughly.

26 The reading passage **How Safe is a Cup of Tea?** will be followed by multiple choice questions. While you are reading, try to distinguish between the main points the author is making, and the supporting points.

Note the time you started reading.

How Safe is a Cup of Tea?

People all over the world drink tea. It is a mild beverage which people enjoy in the morning when they start their day, and for years it has had a reputation for being both safe and almost always beneficial, a drink which will give its consumer a lift without dangerous side-effects. It was a drink favoured by temperance organizations who saw far more to fear in alcoholic beverages.

Now scientists are suggesting that tea may not be as safe as we had previously believed. Tea contains caffeine, and caffeine has been linked to sleeplessness, and to the unpleasant jumpy feeling some people get when stressed. More seriously, there is a link with miscarriages, and pregnant women are advised to reduce their intake of tea until after their baby is born.

Caffeine is found in tea, but it is a larger component of other drinks. Six hundred mg of caffeine is found in six cups of percolated coffee, eight cups of instant coffee and twelve cups of medium strength tea. Chocolate drinks contain about 30 mg of caffeine per glass, so it takes 20 glasses to reach 600 mg.

The comparison demands that we know how strong 'medium strength' tea actually is, but medium strength to one person is weak to another. It would, of course, be possible to devise an objective test which prescribed the exact amount of tea in the pot, the time taken for it to brew, and the differing effects of adding (or not adding) milk or lemon. Most tea drinkers would rightly regard this as a foolish waste of time, and would continue to judge the strength of the tea they drink by its colour.

Many people who drink a lot of tea solve the problem by drinking a beverage from which the caffeine has been removed, decaffeinated tea, but others claim that it simply doesn't taste right. The sensible course is probably one of moderation: continue to enjoy your cup of tea, but don't enjoy too many!

Note the time you finished reading and the time elapsed.

Answer the following questions by choosing the appropriate letter **A, B, C** or **D.**

1. Tea used to be considered to be
   A beneficial in moderation
   B beneficial in all situations
   C more dangerous than alcohol
   D less dangerous than alcohol

2. Scientists say tea may be dangerous because it

    A contains caffeine
    B makes all its drinkers nervous
    C reduces miscarriages
    D irritates babies

3. There is more caffeine in tea than

    A instant coffee
    B chocolate drinks
    C percolated coffee
    D cola drinks

4. Tea drinkers usually assess the strength of tea by

    A its colour
    B how long it is brewed
    C its milkiness
    D a measured amount

5. The author suggests the best solution is to drink

    A decaffeinated tea
    B instant coffee
    C tea in moderation
    D no tea at all

Talk to your partner. Would it have been easier to read the questions first? Why?

27 Read the passage **Art Lovers Enjoy New, Decorative Lights** and answer the questions that follow.

Note the time you started reading.

Art Lovers Enjoy New, Decorative Lights

by Janet Smith, writing in the *Westender*, Vancouver, Canada

On rainy Vancouver nights, Bute Street's corridor of towers between Georgia and Robson has always been a dark place. But now, dozens of glowing, fan-like orbs in electric red, yellow and blue light up the sidewalk.

The glass display at 1200 Georgia is internationally renowned artist Dale Chihuly's first public art installation in Canada.

'I've never done a piece that's this public before. I've only recently started doing this sort of thing. People don't think of glass being outside,' said Chihuly, in town to unveil his new work, and an artistic vision himself in paint-spattered boots, eye-patch and curly shock of copper hair. 'So many people are going to be able to see it, driving by or walking around the building.'

Chihuly and his team of young artists created the $500,000 installation with pieces of colored glass blown open using centrifugal force. Each measures three or four feet in diameter. The overlapping orbs are protected by a sturdy glass encasement and a surrounding, reflective pool.

Chihuly has revolutionized an art form that was relegated for 2,000 years to glassblowing factories and practical pieces. Lately, the artist has been venturing into more architectural installations, and he enjoys the interaction of the forms. He said his fanciful fans brighten Bute Street's stark, modern architecture. 'When I saw it for the first time today, it really seemed to fit into this street. I'd like it to be a real meeting point for the city.'

For passers-by, the blown glass may seem a fragile medium for an outdoor exhibit. But anyone who has seen Chihuly and his team work with molten glass knows they treat their medium with little delicacy.

Chihuly is confident the piece will be respected, regardless of its materials: 'Interestingly enough, people tend to vandalize art a great deal less than anything else'.

Note the time you finished reading and the time elapsed.

Answer the following questions by choosing the appropriate letter **A, B, C** or **D.**

1. The glass is displayed in
   A an art gallery
   B a museum
   C an architectural installation
   D a street

2. The artist, Dale Chihuly, is
   A world famous
   B well known only in Canada
   C as yet unknown
   D seeking fame in Bute Street

3. Chihuly believes the location of the glass will
   A anger people
   B surprise people
   C disappoint people
   D not matter to people

4. Chihuly regards his glass installation as
   A part of the streetscape
   B purely a thing of beauty
   C a once-only event
   D a practical joke

Read multiple choice questions carefully. You will often find that more than one answer might seem correct. Look for the most precise answer.

Sometimes they seek the most <u>appropriate</u> answer or even the most <u>accurate</u> answer.

5. Chihuly believes the glass is likely to be
   A torn down by the council
   B stolen
   C undamaged
   D broken

What does <u>appropriate</u> mean? What does <u>accurate</u> mean?

Short-answer questions

28 Look at the advertisements for different museums that follow. Identify the letter of the appropriate museum.

1. Which museum includes exhibits from a gaol? ____

2. Which two museums have exhibits about medicine? ____

3. Where can you learn about wine making? ____

4. Which museum is concerned with education? ____

5. Which museums will permit visits after hours? ____

Note the time you started reading.

CAPE TOWN & PENINSULA REGION		
Museum	**City/Town/Times**	**Comments**
A Bo-Kaap Museum	Cape Town Mon. – Sat.: 09:30–16:30	1760 House
B Cape Medical Museum	Green Point Tues. – Fri.: 09:00–16:00 Mon., Sat., after hours on request	Early Cape medical history
C CP Nel Museum	Oudtshoorn Tues. – Fri.: 09:00–16:00 Some public holidays: closed	Was the home of medical superintendent of now defunct City Hospital, 100 years ago. Early Cape medical history, artefacts, reconstructions, photographs, books, documents of cultural heritage
D District Six Museum Foundation	Cape Town Mon. – Sat.: 10:00–16:00 After hours on request	Oldest residential area of the inner city which fell victim to the Group Areas Act, 1966. 50 000 people were relocated
E Education Museum	Wynberg Mon. – Fri.: 09:00–15:00	Victorian and Edwardian school furniture. Teaching aids before computers
F Fish Hoek Valley Museum	Fish Hoek Tues. – Fri: 09:30–12:30 After hours on request	Stories about the early inhabitants of Peers Cave, whaling in Fish Hoek and the community
G Groot Constantia	Constantia Daily: 10:00–17:00	South Africa's oldest producing wine estate
H Josephine Mill	Newlands, Cape Town Mon. – Fri.: 09:00–16:00 Sat. & Sun.: 10:00–15:00	Cape Town's only surviving and operational watermill, built in 1840
I Koopmans De Wet House	Cape Town Tues. – Sat.: 09:30–16:30	19th century home of politically prominent Marie Koopmans De Wet
J Knysna Museum	Knysna	Four buildings with relics of Knysna's past: Old Gaol Complex, Millwood House, Parkes Shop, Parkes Cottage
K Le Roux Townhouse	Oudtshoorn Mon. – Fri.: 09:00–17:00 Closed 13:00–14:00 Sun. After hours: on request Public Holidays: closed	Annex to CP Nel Museum South African Arts, Culture and Heritage: 1997 Calendar page 121

Note the time you finished reading and the time elapsed.

What was the best way to answer these questions?

29 Look at the six advertisements for different courses in oral communication skills. Identify the appropriate courses for each question.

1. Which four courses are conducted on Saturdays? ____

2. Which course will teach you how to deal with hurtful language? ____

3. Which two courses will help improve the quality of your voice? ____

4. Which course is designed for people who employ others? ____

5. Which course will increase your listening skills? ____

6. Which is the most expensive single session course? ____

Note the time you started reading.

ORAL COMMUNICATION SKILLS

A Step Out and Move Ahead - Effective Communication
This course is for anyone who wants to step out and move ahead in their communication skills. In the next five weeks, learn some basic tools that will help you avoid some common communication pitfalls. Learn about communication styles. Follow four simple steps toward presentation power. Find out how to impact your listener and become a more effective communicator. Fluency in spoken English required.

#CM10: Wed 7:00–9:30 pm $92
6 sess.   Jan 14-Feb 18

B Public Speaking For Success
In this hands-on, high-energy workshop, you will learn about image projection, setting goals and meeting objectives, leadership and protocol, impacting your audience, and confidence building and attitudes for success. Build skills that are timeless and invaluable in both your business and personal life. Why put it off? Do it NOW!

#CM61: Sat 9:00–4:00 pm $65
1 sess.   Apr 25

C Defusing Verbal Abuse In Your Professional and Personal Life
We experience verbal abuse when the language we hear causes us distress and pain. Hurtful language may occur at work, between loved ones, at school, in the community. Learn how to set communication goals designed to create language harmony without loss of face on either side.

#CM11: Sat 9:00–1:00 pm $29
1 sess.   Jan 31

D Developing Verbal Communication Skills
Let's talk and unfold your personal power. Discover ways to achieve positive results through developing successful listening and communication techniques. Create presence through personal presentation. We will look at your voice, appearance and attitude and how you can build for success. An action workshop designed to create a value-added you.

#CM12: Sat 9:00–4:00 pm $65
1 sess.   Jan 31
#CM62: Sat 9:00–4:00 pm $65
1 sess.   Apr 25

E How To Be A Successful Interviewer
Learn how to expedite the interview process and hire the right people to do the job. This workshop will assist you in developing an efficient interview process and guide you in hiring the right people.

#CM14: Wed 6:30–10:00 pm $25
1 sess.   Feb 4

F Change Your Voice: Make A Choice For Success
Participate in an exciting, dynamic program that will totally involve you. The voice you have may not be your own. Find your TRUE or OPTIMUM VOICE rather than your habitual voice, which may be physically damaging. Voice quality creates a voice image that people remember. Obtain the necessary techniques to help you for a lifetime. Taught by a certified speech language pathologist. Please bring a battery-operated cassette tape recorder and a tape to class.

#CM15: Sat 9:00–4:00 pm $137
1 sess.   Jan 31

Course Calendar, North Shore Continuing Education, Vancouver, Winter/Spring '98

Note the time you finished reading and the time elapsed.

Which was the most difficult question? Why?

To answer these questions successfully you need to skim and scan effectively.

How can you use the titles to help you?

Sentence completion

30 Answer the questions that follow the passage **Nesting Habits**.

Note the time you started reading.

Nesting Habits

Singapore's Jurong Bird Park is home to extraordinary creatures including the Great Hornbill, a large bird with an ornamental growth called a casque on the top of its head. Perhaps the most remarkable thing about this bird is the way it goes about nesting and raising its young. The pair find a hollow tree, and, after the eggs are laid, the female is sealed inside with a cement-like substance made of saliva and mud. She may stay inside for the entire incubation and fledgling period of 100 days. While she is incarcerated she depends entirely upon the male bird, which delivers food through a small slit left in the seal. The hornbills are noted for their affection as a pair, which may be fortunate for the female sitting helplessly in her nest, alone at first, then accompanied by her hungry brood.

The bird park has developed an artificial nesting tree and the Great Hornbills have been bred in captivity.

Another good family bird is the male King Penguin, which incubates the fertilized egg by resting it on his feet, thus protecting it from the Antarctic ice. There is a fold of skin to help protect the egg. The female King Penguin also takes her turn, and the egg is passed swiftly between them to preserve its warmth. The Humbolt Penguin, however, makes a nest which resembles a cave. The pair zealously guard the nest together.

Not surprisingly, the Antarctic birds in the Jurong Bird Park live in an airconditioned enclosure. They are entirely adapted to life in the bitter cold of Antarctica, and would find it hard to survive in the tropical warmth of Singapore.

The penguin is a flightless bird, and so is the emu. The female emu lays a clutch of approximately nine eggs which weigh about 750 grams each, and the male sits on the eggs for eight weeks. During this time he may lose between 5 and 10 kilograms.

One may generalize that most birds follow the pattern of the female staying by the nest while the male goes out to forage, but these birds at Jurong Bird Park show that there are interesting variations to the pattern.

Note the time you finished reading and the time elapsed.

Complete the sentences below with words taken from the passage. Use **NO MORE THAN THREE WORDS OR NUMBERS** for each answer.

1. The female Great Hornbill is inside her nest for all of the incubation and fledgling period of _____

PREPARE FOR IELTS: The IELTS Preparation Course
Unit 3 The Reading Test

2. The male Great Hornbill brings food to his family and passes it through _____

3. King Penguins rest the egg on their feet where it is additionally protected by a _____

4. The male emu hatches the eggs for _____

Is it easier to answer this exercise if you read the questions first? Why?

Notes/summary/diagram/flow chart/table completion

This type of question tests your ability to understand the overall meaning of a passage, and to extract particular information from it.

31 Read **Bondi and Bay Explorer Bus Terms and Conditions.**

Note the time you started reading.

Bondi and Bay Explorer Bus Terms and Conditions

Sydney is a busy, vibrant city of over four million people. From time to time, due to circumstances beyond the control of Explorer Buses, the city streets may be temporarily closed for street parades, celebrations and road works. These closures may affect the running time of Explorer Bus services.

Busy streets may become very crowded, and this congestion affects the Explorer Bus services, especially the Bondi and Bay Explorer Bus during the hot summer months from December to February, when everyone wants to go to the beach. In August every year many streets close for the City to Surf Fun Run which attracts huge crowds.

The information, prices, conditions and times are correct at the time of printing but are subject to change at any time. They apply as far as circumstances will permit; however, the State Transit Authority which runs the buses shall not be responsible for any consequence arising from any variance.

State Transit reserves the rights to cancel, without notice, wholly or in part, any of the bus services. The State Transit Authority shall not be held responsible for property left on buses.

During peak times (including school holidays), services become very popular, and all seats are sold on a 'first in - first seated' basis. Reservations cannot be made, so be early to avoid disappointment.

Note the time you finished reading and the time elapsed.

Complete the summary below. Choose **ONE OR TWO WORDS** for each answer.

Sometimes the buses of the Explorer Service cannot follow their usual timetable because of road _____(1)_____ There may also be a problem with _____(2)_____ streets during the summer.

The information in this brochure is correct now but circumstances may change. If this happens, the State Transit Authority accepts no _____(3)_____ for anything resulting from a change.

Be careful to answer
using only the
number of words
suggested.

The State Transit may cancel all or part of a bus service, and is _____(4)_____ for things left behind on its vehicles.

There are no reservations so it is wise to arrive _____(5)_____ particularly during times when the service is very popular.

The examiners are checking for overall comprehension, so you cannot simply scan the passage for words to go in the gaps. You must understand what you have read. How can this be achieved quickly?

- Read the passage quickly to get an overall idea of meaning. Don't worry about unknown words.

- Read the question.

- Read the passage again and answer the question.

Sometimes the question asks students to 'Choose **ONE OR TWO WORDS** from the passage for each answer'.

32 Complete the notes that follow the passage **The West and American Unity.**

Note the time you started reading.

The West and American Unity

from *FRONTIER AMERICA*
published by the Buffalo Bill Historical Center, Cody, Wyoming

The men and women who struck out for the western territories did not leave their culture behind. Citizens of the United States—even in the late eighteenth and early nineteenth centuries, when there scarcely was a United States—were conscious of their American identity.

Americans, like people from other nations, adopted certain cultural symbols that helped them identify with their country and their fellow countrymen. Their symbols of unity were newer and fewer than those of Englishmen. They were also mainly political symbols at first, since the United States was (or 'the United States *were*', as people of the era would have said) a political rather than a racial or cultural or geographical union. The most important symbols were the Fourth of July, the Constitution, and George Washington.

East and West, Independence Day was celebrated with gusto. It was a national festival, the reminder of America's origins. It was both a martial and social occasion. Wherever they found themselves on that day, Americans fired guns and drank toasts, acknowledging that independence was won by force of arms and expressing fellowship with their countrymen.

The U.S. Constitution was tangible proof of the ascendance of law and reason. For those moving West, who could and did carry copies of the document, it was particularly important because it provided for the extension of the nation and the creation of new states. Its power to unite people was such that, as early as 1812, Louisiana could join the Union despite being separated by hundreds of miles from the nearest state.

The most widely honored symbol of all was George Washington. Newspapers in the 1790s called him 'the eighth wonder of the world'. His steadfast republicanism, his integrity, and his heroic deeds made him a model for all Americans. In fact, it was a source of pride for citizens of the new nation to be able to call themselves the countrymen of George Washington. Furthermore, his own pursuits and youthful career in the Ohio Valley West made him the inspirational patron for westering America. Whether toasting the Fourth of July or their safe arrival in a new place, Americans would raise their cups first to George Washington.

Pioneers in the western territories were not trying to create new societies. Usually they set out to replicate the social and political forms they had left behind. Their homes and towns were practical adaptations of the styles and technologies with which they were most familiar. Even those Easterners most fearful of expansion were generally reassured when they saw the rapid strides Westerners made in building American institutions. The common bonds were apparent.

Note the time you finished reading and the time elapsed.

Skim the passage to find the paragraphs which will give you the answers, and then scan for the information you need.

This activity may be photocopied

Complete the notes below with words taken from **The West and American Unity.** Use **NO MORE THAN ONE OR TWO WORDS** for each answer.

How many words may you use in each answer?

SYMBOLS OF AMERICAN UNITY		
Independence Day	**(1)**	**(2)**
celebrated by festivities, gun fire	deeply respected, carried westward	'inspirational patron'

Choosing from a 'heading bank' for identified paragraphs/sections of the text

To answer a question using a list of headings, or heading bank, the student must:

- understand the detail and gist of the article
- understand how the article progresses.

How can this be achieved quickly? Choose whichever approach below suits you best:

- read the article and then the headings. Some of the headings will fit to the paragraphs or sections quite quickly. Make a note of these headings and pencil them in. Then, read the passage. As you read the passage, think about what each section means, and match it to a heading.

or

- read the headings first and then read the article with the headings in mind.

The reading passage **A Good Night's Sleep** has 7 sections **A-G**.

Note the time you started reading.

A Good Night's Sleep

A. There's nothing quite like the refreshment of a good night's sleep; conversely there is much misery which comes from a restless night. The whole of the next day can be disturbed by a bad night, as the poor sleepless one drags him or herself through the day, snapping at friend and colleague alike. Hopefully the problem can be solved quickly so the next night is not so bad, because entrenched bad sleeping habits may lead to serious problems.

B. Why do we have bad nights? In some cases it is because of some traumatic event or emotional upset which deprives us of sleep. A good example would be if we are waiting for someone who is late coming home, or we are anticipating a serious examination, or are worried about some event which will occur the next day. The event may equally be something we are looking forward to, like a party or a celebration, so we cannot get to sleep for thinking about it. These bad nights are limited by the temporary nature of the events which cause them.

C. Anxiety is a great thief of sleep, and may settle into a pattern where the sufferer gets to bed and to sleep only to awaken in the early hours of the morning. This sort of chronic pattern may go on for a long time, and is a serious health issue. Opinions differ on the best way to handle this sort of sleep deprivation: the early morning is probably no time to try to resolve the issue which is causing the concern. The immediate solution at 2 am may be to get up and move around a little and then return to bed, ready to sleep. This method is advocated by people who have running nightmares about their problems if they just try to lie in bed and go back to sleep.

D. People may lose sleep because they are in greater or lesser degrees of pain. Here the problem becomes medical, and is beyond the scope of this article. Suffice it to say that a whole array of medicine is out there, and should be administered by the experts.

E. People may find it hard to sleep because they are too hot or too cold. In hot, airless conditions even a standard fan will help immensely, and if there is a ceiling fan it should be set to move the air gently. Many people prefer to sleep with a window open to allow plenty of fresh air into the room, although in some places the fresh air may be accompanied by noise and mosquitoes.

F. The topic of bedding is often neglected. Bed clothes should be light and clean, and in summer they should be minimal. In winter people can resort to heavier blankets or the self-indulgence of the electric blanket, best used to heat the bed before anyone gets into it and then turned off. It is quite easy to over-estimate the number of blankets needed in winter, and many people make themselves too hot, kick the bedclothes off, and then wake up cold.

G. Finally, one must consider the part habit plays in our lives, and our sleep. People often claim they cannot sleep in a strange bed. When we settle down for the night a powerful part of us demands to feel secure, and to know that nothing has changed since the last time we slept. Lead me to my bed!

Note the time you finished reading and the time elapsed.

Choose the most suitable heading for sections **A-G** from the list of headings below. Write the appropriate numbers **(i-x)**.

NB There are more headings than paragraphs so you will not use all of them.

You may use any of the headings more than once.

```
                        List of Headings

    (i)     Sleeplessness and discomfort
    (ii)    How sleep habits have changed
    (iii)   Long-term anxiety
    (iv)    Staying cool in summer
    (v)     Sleep and security
    (vi)    Comparisons between good and bad sleep
    (vii)   The importance of sleep
    (viii)  The correct temperature for winter
    (ix)    Temporary problems
    (x)     The full moon
```

Section	Answer
Section A	
Section B	
Section C	
Section D	
Section E	
Section F	
Section G	

34 Work with another student. Look at the reading **The West and American Unity** on page 82 and make up headings for the paragraphs. Your heading should indicate to the reader what the paragraph is about.

Compare your headings with those written by other students.

Identification of the writer's claims, views and attitudes: Yes, No, Not Given

 Answer the questions that follow the passage **Culture in Action – Table Manners.**

Note the time you started reading.

Culture in Action – Table Manners

Victoria Strutt, writing in *Boomerang*

Food is one of the first things we notice about a different culture. It is also one of the first aspects of a different culture we feel free to adopt. The table manners that accompany the food are not so obvious. When the behaviours of a culture are invisible, when we are not even aware we have them, they are most powerful. What are some of the different table manners we might encounter at a class dinner when a range of cultures is represented?

In Australia, it is expected that everyone will talk during a meal. The talking passes from one person to another and is often about an issue that has been in the news, a new movie or some other neutral and safe topic. In many Eastern cultures it is considered impolite to speak while the meal is in progress. Conversation is held before or after the meal itself.

After the meal, the way we place our eating tools, our knives, forks, spoons or chopsticks, is also culturally defined. In Australia, when we have finished eating the main course we put the knife and fork across the middle of the plate parallel to each other with the handles facing towards us. When we are resting during the meal, we put the knife and fork across each other on the middle of the plate. In China the chopsticks go crossways across the top of the plate with the handles facing towards the right as that is the hand that holds the chopsticks. In Indonesia, some students tell me, the fork and spoon are crossed as in the Australian resting position. But not all Indonesians may do this. Indonesia is itself a very multicultural society so there may be a number of different customs for this within the country.

Consider further where the dishes are positioned on the table. The Chinese custom of all the diners eating from a range of central dishes is different from the Western way of having servings on separate plates. This expresses a different relationship between people and shows lines of community in contrast to the Westerner's separate plates. Even the way the knives and forks fence in the plates makes a little frame for the plate and defines separate arenas of action all around the table, rather than one common arena of action as is the case of cultures where all the diners share from the common dishes in the middle.

Then there is the complex issue of accepting or declining an offer. Ritual refusals also differ from one culture to another. If you decline the offer of a drink in Australia, you may not be offered another for some time as the 'no' is taken to mean 'no'. In some cultures however, the first 'no' is a recognised step in the polite way of accepting a drink, while saying 'yes' straight away is seen as impolite and too direct.

Even leaving food on a plate at the end of the meal tells us something about our culture. Are we accustomed to leave a small amount to indicate we have been provided for well? Are we accustomed to eating everything on the plate to indicate we have respected the food and so wasted nothing? Are there rules in your culture for where you put any scraps or leftovers on the plate? Can you leave them scattered on the plate or should you put them together in one tidy heap?

We need to remember too that table manners change within cultures. First, they change across time; from one generation to another what is considered polite, marginal or uncouth shifts and alters. What were bad manners to one generation may be unimportant to another. Manners also vary according to the occasion. Just as in language, where the level of formality we use must fit the social context, so the manners we use for eating will change depending on how formal the eating event is. A barbecue or a dinner with a few friends will have different rules and conventions from a big family gathering or the formal dinner of a professional group.

Table manners are mostly invisible but bringing them to consciousness can be an intriguing way of becoming more familiar with another culture. They can also be a rich topic of conversation as everyone is an authority with a lifetime of first hand experience.

Note the time you finished reading and the time elapsed.

Do the following statements agree with the attitudes of the writer in the reading passage **Culture in Action – Table Manners?**

- A claim is a statement of something as fact.

- A view is a personal opinion, belief or idea about something.

- An attitude is a way of feeling, thinking or behaving.

Select:

YES	if the statement agrees with the writer
NO	if the statement does not agree with the writer
NOT GIVEN	if there is no information about this in the passage

1. Unrecognized cultural differences are more powerful than recognized ones.

2. It is always polite to talk during the meal.

3. The writer has never visited Indonesia.

4. The writer prefers the idea of eating from dishes in the middle of the table.

5. It is rude to refuse a drink in Australia.

Discuss your answers to questions 1-5 with other members of the class.

Why is it essential to answer using only the information in the passage?

Make up a yes/no/not given question on any part of the last three paragraphs in the passage.

Answer the questions that follow the passage **The University of Hong Kong Museum Society.**

Note the time you started reading.

The University of Hong Kong Museum Society

The University Museum and Art Gallery is one of the oldest and most distinguished museums in Hong Kong. It is housed in the Fung Ping Shan Building and the lower three floors of the new T. T. Tsui Building. Both are located on the campus of the University of Hong Kong on Bonham Road. The Museum primarily displays traditional Chinese art: painting and callligraphy, bronzes and ceramics. The Art Gallery features both Chinese and Western modern art. Special exhibitions are organised throughout the year.

The Museum and Art Gallery is open to the public free of charge on Monday to Saturday, 9.30am – 6.00pm. Both buildings are closed on Sundays and public holidays.

Objectives

- To support and assist the University Museum and Art Gallery

- To promote the understanding and appreciation of art, particularly Chinese art

- To raise funds, enrich the collections and finance exhibitions and cultural activities

- To promote friendship among members

Activities

- Lectures, seminars, museum and art gallery tours

- Overseas tours to museums, galleries and other places of interest

Membership

Membership of the Society is open to all. Categories of membership are:

- Ordinary Membership
  HK$250 per annum (single)
  HK$300 per annum (joint)

- Full-time Student Membership
  HK$100 per annum (most lectures are free)

- Life Membership
  HK$2,500 (single)
  HK$3000 (joint)

The membership year runs from June to May. Anyone joining after 1st March receives membership until May of the following year.

Benefits

- Museum Society newsletters and invitations to lectures and seminars

- Invitations to previews of exhibitions at the University Museum and Art Gallery

- 20% discount on University Museum and Art Gallery publications

Please send your application to:

Honorary Secretary
The University of Hong Kong Museum Society
University Museum and Art Gallery
The University of Hong Kong
Pokfulam, Hong Kong
Tel: 2975 5600
Fax: 2975 5610

Note the time you finished reading and the time elapsed.

Look at the following statements and decide if they are correct or wrong, according to the information in the reading passage on the University of Hong Kong Museum Society.

Select:
TRUE	if the statement is true
FALSE	if the statement is not true
NOT GIVEN	if the information is not given in the passage

1. The University Museum and Art Gallery is on the university campus on Bonham Road.

2. The Museum and Art Gallery are open every day of the year.

3. The University of Hong Kong Museum Society aims to raise money for travel grants for artists.

4. Membership of the University of Hong Kong Museum Society is free and open to all.

5. Members may take part in overseas tours to museums.

Discuss your answers with other members of the class.

37

Answer the questions that follow the passage **Staff Value a Career Path Above Salary.**

Note the time you started reading.

Staff Value a Career Path Above Salary

from **People Management**

Companies are learning that they will hold on to staff only if they give them the chance to develop.

Ruth Prickett reports.

Staff retention is once again a key concern for almost two-thirds of UK companies, while turnover in the retail sector is twice as high as the national average. But firms wishing to buy their employees' loyalty would be well advised to offer career opportunities rather than money, according to a survey by Reed Personnel Services.

With staff turnover at 26 per cent, it is not surprising that three out of four retailers have introduced, or are considering introducing, measures to retain people. Less predictably, however, respondents put a higher salary second to the chance of career progression in a list of the top five reasons why people change jobs.

Employers' responses to the problem vary widely, from staff recognition programmes to multi-skilling and team-building exercises, but 70 per cent of those surveyed listed training as their primary solution. 'This research emphasises how effective it can be to concentrate on increasing staff morale rather than pay,' said James Reed, chief executive of Reed.

Tesco, one of the retailers featured in the survey, began a staff retention programme some years ago. Although turnover was 33 per cent last year, the company is confident that morale is rising and long-term loyalty has increased.

Employees in every store have recently gone through a management programme focusing on improving core skills and process development. Managers scrutinised jobs and attempted to eliminate unnecessary or bureaucratic processes so that staff were able to concentrate on the main business.

The company has been running a programme called Project Future since early 1997 and, according to Cartwright, it is now an ongoing process. Managers attend short core skill workshops in their stores, together with shopfloor staff who are earmarked for promotion.

This training fits in with managers' individual career development plans, and the company is also keen to encourage employees to apply for jobs in different functions. 'I've been here for 12 years, but never in the same job for more than two,' Cartwright said. 'It's almost like working for a different company each time you move.'

Tesco's expansion into central Europe has opened up new possibilities for long-term posts abroad. More than 100 of its British managers are working in Poland, Hungary and the Czech and Slovak republics, and 31 more central European hypermarkets are planned for the next few years.

Back at home, the company has introduced more flexibility to encourage the store's predominantly female workforce to return to work after maternity leave. More people are taking career breaks and returning to part-time management positions.

'We are operating a 24-hour, seven days-a-week business,' Cartwright said. 'If a mother wants to fit her work around her kids or her husband's shifts, then we can accommodate that.'

Note the time you finished reading and the time elapsed.

Look at the following statements in questions 1–7 and decide if they are correct or wrong, according to the information in the reading passage.

Select:
TRUE   if the statement is true
FALSE   if the statement is false
NOT GIVEN   if the information is not given in the passage

1. Employee groups say that a career path is more important than money.

2. Staff turnover in the UK in general is 26%.

3. Retailers are attempting to keep their staff.

4. Most employers in the survey prefer training to encourage staff to stay.

5. Tesco has reduced staff turnover.

6. Managers in each Tesco store designed the training programme.

7. All Tesco employees take part in Project Future.

Classification

Read the passage **Safety Information for Guests,** and answer the questions that follow.

Note the time you started reading.

Hotel Sofitel

Safety Information for Guests

Please assist us in ensuring your safe stay at Hotel Sofitel by taking a moment to carefully read the following safety instructions:

- **Prepare**
  If you have a disability that might prevent you from responding to a fire alarm notify the reception desk.

- **Know Where the Exits Are**
  On the back of the door to your room is a map showing the location of emergency exits, fire extinguisher and alarms. Walk down the hall and check the locations so that you could easily find them under adverse conditions.

- **Don't Use the Elevators**
  In the event of a fire or earthquake, don't use an elevator. It may take you to a floor filled with smoke or flames, or it may be mechanically unsafe.

- **Know How to Turn Off the Air Conditioner/Heating Unit in Your Room**
  Familiarize yourself with the Air Conditioning/Heating System instructions. In case of fire, turn off the air conditioner. It may suck smoke into your room.

- **If There is a Fire, You'll Smell Smoke**
  Call the Operator (press '0')
  If there is no answer, press '9' and then '911'. Tell them there is an emergency at Hotel Sofitel. Give them your room number and tell them you are staying in your room, if that is the case.

- **Touch Your Guest Room Door**
  If it feels hot, do not open it. Fill your bathtub, waste basket and ice bucket with water.

- **Stuff Wet Towels, Sheets or Blankets into the Cracks Around Your Door**
  Use them to cover all air vents. Keep several wash cloths moist so that, if your room fills with smoke, you can put the wet cloth over your nose and mouth.

- **If Your Door and/or Walls Feel Hot**
  Use your waste basket or ice bucket to throw water on them. Keep them damp.

- **Know Where Your Room Key is at All Times**
  Always have your room key within easy reach. This is especially important at night. If you leave your room during an emergency, take your key with you. Exits may be blocked and you may need to return to your room.

- **If You Leave Your Room**
  Go to the fire exit. Before opening the door, check to make sure it is not hot. If it is not hot, enter the stairwell and if possible, go downstairs and out of the building. If you cannot go down and out, use your judgement; consider whether to try another exit, or return to your room.

Note the time you finished reading and the time elapsed.

Look at the list of safety instructions. Write:

    A   if the action should be taken before a fire has started
    B   if the action should be taken during a fire
    C   if the action is not mentioned by the author

1. inform reception desk of disability

2. use fire extinguishers

3. shout from the open window

4. telephone for help

5. turn off air conditioner

6. moisten wash cloths

7. crawl through the smoke

> Be careful to answer using the information in the passage.

To perform this task quickly and effectively the reader must be able to skim and understand both the gist and the detail of the question.

Discuss your answers with your classmates. Which answer was most troublesome? Why?

When answering a question like this, you could:

- read the questions before the text
- skim the text, read the questions, scan the text
- read the text carefully before reading the questions.

How can you use the headings to help you to understand quickly?

Matching

Answer the questions that follow the passage **Smoking a Problem for Occupational Health Nurses.**

Note the time you started reading.

Smoking a Problem for Occupational Health Nurses

from *Occupational Health*

Occupational Health (OH) nurses responsible for staff in nursing homes face a dilemma on managing the risks of passive smoking following a test court case.

In the first case of its kind, a nurse who has never smoked is claiming damages against a private old people's home in Manchester, England.

Sylvia Sparrow alleges that inhaling smoke in the residents' lounge gave her asthma, to the extent that she was forced to give up work as a nurse. Legal experts say a successful outcome is likely to lead to many other claims. A ruling from Manchester High Court was due as *Occupational Health* went to press.

The Royal College of Nursing's (RCN) Society of Occupational Health Nursing chairwoman Kit Artus said OH practitioners face a moral dilemma. 'The people in these homes are lifelong addicts, and OH nurses already do what they can to encourage staff as well as residents to try to stop smoking,' she said.

Artus argues that OH staff can only be as effective as management will allow. 'They can give advice on providing a safe place of work but it is the duty of the employer to ensure any staff are told of possible hazards, so that they can make an informed decision before taking up employment,' she said.

Sparrow has not worked since February 1992 and, backed by the RCN, is suing St Andrew's Homes for failing to provide a safe place to work, and is claiming for injury and loss of earnings.

Note the time you finished reading and the time elapsed.

Choose one phrase (A–H) from the list of phrases to complete each key point below.

The information in the completed sentences should be an accurate summary of the points made by the writer.

NB   There are more phrases than sentences so you will not use them all. You may use any phrase more than once.

1. People who run nursing homes are concerned about passive smoking and _____

2. If Sylvia Sparrow wins _____

3. At the time of writing _____

4. The old people _____

5. Employers should explain the risks so _____

     A.   employees can prepare a good court case.

     B.   the judge's decision was available.

     C.   the incidence of asthma.

     D.   people can decide to work elsewhere.

     E.   the court case will lead to many others.

     F.   cannot stop smoking

     G.   the case was still before the court

     H.   its effect on the health of their staff.

Reading activities answer sheet

You may photocopy this page.
In this IELTS test, candidates will write their answers on an Answer Sheet similiar to this.

1		21	
2		22	
3		23	
4		24	
5		25	
6		26	
7		27	
8		28	
9		29	
10		30	
11		31	
12		32	
13		33	
14		34	
15		35	
16		36	
17		37	
18		38	
19		39	
20		40	

Unit 4
The Writing Test

ACADEMIC AND GENERAL TRAINING WRITING MODULES

The writing test takes one hour and is divided into two tasks in both the Academic and General Training writing modules.

In the first task of the Academic module candidates are expected to describe some visual information such as a graph, writing at least 150 words. The second task is to write an essay of at least 250 words.

In the first task of the General Training module candidates write a letter of at least 150 words and then write an essay of at least 250 words for the second task. In each module the first task should be completed in 20 minutes, leaving 40 minutes for the second task.

Writing Task 2 counts more than Writing Task 1 towards an IELTS band score. It may be a good idea to answer Task 2 first. However, candidates must complete both tasks so it is important to allow adequate time to do Task 1. The recommended 20 minutes to complete Task 1 and 40 minutes for Task 2 are good guidelines.

There is a Correction Key at the end of this Unit which may be useful to students in giving feedback on written work.

WRITING TASK 1
Introduction to Academic Writing Task 1

Task 1 of the Academic Writing Module measures the candidate's ability to describe information presented as a graph, or a picture, or a table. You are expected to be able to:

- organize, present and possibly compare data
- describe the stages of a process or procedure
- describe an object or event or series of events
- explain how something works.

(*The IELTS Handbook*, 1998, p. 12)

The topics in Academic Writing Task 1 will be of general interest. There will be no bias toward any field of study, and the candidate will not need any special knowledge. Candidates will be asked to write about things that people entering tertiary study should know about. They might, for instance, be asked to describe basic physiological processes (like the circulation of the blood) or simple physical processes like the way rain occurs.

Understanding and describing visual information

This practice writing task is similar to a question which might be asked in the IELTS test. Look at the question.

The graph below shows the rates at which cars were stolen in four countries between 1980 and 1989.

Write a report for a university lecturer describing the information shown below.

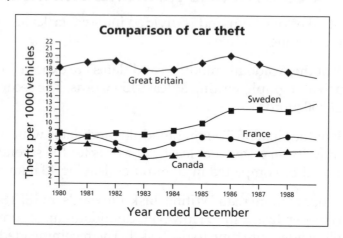

What are the topic words?
Topic words are words in the question which tell you the topic you should write about. In this question they are: *cars stolen, four countries, between 1980 and 1989.*

What are the dimensions?
The dimensions refer to the way the material is presented, perhaps as a graph, or a table, or a map. The dimensions also refer to the amount of information given. In this case there are four lines in the graph representing car theft in Great Britain, Sweden, France and Canada.

What are the striking features/general trends?
You should look for the most obvious information. In this case it is easy to see that Great Britain suffered the largest number of car thefts, Canada the least, and that thefts were rising in Sweden but falling everywhere else.

What are the task words?
The task words are words in the question which tell you how you should present the information. In this case the task word is *describing.*

Who are you writing for?
A university lecturer.

The answer must:
Look for the most important things you can say about the graph. In this case, you should bring out all the striking features.

It's a good idea to:
Work out how to express the numerical information. *Ten cars stolen per thousand vehicles* could be expressed as *1%.* Watch your time carefully.

1 Write an answer to the practice writing task on car theft.

You should spend about 20 minutes on this task, and you should write at least 150 words.

Planning your answer
When you are writing numbers and amounts you must consider whether you are using the adjectival form. In the exercise below amounts are expressed in the noun form *millions of tonnes* but in the description you are more likely to use the adjectival form *x million tonnes*.

2 Work through these five steps with another student to identify the nature of the graph below and the most important features.

1. Identify the form of the information.

2. Identify the overall subject of the visual information.

3. Identify the main factors being measured.

4. Decide the main comparisons.

5. Concentrate on any obvious correlations or contrasts in figures.

Year	Raw coal					
	NSW	Qld	SA	WA	Tas./Vic.	Australia
1950-51	12.9	2.3	0.3	0.9	0.3	16.7
1955-56	14.8	2.7	0.5	0.9	0.4	19.3
1960-61	18.5	3.1	1.0	0.8	0.3	23.7
1965-66	25.4	5.6	2.0	1.1	0.1	34.2
1970-71	35.7	14.3	1.6	1.2	0.2	53.0
1975-76	40.6	32.4	1.8	2.1	0.2	77.1
1980-81	58.3	42.8	1.7	3.1	0.3	106.2
1985-86	77.2	80.0	2.2	3.8	0.5	163.6

Table 1: Australia: Coal Production by states, 1950-51 to 1985-86 (millions of tonnes).

How will you organize the information contained in the table?

Write a description of the information you have learned from the table.

Organizing your answer

Your answer should be constructed so that the important information in the graph or table can be easily gained from your text. For example, similar information may be grouped together, or the most important changes highlighted, supported by data from the graph. Good organization makes your answer easier to write, and the reader will find it easier to understand.

3 Look at the table below and read the two sample answers that follow. What is the organizing principle for each essay?

Market Research Survey

Use the information below to write a short report on the destinations favoured by tourists in the city of Llorente.

TOURIST DESTINATIONS	AGE GROUPS			
(Figures are percentages which show places tourists said they visited on their last holiday)	21-30	31-40	41-50	51 +
Beaches	47	41	32	25
Night Clubs	78	62	41	15
Discotheques	87	75	33	5
Art galleries	21	48	62	81
Shopping centres	91	83	95	83
Zoos	12	36	46	49
National parks	28	37	24	21
Cinemas/Theatres	83	85	69	42
Museums	8	16	28	29
Sporting events	22	29	27	43

Sample answer 1:

The table shows clearly that different age groups favoured different destinations in the city of Llorente, although some destinations were popular with all ages.

Shopping centres, discotheques, night clubs, and cinemas and theatres were the preferred places for the youngest age group in the study, the 21–30-year-olds. This group visited museums and zoos least, with only 8% visiting museums and only 12% visiting zoos. Shopping centres and discotheques were also popular with the next group in the study, the 31–40-year-olds, and 85% of this group also visited cinemas and theatres.

For the next group, who were aged 41–50, shopping centres were far more popular than any other location, with 95% visiting them. Art galleries and cinemas and theatres were visited by 62% and 60%, respectively, of this group. The most popular location for the oldest group, people over 51, was also shopping centres, with 83% visiting them, but art galleries were visited by 81%.

Thus, while shopping centres were popular with all age groups, discotheques were far more popular with the youngest group and art galleries with the oldest group.

183 words

Sample answer 2:

The table shows clearly that different groups favoured different destinations in the city of Llorente, although some destinations were popular with all ages.

Beaches, night clubs and discotheques were most popular with the youngest age group, of 21–30-year-olds. The popularity of these activities declined noticeably as the age increases. Art galleries, on the other hand, increased in popularity from 21% of 20–31-year-olds visiting them, to 81% of people over 51. Shopping centres were highly popular with all age groups.

Zoos were more popular with older age groups; 36% of 31–40-year-olds, 46% of 41–50-year-olds, and 49% of over 51-year-olds visited them, compared to only 12% of 21–30-year-olds. National parks were most popular with the 31–40-year-olds, and so were cinemas and theatres although the 21–30-year-olds went to them in similar numbers. Museums were not popular with any age group, but the interest in sporting events remained fairly steady at 22–27% in people from 21 to 50 years, rising to 43% in people over 51.

Thus, shopping centres were clearly the preferred location for all age groups, with museums being the least preferred place.

189 words

Skills for Academic Writing Task 1

The language of data analysis and comment

Phrases like these are often used when describing information presented in graphs and tables:

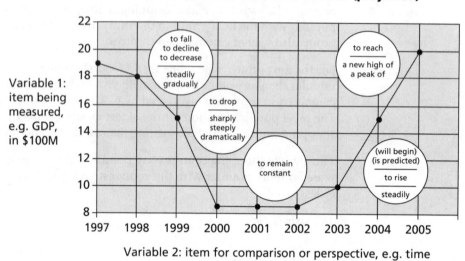

Gross Domestic Product, 1997 to 2005 (projected)

Variable 1: item being measured, e.g. GDP, in $100M

to fall
to decline
to decrease
____
steadily
gradually

to reach
____
a new high of
a peak of

to drop
____
sharply
steeply
dramatically

to remain
constant

(will begin)
(is predicted)
____
to rise
____
steadily

Variable 2: item for comparison or perspective, e.g. time

4 The description below is written in the year 2000. Complete the description using the correct tenses.

GDP _____(1)_____ in the years 1998 and 1999. In the present year, 2000, it _____(2)_____ and _____(3)_____ at least until 2002. A rise is forecast by 2003 and after that GDP _____(4)_____ It is predicted that GDP will _____(5)_____ by 2005.

Describing trends

5 The verbs in the boxes below are often used to describe trends or changes. Draw an arrow next to each verb to indicate whether they show an upward (↑), downward (↓) or horizontal (→) movement.

remain constant	plunge	remain unchanged
fall	climb	rise
increase	even out	drop
decline	go down	go up
level off	remain stable	decrease

Do these verbs indicate that things are better, or worse?

recover	deteriorate	pick up
improve	slip back	

What do you think these words mean?

| reach a peak | reach a high | hit a low | fluctuate |

What are the past participles of the verbs in the boxes above?

Which of the verbs above can be made into nouns?

Example: to fall .... *a fall*

The following adjectives can be used to describe the speed or the size of the change. What is the appropriate adverb for each of the adjectives below?

Speed of Change		Size of Change	
rapid	*rapidly*	slight	*slightly*
gradual		substantial	
slow		considerable	
steady		dramatic	
quick		noticeable	
		negligible	

Classroom Exercise: Draw horizontal and vertical lines on the board. One student goes to the board and draws a line and other students describe it: *a dramatic fall*, *a steady increase*, and so on. Another student adds more lines. Students should be sure they use as many different vocabulary items as possible.

'Trend' and 'tendency'
A trend is a pattern. If the numbers seem to be consistently going downwards, there is a downward trend. The verb form *to trend* (upwards or downwards) is little used. The adjectival form, *trendy*, and the adverbial form, *trendily*, refer to clothes and fashionable objects and are not used when describing numbers.

A tendency is very like a trend. If the numbers are consistently going downwards, we can say: *there is a tendency to fall.*

The verb is *to tend*. We can say that numbers *tend to fall*. There is no adjectival or adverbial form.

Percentages and numbers

6 What is the difference in meaning between these two sentences?

10% of the students ate bread for breakfast.
10 students ate bread for breakfast.

What is the difference between a percentage and a number?

7 Choose ten of the words used in the section, 'The language of data analysis and comment' and use them in sentences.

Appropriate register

When you write your answer you should be careful to use the appropriate register. You are writing a report for a 'university lecturer'. The language should be formal and respectful, and is unlikely to include many personal pronouns (I, you, we). It should not include unnecessary words and phrases.

All these informal sentences can be rewritten as *The table shows ...*

> *As you can see from the table, ...*
> *As we know from the table ...*
> *I can see in the table that ...*
> *We can tell from the table ...*

Guided practice

Academic Writing Task 1: Practice 1

The table below shows the number of computer terminals available to students in different faculties of a university.

Write a report for a university lecturer describing the information shown below.

You should write at least 150 words.

Faculty	Computer terminals	Number of students	Average number of students using one computer terminal
Agriculture	17	240	14
Arts	35	730	21
Education	25	890	36
Engineering	41	317	8
Law	43	473	11
Science	74	241	3
TOTAL	235	2891	12

First, prepare your answer.

> Look at the table. What is the first thing that you notice?
> Can you make any comparisons? What are they?
> Which tense will you use? Why?

Write three paragraphs describing the number of computer terminals available to students in different faculties at the university.

> Paragraph 1: Describe the table. What does it say? Do NOT re-write the question.

> Paragraph 2: Compare the availability of computer terminals for groups which are obviously different.

> Paragraph 3: Write a brief conclusion.

Remember: it is useful to relate information to the average for the group.

Academic Writing Task 1: Practice 2

Use the vocabulary you have learned to describe the information in the graph about seasonal water consumption in four towns.

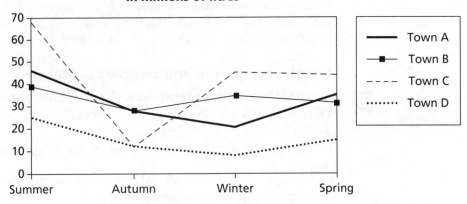

Seasonal water consumption in millions of litres

Use these strategies to assist you to write your description:

- Identify the main features of the graph.
- Decide how you will organize the information.
- Vary the words you use.
- Time your writing and do not take more than 20 minutes.

Varying the types of sentence used

Look again at the sample answers on the **Market Research Survey** on page 101, and note the different sentence types used.

8 Look at this part of an essay on the **Market Research Survey** and say what is wrong with it.

This table shows that different age groups like going to different places in Llorente. Some places are popular with all age groups.

The 21–30-year-olds liked to go to beaches more than the 51 plus age group. The 21–30-year-olds liked to go to night clubs more than the 51 plus age group. The 21–30-year-olds liked to go to discotheques more than the 51 plus age group. The 21–30-year-olds liked to go to shopping centres and so did all the other age groups. The 21–30-year-olds liked to go to cinemas/theatres and so did all the other age groups. The 21–30-year-olds did not like to go to museums. The 21–30-year-olds did not like to go to zoos.

The 31–40-year-olds ...

You can add variety to your writing by:

- using a mixture of simple sentences, compound sentences and complex sentences (see below)
- using sentences which are different in length
- using some sentences which do not follow the subject - verb - complement pattern
- using the passive voice in a few sentences
- varying the vocabulary you use.

Rewrite the following passage to make it more interesting.

Nowadays most people travel by air if they have to travel a long distance. This was not always so. If people had to go on a long overseas trip fifty years ago they went by boat. The trip took a long time and was often quite rough and uncomfortable. First class passengers were far more comfortable than second class passengers. Second class passengers were not allowed into first class areas. Many people preferred to travel on a ship which only had one class. Even thirty years ago many people were travelling by sea. Air travel has only become popular in the last twenty years. This is because it is safe, convenient and quick.

Simple, compound and complex sentences

9 Look at these **simple sentences.** What are the underlined words? Why is each sentence a simple sentence?
a) Many tourists <u>visit</u> Canada.
b) Canada <u>offers</u> tourists many interesting sights and experiences.

c) Hong Kong <u>has</u> no natural resources except people.
d) Hong Kong <u>is</u> a prosperous city.

e) Japan <u>imports</u> raw materials from Australia.
f) Australia <u>imports</u> manufactured goods from Japan.

g) I <u>heard</u> about his promotion.
h) I <u>congratulated</u> him.

i) This summer, my friend is <u>coming</u> to California.
j) She <u>might stay</u> for three months.

Look at these **compound sentences.** Why is each sentence a compound sentence? What is the classification of the words *because, but, and, when,* and *while?* What other words can you use to make compound sentences?

a) Many tourists <u>visit</u> Canada because it <u>offers</u> them many interesting sights and experiences.

b) Hong Kong <u>has</u> no natural resources except people but it <u>is</u> a prosperous city.

c) Japan <u>imports</u> raw materials from Australia while Australia <u>imports</u> manufactured goods from Japan.

d) When I <u>heard</u> about his promotion, I <u>congratulated</u> him.

e) This summer, my friend <u>is coming</u> to California and she <u>might stay</u> for three months.

Write a rule which describes the difference between a simple and a compound sentence.

Look at the following examples of simple sentences. Why are these sentences interesting to read?

f) With its offer of many interesting sights and experiences, Canada <u>attracts</u> many tourists.

g) Despite having no natural resources except people, Hong Kong <u>is</u> a prosperous city.

h) Hearing about his promotion, I <u>congratulated</u> him.

i) This summer, my friend <u>is coming</u> to California for perhaps a three months' stay.

A **complex sentence** consists of one main clause and one or more dependent clauses. For example, in the sentence below, *The artist ... comes from India* is the main clause, and *who won the prize* is the dependent or subordinate clause.

The artist who won the prize comes from India.

Identify the main and dependent clauses in sentences a) and b).

a) My favourite teacher, who is an expert in Arabic literature, has left the country.

b) The bank clerk who usually works here has retired.

Which of the following sentences are simple, compound or complex?

c) The Malaysians have built the tallest building in the world in Kuala Lumpur.

d) Although my uncle was very rich, he lived a simple life.

e) London and Edinburgh are extremely interesting capital cities in Britain.

f) Bangkok, with its many canals, was once called 'the Venice of the East'.

g) The river Danube runs through Budapest and divides the city in two.

h) Realizing the importance of public transport, the government introduced more train and bus services.

i) The tide is high when the moon is full.

j) Although Australia is a big country, it has a small population.

k) I sold my car since I didn't need it.

l) The people in Chicago are surprised that the tallest building in the world is in Kuala Lumpur.

Paragraphing

10 The graphs below show the number of schools, enrolments and teachers for the years 1905 to 1985.

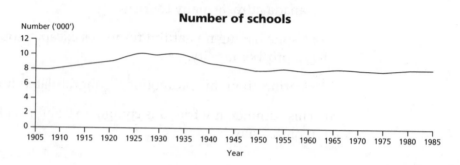

Number of schools

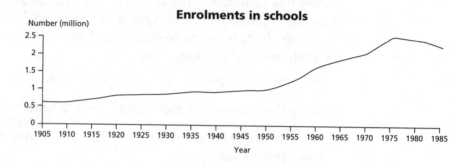

Enrolments in schools

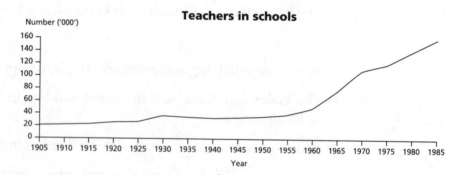

Teachers in schools

Sentences 1 to 8 below describe the information shown in the graphs, but not in any order. Rewrite the information taken from these graphs and jumbled sentences into a total of five paragraphs, including an introduction of one sentence and a conclusion.

How will you know what order to use?

1. Numbers fell slightly to 1945, rose gently to 40,000 in 1955 and then rose dramatically to 160,000 in 1985.

2. The graphs reveal that although the numbers of teachers and students rose, particularly between 1955 and 1975, the number of schools declined. After 1975 student numbers fell but the number of teachers continued to rise.

3. These graphs shows the relationship between the number of schools, enrolment of students, and teachers in schools between 1905 and 1985.

4. Numbers rose dramatically between 1945 and 1985, with more than 2.25 million students at school at the end of the 1970's.

5. Although there was a return to 8000 in 1965, this was not maintained and in 1985 there were again fewer than 8000 schools.

6. There were almost 8000 government schools in 1905, rising to 10,000 in 1924 and remaining around that figure until 1935 when a steady decline began, falling to less than 8000 schools in 1955.

7. Enrolments climbed steadily from more than half a million students in 1905 to almost a million in 1945.

8. Teacher numbers climbed steadily from fewer than 20,000 in 1905 to almost 40,000 in 1930.

Open practice

Academic Writing Task 1: Practice 3
You should spend about 20 minutes on this task.

The graph below shows the writing technology used by undergraduate students to prepare assignments at a university in 1970, 1982 and 1994.

Write a report for a university lecturer describing the information shown below.

You should write at least 150 words.

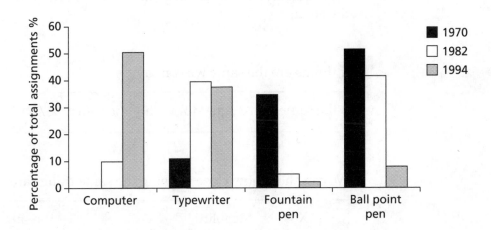

Checklist:
- Have I answered the question?
    What are the topic words?
    What are the task words?
- Have I organized my information?
- Is my work arranged in paragraphs?
- Have I used a variety of sentence types?
- Have I written in the correct register?
- Is my vocabulary appropriate and interesting?
- Is my spelling accurate?

Comparing and contrasting

11 Choose one of these five chairs, and describe it to your partner. Do not name the chair. Your partner must tell you as soon as he/she knows which chair you are describing.

What did you say to make sure your partner would recognize the chair quickly? Try to identify the most important differences between the chairs.

If things are the same we can say:

the same as	equal to/with	identical to/with

We can show how close to being the same things are:

X is	absolutely	the same as Y.
	just, exactly, precisely	
	almost, nearly, practically	
	more or less	
	about	
	not quite	

12 Arrange the phrases in the box below to show by what degree X is greater than Y. Start from the biggest difference and work to the smallest. In some cases two phrases may be almost the same.

hardly	a great deal	very much	infinitely
barely	a lot	a little	many times
much	slightly	not very much	far
scarcely			

Example:

X is ——— *infinitely*

barely

→ **greater than Y.**

Choose two chairs from those illustrated and <u>compare</u> them (say what they have in common).

Choose two chairs and <u>contrast</u> them (say what makes them different).

Distinguishing features

When something is being described to contrast it with another object we talk about the important features which make the two objects distinct.

13 Describe the differences between a mug and a tumbler.

What is the biggest difference?

What do they have in common?

> *Example:* A mug is a drinking vessel with a handle on the side, while a tumbler has no handle. The handle on the mug makes it easy to hold it when it is full of hot fluid. People usually put cold drinks in a tumbler, but it is possible to drink hot tea from a tumbler if you hold it by the bottom and the top.
>
> A mug is usually made of pottery or china, while a tumbler is usually made of glass.

Describe the differences between a mug and a cup.

Do not try to give detailed information about every aspect of the graph.

Be careful to vary the types of sentence you use.

Academic Writing Task 1: Practice 4

You should spend about 20 minutes on this task.

Write a description comparing the information contained in the pie charts below.

You should write at least 150 words.

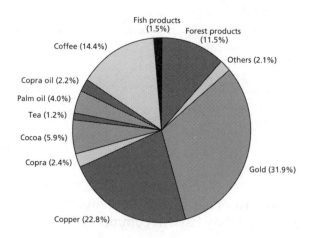

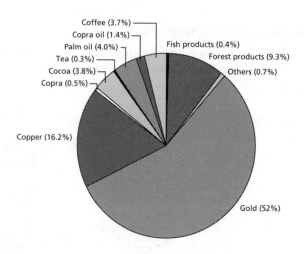

Figure 1: Composition of exports of Papua New Guinea, 1982 (top) and 1991 (below).

Source: Te'o Ian Fairbairn, Chapter 1, 'Recent Developments', *The Papua New Guinea Economy*, AIDAB, Commonwealth of Australia, 1993.

Checklist:

- Have I answered the question?
    - What are the topic words?
    - What are the task words?
- Have I organized my information?
- Is my work arranged in paragraphs?
- Have I used a variety of sentence types?
- Is my vocabulary appropriate and interesting?
- Is my spelling accurate?

Academic Writing Task 1: Practice 5

You should spend about 20 minutes on this task.

Write a report comparing the information in these two graphs.

You should write at least 150 words.

Median house prices in four cities A, B, C and D (000's)

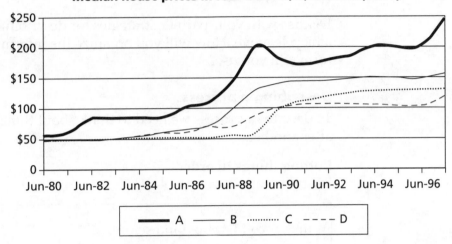

Median unit prices in four cities A, B, C and D (000's)

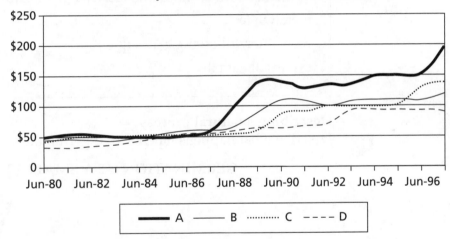

Source: 'REI (JLW research)', *Australian Property Digest* # 38, Third Edition 1997, p. 34.

Glossary: A *unit* is a flat or apartment.

Checklist:

- Have I answered the question?
  What are the topic words?
  What are the task words?
- Have I organized my information?
- Is my work arranged in paragraphs?
- Have I used a variety of sentence types?
- Have I written in the correct register?
- Is my vocabulary appropriate and interesting?
- Is my spelling accurate?

Describing objects with moving parts

14 Draw a bicycle.

When you were drawing the bicycle what parts did you draw first? Do you think they were the most important parts of the bicycle? Will the way you drew influence the way you write about the bicycle?

Describe how you make a bicycle move.

Discuss with your partner strategies for describing how you make a bicycle move. How will you organize the information? What verb form will you use?

Describing a process

To describe a process we need to think about things happening one after another.

Putting things in order
Useful vocabulary:

first, second, third, (and so on)

before, prior to

at the same time, simultaneously, as, while, during, meanwhile

then, after, following, subsequently

eventually, finally

Describing a natural process

15 Describe what happens when a seed germinates.

GERMINATION OF A SMALL PLANT

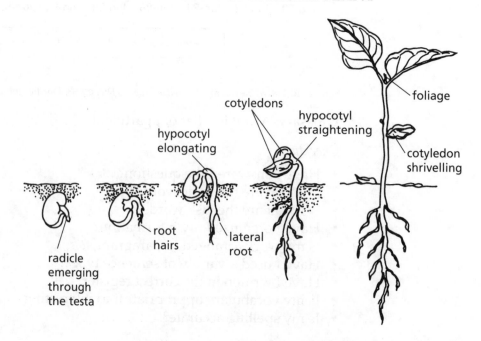

cotyledons

hypocotyl straightening

foliage

hypocotyl elongating

cotyledon shrivelling

root hairs

lateral root

radicle emerging through the testa

We do not have to use the passive when describing a natural process.

How did you cope with the specialist vocabulary?

Homework: Find out about the rainfall cycle.

Next class: Work in groups and describe the rainfall cycle. Put your description on an OHT for discussion in class.

Useful vocabulary:

rain	evaporate	evaporation	condense
vapour	precipitate	oceans	lakes
sunshine	clouds	storms	altitude
cold air			

Describing a mechanical process

16 Which of these 2 drawings, A or B, is described here? Be prepared to say why.

A

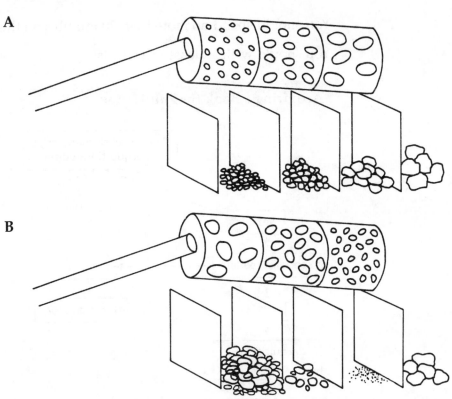

B

A Simple Method of Sorting Stones According to Size

The stones are carried up a conveyor belt and enter a revolving cylinder which is about three metres (ten feet) above the ground. The cylinder rotates in a clockwise direction and slopes at 7° away from the conveyor end.

The stones enter the first part of the cylinder which has the smallest holes, and the small stones fall to the ground below. The remaining stones enter the next part of the cylinder under gravity. This section has medium-sized holes, and the medium-sized stones fall to the ground. The largest stones then pass into the third part of the cylinder and either fall through large holes or, if they are too big, are propelled to the open end of the cylinder where they fall out of the machine and onto the ground. At this final stage the operator must decide whether to break the stones and put them back through the process or to use them in their current state.

Describing a process which is not mechanical

17 What is required in the question below? How should you answer it? Talk to your partner.

The diagram below shows what happens when a manuscript is delivered to an educational publisher.

Using the information in the diagram, describe how the manuscript moves through the publishing house, and the people who are involved.

You should spend no more than 20 minutes on this task.

You should write at least 150 words.

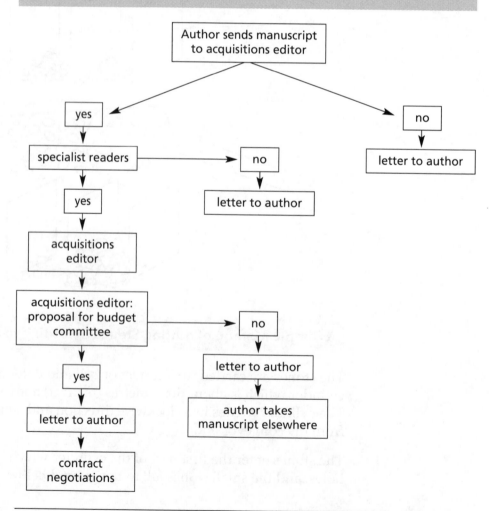

Acquiring a Book for Publication

Vocabulary of time and direction

Some of the words below relate to time, others to position or direction. Some relate to both time and direction.

18 Identify the words which relate to time.

up	over	before	since	north
vertical	across	centre	middle	outside
laterally	after	diagonally	prior to	horizontal
later	upward	downward	eastward	sideways

Choose ten of the words above and use them in sentences.

When you are reading diagrams or cartoons in English, from which direction should you read?

left to right	right to left
bottom to the top	top to the bottom.

Indicating relationships of cause and effect

We use the passive in describing cause and effect to distance ourselves from the process.

Compare:

Scissors are used for cutting.   (no personal pronoun, passive)
You use scissors to cut fabric or paper. (personal pronoun, active)

Useful vocabulary:

thus	as a result	and so	thereby

19 Describe how a pair of scissors works.

Useful vocabulary:

hinge	blade	finger holes
cutting edge	screw	

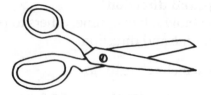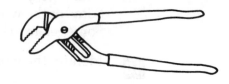

Compare and contrast a pair of scissors with a pair of pliers.

Useful vocabulary:

handles	serrated	grip

How will you organize the information?

Write the comparison.

Open practice

Academic Writing Task 1: Practice 6
You should spend about 20 minutes on this task.

> *Use the information in the diagram below to explain how a fire extinguisher works.*

You should write at least 150 words.

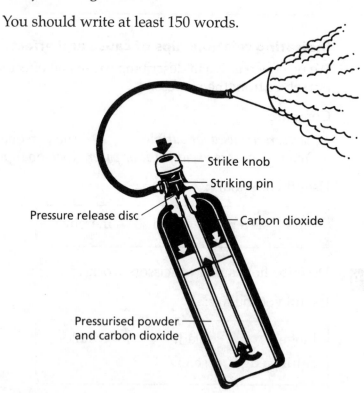

Checklist:

Look back over your work and check for:
* verb/noun agreements
* use of the passive
* use of devices which indicate cause and effect
* use of devices which indicate the sequence of events
* correct paragraphing.

Academic Writing Task 1: Practice 7

First, analyse the task below, then write your answer.

What are the topic words in the question?

What are the task words?

What are the dimensions of the diagram?

What are the striking features/general trends?

After you have written your answer, look at the Sample answer that follows.

You should spend about 20 minutes on this task.

The diagram below shows how sewage passes through a sewage treatment unit.

Write a description of the process shown in the diagram.

You should write at least 150 words.

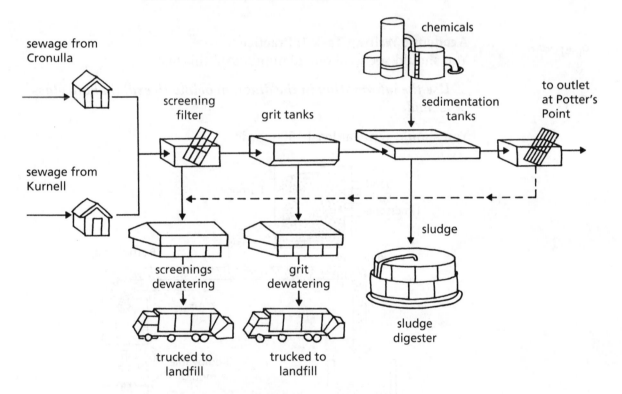

Sample answer:

The sewage passes through a number of treatment procedures after it enters the sewage treatment plant.

Firstly, sewage from Cronulla and Kurnell passes through screens which separate large objects or debris from the water. These screenings are then transferred to tanks where the water is removed, and are taken by truck to a landfill site.

Sewage that has passed through the first screen enters the grit tanks where grit, or fine particles, is removed. The grit is then taken to be dewatered and subsequently trucked to a landfill site. Meanwhile, the sewage still in treatment flows from the grit tanks to sedimentation tanks in which chemicals are added to assist the separation of sludge from waste water. The sludge is then transferred to a sludge digester.

From the sedimentation tanks the waste water continues through fine screens which filter out any remaining solids. The solids are sent back to the screenings dewatering unit and also trucked to a landfill site. The treated waste water is released at Potter's Point.

This completes the process of sewage treatment at Cronulla.

178 words

Go through the sample answer.
Identify passive verbs.
Identify the words and phrases which express the order in which things occur.
Take note of the conclusion.

How do the paragraphs relate to each other?

What were the best things about the answer?

Open practice

Academic Writing Task 1: Practice 8
You should spend about 20 minutes on this task.

Use the information in the diagram below to explain how glass is made.

You should write at least 150 words.

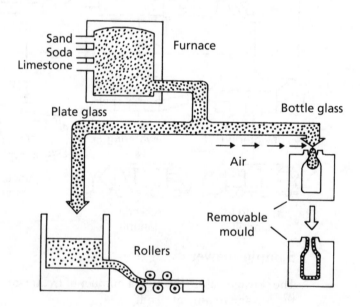

How will you order the information?

Checklist:

When you have finished, look back over your work and check for:
- verb/noun agreements
- use of the passive
- use of devices which indicate cause and effect
- use of devices which indicate the sequence of events
- correct paragraphing
- a concluding paragraph.

Introduction to General Training Writing Task 1

General Training Writing Task 1 measures the candidate's ability to respond to a given problem with a letter requesting information or explaining a situation. You are expected to be able to:

- engage in personal correspondence
- seek and provide general factual information
- express needs, wants, likes and dislikes
- express opinions (views, complaints etc.).

(The IELTS Handbook, 1998, p. 13)

Candidates should spend no more than 20 minutes on Task 1, and should write at least 150 words.

The topic in Task 1 will be of general interest. This means candidates will be asked to respond to the sort of things which happen to people every day. They may have to write a letter asking for help with something, or complaining about bad goods or unsatisfactory service.

Writing a letter

Look at this example of a letter task to be written for General Training Writing Task 1.

> *You belong to a group which uses a hall near your home to meet once a month. You have been using the hall for the last three years. You have just heard that the rent will double next month. Your group cannot possibly afford such a large increase.*
>
> *Write to the manager of the hall and explain your problem.*

20 Before writing your answer, follow steps 1 to 5.

1. Identify who you are writing to:
   - somebody of equal status to yourself, like a friend?
   - an older or more important person?
   - somebody you know only through business?

   This will determine the tone of the letter.

2. Identify the overall subject or subjects of your letter:
   - a complaint?
   - praise?
   - a request for information?
   - an expression of needs or wants?
   - an expression of an opinion, likes and dislikes?

3. Identify the main point or points you want to make:
   - think of details to support the main point of the letter.

4. Relate the letter to any information given in the writing task:
   - look for clues in the wording of the task.

5. Think of a suitable ending to the letter.

   After working through steps 1 to 5, write the letter to the manager of the hall in the task above.

Personal letters

These are the general rules for writing letters. A candidate in the IELTS test will not be penalized for deviating from these rules, and the salutation is always given in the rubric which says 'Begin your letter: *Dear Sir/Madam*' or another appropriate salutation.

The letter you are asked to write may be a personal letter. What is a personal letter?

A personal letter is a letter to someone you know relatively well. The letter should be informal in tone and register.

A letter usually begins with a greeting or salutation, like *Dear...* You may begin and end a personal letter with any salutation you think is appropriate to the person receiving it. It could begin *Dear..., Dearest..., My Darling...*

It could end *Love, Best wishes, Yours sincerely, Affectionately, Hugs and kisses, Lots of love, With love...*

21 Discuss appropriate salutations with your teacher. How would you begin and end letters to these people?

- your grandfather
- an ex-boyfriend or ex-girlfriend
- your aunt
- your favourite former school teacher.

This is the way we set out a letter to somebody we know personally, or to a friend:

The writer's address
The date

The salutation: *Dear* ....

A greeting, for example: *I hope you are well*, and the orientation of the letter, indicating what the letter is about.

The body of the letter, recounting the news.

The end of the letter.

The signature.

A personal letter often ends with good wishes to the reader, or a polite request.

Example of a personal letter

You do not need to be precise about the date of a personal letter ——

Opening salutation: we know who Sally is, so we do not use titles in personal letters

Greeting

Orientation of the letter: to talk about the writer's life in London

The body of the letter: giving the writer's news and recounting events

Conclusion of the letter ——

Closing salutation ——

Signature ——

---

55 Bargery Road
London SE6 2LJ

Sunday, June 30

Dear Sally,

How are you? I'm very well, and settling happily into life in London.

The family I am staying with have been very kind, although their little boy can be a problem. He's only ten, but he's very curious and he asks all kinds of strange questions. However, the family lets me have my friends come to visit, and they certainly try to be sure I'm not lonely.

They took me to Greenwich at the weekend. It was quite cold, but I enjoyed it, partly because we went with another family who also have home stay students. I'm going to meet them again at a dance party next week.

Please write to me. I'd love to hear what's happening to all our schoolmates.

With love

Jenny

---

22 Write a letter to a friend, telling them about the way you spend your day, or about a visit you have just made.

Checklist:

When you have finished, check your work.

- Are the salutations appropriate?
- Is the tone of the letter appropriate?
- How can we tell it's a letter to a friend?
- Are the subject/verb agreements correct?

Business letters

This is the way a business letter is set out:

The writer's address
The date

The salutation:

- The recipient's name (if known)
- The recipient's title or position in the company
- The company name
- The company address

The salutation: *Dear* ....

The orientation of the letter.

The body of the letter, giving information.

The end of the letter.

The closing salutation.

The signature.

The printed name and title of the person who is signing the letter.

Example of a business letter

You need to be precise about the date of a business letter ————

Opening salutation: the recipient's name, title, company name, company address ————

Salutation ————

Orientation of the letter: to thank the recipient for something

The body of the letter: a list of the reasons why the writer wants to thank the reader

Conclusion of the letter ————

Closing salutation ————

Signature ————

Printed name and title ————

Language Teaching Centre
10 Robert Street
Sydney NSW 2000

30/06/1999

Robert Jones
Manager
Home Sense Shops
99 Johnson Street
Glebe 2037

Dear Mr Jones,

I am writing to thank you for permitting our students to visit your company's factory.

The students thoroughly enjoyed their visit, and learned a great deal. They particularly enjoyed seeing the new machines working.

It is extremely valuable for students to make these visits, and my students are very keen to read more about what they have seen.

Thank you again. We really appreciate your kindness.

Yours sincerely

Mary Cater

Mary Cater
Senior Teacher

Ending a business letter
Many business letters end with a very brief summary of what has been written earlier in the letter, or an indication of the response the writer hopes the reader will make. There should be no new information in the last paragraph. For example, look at the conclusion of the letter from Mary Cater to Robert Jones above.

23 How would you end the letter below?

Dear Principal,

I am writing to ask you if there is a place at your school for my son, Andrew Chen.

Andrew is in Year 9 at his school. He is interested in Science subjects, so we are keen to find a school with good science laboratories and teachers. I am enclosing a copy of Andrew's school report for last year, which shows his good marks in science and his love of sport, particularly football. He was captain of the under 15's team which plays near our house. He is also interested in music, and is part of the school orchestra. Do you have an orchestra at your school?

We hope to arrive at our new home in January next year, and we are looking for a house in your area. We will be very happy to provide you with more information about Andrew, and we are looking forward to receiving information about your school.

Choose one of these endings, and be ready to explain why you chose it.

a) I do hope you can find room at your school for a boy with Andrew's interests.

b) Andrew would like to go to your school.

c) Although Andrew is fifteen he is extremely tall and mature for his age.

Paragraphs

24 Divide this letter into three paragraphs.

- The first paragraph says why the writer is writing the letter.
- The second paragraph gives details of the writer's feelings.
- The third paragraph closes the letter.

Be ready to say why you placed the breaks where you did.

Dear Miss Brown,

My son tells me that you are in charge of music at his school. I am writing to tell you how much I enjoyed listening to the music the school orchestra played at the concert last Friday night. It is very good for children to understand and be sensitive to music, and your students played as though they really did feel the music. I thought the young man playing the piano was very talented, and I expect he will be very successful. Once again, thank you for a most enjoyable evening.

Yours sincerely

Carlos Martinez

Register and letters

It is important to use the appropriate register. If the letter is to someone you do not know, the language should be respectful, and a little formal. It should not include unnecessary words and phrases.

25 Which of the characteristics below would more likely be found in a personal letter? Which would be found in a business letter?

familiarity	friendliness	precise information	respect

These are some endings for letters. Which ones are appropriate for personal letters? Which are appropriate for business letters? Some endings may be used in both types of letter.

Yours truly	Affectionately	Yours faithfully	Yours sincerely	With love

Which of these requests are suitable for the end of a letter?

Let me know now.
I look forward to your reply.
Please advise me as soon as you can.
I want an urgent reply.
I would appreciate an urgent reply.

Look at the business letter below. The underlined parts show two ways which have been used to say the same thing. Identify which of the underlined words are written in an inappropriate register. Be prepared to explain why you chose as you did.

Dear Manager of Hill Street Swimming Pool / Darling,

I went for a swim at your pool last week. Unfortunately I had <u>a shocker of a time / a very unpleasant experience</u> and I want to tell you about it.

When I came into the pool area there was a group of young men <u>playing / horsing around</u> on the lawn. They were <u>running like wild things / running very fast</u> and bumping into each other. After a while they began to run into the other people who were going to the pool. When I asked them to stop, one of them pushed me hard and I nearly fell over. I could not find <u>a solitary person / anyone</u> who worked at the swimming pool to help me, so I went home.

Please explain to me what you will do to make sure this does not happen again.

<u>Yours faithfully / Love</u>

Jan Andersen

GT Writing Task 1: Practice 1

You should spend no more than 20 minutes on this task.

> *You left a bag of equipment at the gym last night. The gym has closed down for a week, and you can't get in. Your bag contains some notes you need urgently, your driving licence and some important letters.*
>
> *Write to the manager to ask how you can reclaim your bag.*

You should write at least 150 words.

First, prepare your answer.

Who are you writing to? How well do you know them?

What is the subject of your letter?

What is/are the main point/points you want to make?

How can you relate the information in the letter to the task?

What is a suitable ending for the letter?

Write the letter.

You do **NOT** need to write your own address.

Begin your letter: *Dear Sir/Madam*

Skills for General Training Writing Task 1

Seeking and providing factual information

26 What is happening in these pictures? Talk to your partner. Then write a paragraph describing the picture. Say what is happening, and how the people feel.

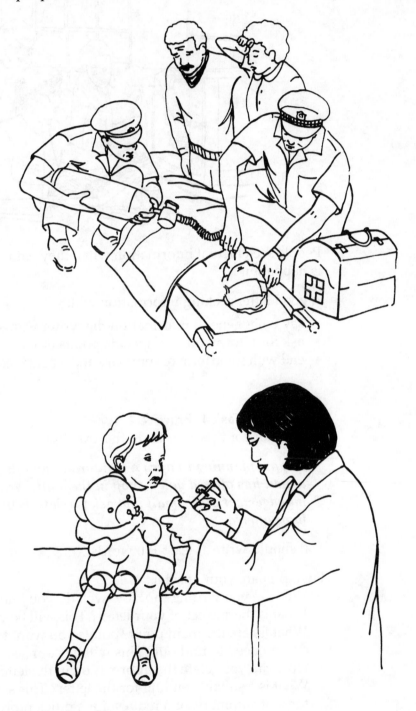

Practise this exercise with pictures from the newspaper. Choose a picture. Describe what is happening in it to your partner, but do not let your partner see the picture.

Work with your partner and ask as many questions as you can about the picture below. Write your questions down, and pass them to another pair of students who will answer them.

Here are some question words: why? how? when? where? who? what? how many?

People seek factual information when they want to find out what is happening.

A good letter seeking information will:

- say what general information the writer wants (first paragraph)
- ask for information on specific points (second paragraph)
- end with some form of summary and a polite request for a swift reply.

Guided practice

GT Writing Task 1: Practice 2

Work with your partner to do this exercise:

> *You are planning to open a restaurant, and the management of a mall has offered you a shop in the mall. Write a letter to the management of the mall and ask for details of the shop they have offered.*

You should write at least 150 words.

First, prepare your answer.
  Who are you writing to? How well do you know them?
  What is the subject of your letter? This will be your first paragraph.
  What is/are the main point/points you want to make? What do you need to find out? This will be your second paragraph.
  How can you relate the information in the letter to the task?
  What is a suitable ending for the letter? This should be some form of summary, or a request for a quick reply.

Write the letter.

You do **NOT** need to write your own address.

Begin your letter: *Dear Sir/Madam*

GT Writing Task 1: Practice 3

You should spend no more than 20 minutes on this task.

> *Your child wants to go on a school excursion to a town about twenty miles away. The children will sleep overnight at a youth hostel.*
>
> *Write to the Principal of the school and ask for details. You are concerned about the facilities at the youth hostel, how the children will be supervised, and whether they will need to bring their own bed linen.*

You should write at least 150 words.

You do NOT need to write your own address.

Begin your letter: *Dear Sir/Madam*

GT Writing Task 1: Practice 4

You should spend no more than 20 minutes on this task.

> *You are organising a class trip to a place of interest a day's drive from the school. You will stay in a youth hostel.*
>
> *Write to the manager of the youth hostel and ask about the conditions at the hostel. You are concerned about the food, entertainment, dress codes and the number of people who can be accommodated.*

You should write at least 150 words.

You do NOT need to write your own address.

Begin your letter: *Dear Sir/Madam*

Expressing needs, wants, likes and dislikes

27 These words all express needs, wants, likes and dislikes.
Which words express needs?
Which words express wants?
Which words express likes/dislikes?

hate	require	want	appreciate
must have	dislike	value	wish
wish for	enjoy	loathe	love
desire	detest	need	admire

What is the difference between something you want and something you need? Make a list of things you want and things you need.

You are going to buy a car. Write two paragraphs. In the first, say what characteristics you <u>need</u> in a car. In the second, say what you <u>want</u> the car to be like.

Write two paragraphs. In the first, write about something you like, and explain why you like it. In the second, write about something you dislike and say why you dislike it.

Expressing opinions and views

To express an opinion means to say what you think of something.

28 Talk to your partner. Choose a topic and give your opinion.

For example, what do you think about:

- something in today's news?
- the place you are sitting?
- the cost of living?

When we talk about somebody expressing their view it is simply a stronger opinion.

Choose something you feel strongly about, and write a paragraph about it.
  Say what you feel strongly about.
  Explain why you hold these views.

Making a complaint

People make a complaint when things have gone wrong and they want to change the situation.

A good letter of complaint will:

- explain what is wrong
- give details
- ask for help to fix the problem

OR

- ask what the person receiving the letter will do to fix the problem.

Guided practice

GT Writing Task 1: Practice 5
You should spend about 20 minutes on this task.

> *You have a neighbour who regularly cooks food on a very smoky outdoor barbecue. The smoke blows directly into your home. You have complained to your neighbour, but he refuses to clean the barbecue.*
>
> *Write to the local police and explain your problem.*

You should write at least 150 words.

You do **NOT** need to write your own address.

Begin your letter: *Dear Sir/Madam*

It is quite all right to make up some extra details.

Work with your partner and think of details you can add when you write the letter. For instance, how old is your neighbour? Does he mean to offend you? How often does he use the barbecue? How did you complain to him? What happened? and so on.

Instructions

We sometimes use the phrase *I want you to... / I would like you to...* when we are asking or telling somebody to do something.

Here are some ways of giving oral instructions:

> *Please shut the door.*
> *I want you to shut the door.*
> *I'd like you to shut the door.*

In written language we could say:

> *I want the door shut, or I want the refrigerator repaired, or I would like the refrigerator repaired.*

When we use the passive form it means that the person to whom we write does not have to fix the refrigerator personally. Another person can be sent to do the job.

Other polite forms to use in written English are:

> *Please arrange to have the refrigerator fixed.*
> *Please have the refrigerator fixed.*
> *Please fix the refrigerator.*

Open practice

GT Writing Task 1: Practice 6

You should spend no more than 20 minutes on this task.

> **You bought an iron at a local shop yesterday. When you got it home you found it does not heat properly, so you cannot use it. Furthermore, the water container in the iron leaks.**
>
> **Write a letter to the shop, and ask for another iron. You would prefer another brand. Explain your reasons.**

You should write at least 150 words.

You do **NOT** need to write your own address.

Begin your letter: *Dear Sir/Madam*

WRITING TASK 2

Introduction to Academic Writing Task 2

To complete Academic Writing Task 2 candidates should be able to:

- present the solution to a problem
- present and justify an opinion
- compare and contrast evidence, opinions and implications
- evaluate and challenge ideas, evidence or an argument.

(*The IELTS Handbook*, 1998, p. 12)

These tasks are often combined: for instance, candidates may need to compare and contrast evidence in order to justify an opinion.

Typically the instruction will read:

WRITING TASK 2

You should spend about 40 minutes on this task.

Present a written argument or case to an educated reader with no specialist knowledge of the following topic:

Concentrate on reading the question and answering it thoughtfully.

The phrase 'a written argument or case' indicates that candidates should explain their views and persuade the reader about the topic that has been given.

The phrase 'an educated reader with no specialist knowledge' indicates that the answer should be written clearly and should avoid jargon or informal language.

Writing Task 2 counts more than Writing Task 1 towards an IELTS band score. It may be a good idea to answer Task 2 first. However, candidates must complete both tasks so it is important to leave time to do Task 1. Whether it is written first or not, it is suggested that candidates should spend about 40 minutes on Writing Task 2.

To do well in Task 2, candidates should try to read as much as possible on subjects of general interest.

Topics

What sort of topics may candidates be asked to write about? *The IELTS Handbook* 1998 says that candidates will be asked to write about general issues. Candidates are not expected to have specialist knowledge.

Task 2 assesses candidates' ability to discuss an issue. The topics chosen will be about issues that every educated person is expected to know something about.

29

This exercise is designed to show you how wide the scope of topics can be.

Some common topics are written below. Try to think of other topics. Remember, there will be no specialist topics.

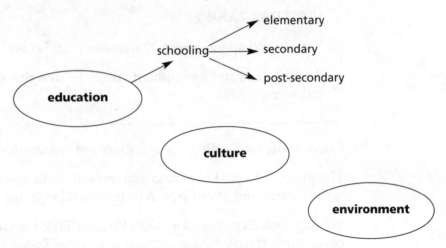

What other possible topics can you think of?

Audience

In Academic Writing Task 2 the instruction will probably be: 'Present a written argument or case to an educated reader with no specialist knowledge of the following topic'.

The audience is educated, but has no specialist knowledge. The writing should be clear, avoid jargon or technical terms, and it should be self-explanatory.

Candidates should be careful not to be too familiar with the audience. The writing should be formal and impersonal. It may help to pretend that the audience is made up of people whom the candidate respects, but does not know personally.

The instructions may conclude: 'You should use your own ideas, knowledge and experience and support your arguments with examples and relevant evidence'.

These ideas should be presented formally.

Introduction to General Training Writing Task 2

To complete General Training Writing Task 2 candidates should be able to:

- provide general factual information
- outline a problem and present a solution
- present and possibly justify an opinion, assessment or hypothesis
- present and possibly evaluate and challenge ideas, evidence and argument.

(*The IELTS Handbook*, 1998, p. 13)

These tasks are often combined: for instance, candidates may need to provide general factual information in order to justify an opinion.

Typically the instruction will read:

WRITING TASK 2

You should spend about 40 minutes on this task.

As part of a class assignment you have to write about the following topic:

Concentrate on reading the question and answering it thoughtfully.

The phrase 'As part of a class assignment' indicates that you should write clearly and avoid jargon or informal language.

Writing Task 2 counts more than Writing Task 1 towards an IELTS band score. It may be a good idea to answer Task 2 first. However, candidates must complete <u>both</u> tasks so it is important to leave time to do Task 1. Whether it is written first or not, it is suggested that candidates should spend about 40 minutes on Writing Task 2.

To do well in Task 2, candidates should try to read as much as possible on subjects of general interest.

Topics

What sort of topics do you think you may be asked to write about? *The IELTS Handbook* says that candidates will be asked to write about topics of general interest.

Suitable topic areas are:

- travel
- accommodation
- current affairs
- shops and services
- health and welfare
- occupational safety and health
- recreation
- social and physical environment.

30 Look at each of these topic areas and think of sub-topics. For instance, in the topic area **travel** you might be asked to write about the ways people travel (road, rail, air, sea), about problems with local transport, about travel in the future, etc.

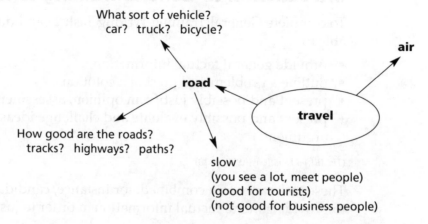

Look at the clusters of ideas around **road.** What ideas might cluster about **air** travel? Work with your partner or a group.

Now try a few more ideas.

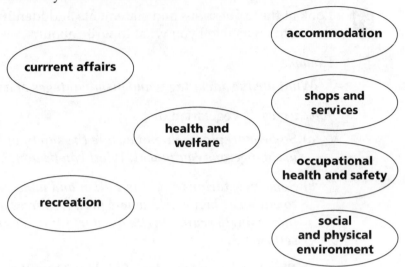

Audience

In Task 2 the instruction will probably be: 'As part of a class assignment you have to write about the following topic'.

The audience will be a teacher and other people in a class. It is a good idea to think of a group whom you do not know well, like a class at the beginning of a term, before you get to know anyone personally.

The writing should be formal and well reasoned, with supporting evidence for any statement made. It should be clear, should avoid jargon or technical terms, and it should be self-explanatory.

Essay writing skills

Writing Task 2 for both the Academic and General Training modules assesses your ability to discuss an issue. You should write an essay which is well organized, with a beginning, middle and end.

It is important to follow a four-stage procedure when writing essays. The procedure is:

1. Analysing the task (understanding the question, brainstorming)
2. Preparing a plan
3. Writing
4. Proof-reading and checking.

At first, you may find that this procedure takes longer than 40 minutes to complete. However, if you keep practising it, you will find that it actually speeds up the writing process. To do this, you need to understand what the question is really asking.

Step 1: Analysing the task

Topic and purpose of the question
First identify the **topic words**.

31 Look at these questions and statements and identify the topic, the words which tell you what to write about.

Example:

> *What are the advantages and disadvantages of a vegetarian diet?*

Topic words: 'a vegetarian diet'.

a) *Some workplaces do not ensure the safety of workers who use dangerous equipment. What can be done?*

b) *Some vegetarians say it is selfish and unnecessary for people to eat meat in a world where food resources are growing increasingly scarce. Write a report for an association which sells meat.*

c) *People who watch a lot of violent TV will find it influences their behaviour when they are angry or upset. Do you agree?*

d) *Some people say that smoking should be permitted in places where people gather to eat and to drink. Others find the smell of the smoke unpleasant, and fear it is bad for everybody's health. What is your opinion?*

e) *What are the features of an ideal television show for children below school age?*

f) *How would you ensure children watch only suitable material on television?*

g) *What do you consider to be the major achievement of the twentieth century?*

h) *The twentieth century has seen more development than any preceding century. What evidence can you offer to support this statement?*

i) *How can society reduce the problems of people with disabilities?*

j) *Many people find it very difficult to balance their responsibilities at home and in the workplace. What advice would you give?*

k) *Students have to absorb a great deal of information. Describe quick and efficient ways to do this.*

l) *It is the responsibility of a government to protect its citizens from natural disasters. How far do you agree?*

Task words

The topic words tell you what to write about. In the first question, 'What are the advantages and disadvantages of a vegetarian diet?' the topic is 'a vegetarian diet'. The words which tell you <u>how</u> to write about the topic are 'the advantages and disadvantages'. These words are the task words which tell you how to do the task.

Look at the questions and statements a)-l) above and identify the task words which tell you how to answer.

Brainstorming

Choose one of the questions a)-l) above and work with your partner to write as many ideas as you can, in any order, that might be relevant to answer the question.

Step 2: Preparing a plan

Choose one of the questions a)-l) above and work with other students to write an outline you can share with the class. If possible, use an overhead transparency (OHT). Use the outline of the typical structure of an essay on the next page to help you.

When you have written your outline, show it to another group or to the class.

Step 3: Writing

Write an answer to one of the essay questions a)-l) above. (This should be done individually. You may use the plan worked out with the group.)

Step 4: Proof-reading and checking

Exchange your essay with another student, or check it yourself. If you are working by yourself, try to let some time elapse between writing the essay and checking it.

Structure of an essay

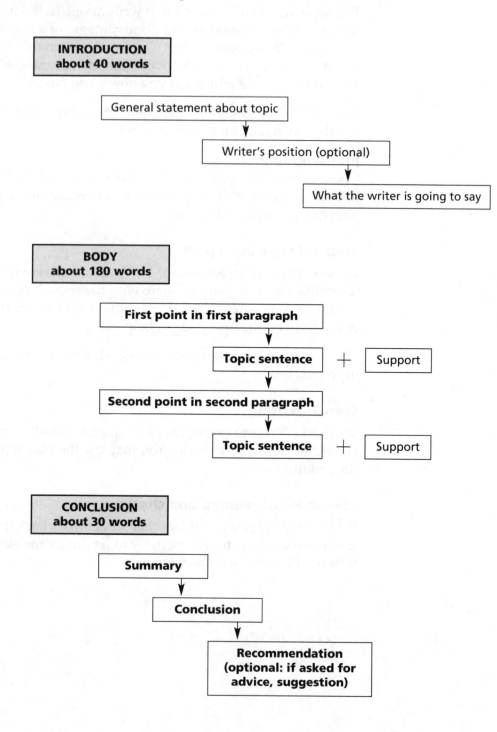

INTRODUCTION
about 40 words

General statement about topic

Writer's position (optional)

What the writer is going to say

BODY
about 180 words

First point in first paragraph

Topic sentence + Support

Second point in second paragraph

Topic sentence + Support

CONCLUSION
about 30 words

Summary

Conclusion

Recommendation
(optional: if asked for
advice, suggestion)

Introduction

The introduction:

- gives a general statement about the topic
- may state the writer's position if the writer is only taking one side in the discussion
- gives an indication of what the writer plans to say.

The general statement says what the controlling idea of the essay will be. The controlling idea is the central idea of the essay.

The writer's position is important in essays where an opinion is sought or a suggestion is asked for.

Students should read the question carefully and use it to start the essay, but they should not simply copy the question.

Look at the example of how the information in a question can be used to start the essay.

Example:

> **Many businesses find it very difficult to assign enough time and resources to research and development. What could a government do to encourage more company spending in this area?**

Topic:
'resources' and 'research and development'.

Task words:
'government ... do to encourage company spending'.

The writer's position:
The writer will make suggestions

General statement:
Research and development is expensive; companies try to avoid spending on it.

What the writer plans to say:
Governments could: offer tax advantages and research grants to companies. These incentives would help to increase employment and creativity.

The introduction will thus read:
'Research and development is very expensive, so companies often try to avoid spending in this area. Governments could encourage work in research and development by offering tax advantages and research grants to companies. These incentives would help to increase employment and creativity.'

32 How can you use the information in this question to start the essay? Work in small groups and write the answers on an OHT where possible.

> *Many people now have personal computers and the use of electronic services such as the Internet is becoming more widespread. Some parents are concerned about children using the Internet to gamble or buy goods on credit.*
>
> *How can access to electronic services be controlled?*

Use these strategies to help you:
- Look for the topic and task words.
- Formulate a general statement.
- Decide the writer's position.
- Formulate what the writer plans to say.

Then, write the introduction.

Use the same method on this question.

> *Some companies say that if an employee wants to smoke they must leave the building and smoke outside. This takes time away from work, and the employers insist that this time be counted as break time.*
>
> *This may not be fair to the smoker who may have to wait a long time to get out of the building.*
>
> *How could this problem be resolved?*
>
> *Give reasons for your answer.*

The body of the essay

The body of the essay is where ideas introduced in the first paragraph are expressed more fully. The body of the essay will follow from what is said in the introduction.

The body should be divided into paragraphs. Each paragraph will consist of a topic sentence and supporting sentences.

The same topic can lead to many different and legitimate answers.

33 Think of a subject you know a lot about: the climate of your country, or a currency you know well.

Write down three things you know about the subject.
Expand one of those three statements into a topic sentence.
Write supporting sentences to go with the topic sentence.

You should now have a well-formed paragraph.

Choose one of the introductions you wrote to the essay questions in **Activity 32** above and write the body of the essay. Be sure the body builds on the introduction.

When you have finished, exchange your work with another student.

Look at the essay you have been given. If you feel the body follows what has been said in the introduction, write a conclusion. If you do not feel the body follows the introduction, speak to the writer.

Conclusion

The conclusion of the essay summarizes what has been said and comes to some sort of conclusion or result. No new information is added at this point.

34 Look at this essay and consider what the writer has said.

> *A balanced diet, or eating balanced meals, is the key to a healthy life. To what extent do you agree or disagree with this statement?*
>
> *Give reasons for your answer.*

Sample answer:

Although a balanced diet is important, there are other factors which contribute to a healthy life. People in some cultures do not eat a balanced diet, but use limited food sources. In addition, lack of stress could well be as important as diet.

One culture-related reason concerns environmental or climatic conditions. The Inuit, in the Arctic Circle, live in harsh surroundings and their major source of food for many months of the year is fish. Nutritionists in industrialized countries would not consider their diet balanced or even healthy, yet Inuit people have flourished on food from the sea for centuries. Another cultural reason is religion-based. Many Hindus are vegetarian because of their religion. Again, many dieticians claim that vegetarianism is unbalanced because humans need protein, especially from animals. Hindus, however, seem to be quite healthy, suffering no ill effects from the lack of animal protein.

The major reason for disagreeing with the balanced diet argument, however, is to do with stress. Even though people in the past did not always have a balanced diet, sometimes existing only on potatoes and bread, they lived healthy lives because there was little or no stress of the kind that afflicts urban residents today. Secondly, there is a large percentage of contemporary people who do their jobs, then relax in front of the TV, and quite often eat junk food, but seem healthy enough. They may be spared disease by their relatively stress-free lives.

240 words so far

Now, write a conclusion to this essay.

35 Choose another of the essay questions a)-l) on page 138 and work with other students to write an outline you can share with the class. If possible, use an overhead transparency (OHT). Then, write the essay you have planned.

Expressing certainty in academic writing

Academic writing rarely reflects absolute certainty. When students or lecturers are discussing difficult or abstract topics, there is always room for discussion. Think of the difference between the absolute statement, *the sky is blue*, and the real sky, which can be blue, black, grey, or even pink.

Useful language: these words are very useful for avoiding absolute statements.

To reduce the size of the group:

a few	some	many	most (countable items)
a little	some	much	most (non-countable items)

To reduce the number of times something occurs:

often	frequently
sometimes	occasionally

To say that something is possible:

may   might   can   could
It is possible that... It is probable that...
It is likely that... (a little stronger)
It is unlikely that...
perhaps   maybe
possibly   probably

You may wish to express doubt about something which, you feel, may or may not be true. These words are useful for expressing these doubts:

seems to	appears to
seems that	appears that

You may wish to express the idea of likelihood rather than certainty:

it is likely that...	it is (very) probable that...

36 Choose words and phrases to reduce the certainty of these statements. Compare your sentences with other people in the class. How does the meaning change?

a) Students find it very hard to settle down in a new country. Later they find it hard to settle down when they go home.

b) Young people are not ready to accept responsibility for the economic well-being of their country.

c) Parents should spend more time with their children.

d) Everyone should learn to cook.

e) Road accidents are the result of reckless driving.

Relationships of meaning

Linking words and phrases

37 Place the words and phrases in the box below in the correct part of the table.

also	although	as a consequence of	as well as
because of	despite	final	for example
furthermore	however	in the case of	now
recently	similarly	subsequently	such as
then	therefore	when	while and

more information is added	a cause and effect relationship is shown	time is indicated	general and particular statements are linked	information is compared or contrasted

Use words and phrases from the box to fill in the gaps in the passages below. Some words or phrases may not be needed, some may be used more than once. There may be more than one possible way to link the sentences.

Computer breakdown may be caused by a number of factors, _____(1)_____ the age of the hardware, human error, or a very recent invention of computer enthusiasts, the computer virus.

Viruses are usually introduced into an office computer system through infected floppy disks. These disks are often brought into an office by the staff, who may be copying office files. These are _____(2)_____ downloaded into their particular personal computer at home. Their personal computers may contain viruses which copy themselves on any new disk inserted into the machine. These machines often do not contain any anti-virus programs which would spot the virus and reject the disk immediately.

Computer viruses have become a threat to the integrity of data stored in personal computers _____(3)_____ large mainframes in corporate and government institutions.

The industry is fighting back; _____(4)_____ the prevalence of these viruses, many anti-viral programs have been developed and can be installed at low cost. Some of the more up-to-date programs will test a disk for a large number of virus types, _____(5)_____ others may not recognize the most recent viruses. It is an ongoing battle, for as fast as the technology to combat a virus is developed, a new virus is created.

The power of the computer is certainly worth defending. Computerized databases provide workers in an organization with the information they need, _____(6)_____ they need it. A good system can allow the free flow of information from one part of an organization to another, _____(7)_____ new information can be quickly assimilated and stored for possible use later.

Computerized personal information is often freely available to government agencies, banks and other institution. This availability has both a benefit and a downside. A good police database will increase the chances of a known criminal being caught by decreasing the clerical side of searching documents, and will _____(8)_____ increase the time police have available to search for and catch their suspects. There is, _____(9)_____, another hazard: this information may be wrong or out of date and lead to the wrong person being arrested. The introduction of a virus to the system might render it useless.

Computerized databases are invaluable in the field of medical health. In a hospital, _____(10)_____, a database for information on diseases, drugs, case studies, surgical procedures and other records will be invaluable to a doctor trying to diagnose many different cases. For the clerical staff, many accurate records can be updated quickly.

It is alarming, _____(11)_____, to consider the damage which might be done to a hospital database by a computer hacker. Such a person might gain entry to a database and then give or sell the information to people who have no right to see it.

So we can see that _____(12)_____ their power, computer systems are highly vulnerable.

Sequencing
Text can also be held together by the order in which things occur.

38 Identify the words which show the order in which things occur.

Public Holidays in Singapore, 1998

The first public holiday in Singapore in 1998 was New Year's Day, celebrated on the first of January. This was followed on January 28 by the Lunar New Year, often called Chinese New Year, and the day following it, the Second Day of New Year. The next holiday, Har Raya Puasa, occurred the next day, on January 30.

There were no more holidays until Hari Raya Haji, which fell on the second Wednesday in April, followed by Good Friday on April 10. Labour Day fell on Friday, May 1, and Vesak Day fell on Monday May 11.

August saw the National Day holiday on Monday August 10, giving the citizens of Singapore a long weekend. Two more holidays remained: Deepavali in October and Christmas Day in December.

What are the public holidays in your country? Write one to three paragraphs describing the order in which they occur.

Time management

39 Remember the four stages of writing an essay below. Talk to a partner or in a small group.

- Think about <u>how much of your 40 minutes</u> you should spend on each stage.
- Think about <u>what</u> you should do in each stage.

1. Analysing the task (understanding the question, brainstorming)
2. Preparing a plan
3. Writing
4. Proof-reading and checking.

Use the skills discussed above to plan and answer the following essay task.

> *Modern life is very stressful. People have to manage their time and other resources very carefully. How can they look after themselves when they are so busy?*

Talk with your partner, analyse the task and prepare a plan together. You may have 10 minutes.
Write the essay and proof-read your work. You may have 30 minutes.
After 40 minutes, exchange work with your partner.
Read your partner's essay. Discuss your essays using the checklist on page 156.

Different approaches in an essay

40 Look at the essay questions below.

Decide whether the question asks you to:

- provide general factual information
- examine cause and effect
- outline problems and give a solution
- give and justify an opinion
- agree/disagree with an argument
- evaluate/challenge ideas, evidence and argument
- compare and contrast evidence and ideas.

More than one of these approaches may be useful to answer each essay question.

> 1. *The rising road toll is due to three factors: vehicle roadworthiness, road conditions and human error. Do you agree?*
>
> 2. *In recent years there has been an increase in the number of people killed on the road. Traffic designers blame drivers for driving too fast and drivers say the roads are bad. Which group do you agree with?*

3. *The highways department blames the high road toll on poor vehicle maintenance. However, there are strict laws regarding vehicle maintenance and roadworthiness, and there are frequent inspections. The roads are very poor and badly maintained.*

4. *Write a report on the state of the roads in your country for a motorists' organization.*

5. *The high road toll is robbing our society of many people who could otherwise be leading useful and productive lives. How can society protect itself from these losses?*

Providing general information

In the test you are expected to provide general factual information.

This means you must be able to describe and explain a situation.

41 Write a paragraph saying why you are preparing for the IELTS examination.

Describe your situation and say why the IELTS test is important to you.

Exchange your paragraph with another member of the class. Read the paragraph and ask your partner questions.

Write the information again so that it includes the answers to your partner's questions. (You may need three or four paragraphs).

Useful language:

I am doing this because	this is because
this is the result of	I need to
I want to	I wish to
I would like to	I hope to

Examining cause and effect

It is important that you can clearly recognize and express cause and effect.

42 Use an OHT or the board and write down every word you can think of which relates to cause and effect. Copy the words your teacher agrees with.

Look at the cause and effect constructions in the table:

CAUSE AND EFFECT

Active voice

Cause		Effect
Drunken driving and excessive speed	cause are a cause of result in lead to	road accidents.
Vehicles are driven by drunken drivers, and at excessive speed.	As a result, Consequently, As a consequence, Therefore, So	accidents can occur.

* Note that when we use a passive construction to describe cause and effect, the effect is placed before the cause.

Passive voice

*Effect		Cause
Road accidents	are caused by are the result of are the consequence of	drunken driving and excessive speed.

Use the above structures to write sentences about:
- road accidents – slippery roads
- drunken driving – drivers losing control of their vehicles
- defective brakes – increase in vehicle stopping time

Outlining a problem and presenting a solution

To outline a problem and present a solution, you must:
- identify the problem
- describe it
- say how it can be solved.

43 Think of a problem; it may be your problem or somebody else's.

Write a paragraph saying what the problem is, and describing it. When you describe the problem you may also have to say what is causing the problem.

Exchange your paragraph with another member of the class.

Write a paragraph or two suggesting how your partner's problem could be solved.

Useful language:

The problem is	might be able to	it should be possible to
could	should	suggest perhaps

44 Look at the essay question below, and work through steps 1–4. (This work may be done individually or with a partner or group.)

A large number of deaths are caused by road accidents. Why do so many road accidents occur? Make recommendations that would help to reduce the number of road accidents.

Step 1: Analysing the task, brainstorming
Look for topic words: 'large number of deaths' ... 'road accidents'
Look for task words: 'why ... occur?', 'make recommendations ... help reduce ... road accidents'
What is the purpose of the essay? (What do you have to say about the topic?)
Check the audience: ('An educated reader with no specialist knowledge / a class assignment')

Step 2: Preparing a plan
Questions I should ask myself: What can be done? Do I know any examples?
Note down in any order as many possible causes of road accidents, and as many ways to stop them, as you can.
Do not organize these ideas until you have written as many as you can, then decide the order in which you will write up each point.

Step 3: Writing
Remind yourself: the answer must make recommendations which will help cut the road toll.

Step 4: Proof-reading and checking
Check for grammar, spelling, vocabulary.

Read this sample answer, and answer the questions below.

Sample answer:

Road accidents are responsible for the deaths of an ever-increasing number of people. Before solutions to this problem can be found it is necessary to examine the main causes of accidents: vehicle roadworthiness, road conditions and human error.

Many accidents are caused by inadequate vehicle maintenance, for example driving with defective brakes or bald tyres which increase the stopping time. Regular mechanical inspections would help reduce the number of unworthy vehicles on the road.

Road conditions also contribute to accidents. Heavy rain, fog or snow, can make roads slippery and accidents can occur. In addition, narrow, winding roads and road surfaces which are in a state of disrepair contribute to the number of road fatalities. A greater proportion of money needs to be designated to improving roads and providing clear road signs.

The third cause of accidents is driver error. Drunken driving and excessive speed are frequently the cause of drivers misjudging distance and losing control of their vehicles. Other examples are drivers failing to signal a turn and overtaking other cars without due care. Although these problems of human error are the most difficult to resolve, advertising campaigns have proved effective in educating drivers about road hazards. Furthermore, harsher penalties such as heavy fines and suspension of licences could be applied to discourage such dangerous behaviour.

In conclusion, although it is inevitable that some accidents will occur, there are ways to reduce their frequency. Governments need to put in place stricter vehicle tests and penalize careless drivers more severely. It is also necessary to allocate more money to maintaining and upgrading roads and educating drivers. By implementing these measures, the roads will be safer for everyone.

277 words

What is the controlling idea of the essay? Where is it expressed as a general statement?

What approach or approaches are used to answer the question?

Identify the topic sentence in each paragraph.

Giving and justifying an opinion

To present and possibly justify an opinion:

- state your opinion
- be sure you can support your opinion with relevant detail.

It is permissible to use personal pronouns because when you express an opinion you say what you, personally, think about something.

 Think of a topic you have a strong opinion about. People often have opinions about taxation, or children, or animals...

Write a paragraph saying what your opinion is.

Exchange your paragraph with another member of the class.

Ask questions about the opinions your partner has expressed, and answer your partner's questions about your opinions. Be ready to justify your opinion: have reasons for saying what you say.

Write your opinion again so that it includes the answers to your partner's questions. (You may need three or four paragraphs).

Useful language:

I think	I believe	I am sure that
it is my opinion that...		it seems to me that
it seems		it is evident that
it is obvious/clear that		obviously
clearly		evidently

The expression *it is obvious that* indicates a very strongly held opinion. It is essential that the supporting details be powerful and relevant if this expression is used.

46 Work with a partner or group. Discuss how you would answer this question.

> *Schools and libraries should ban computer games from their premises to stop students from wasting time. Do you regard this as a good idea?*

You do not need to agree about the topic, but you must be able to support your argument. The critical issue lies in <u>justifying</u> the opinion. Here is a recommended plan:

Introduction: Introduce the issue in the first paragraph. Do NOT re-write the question: paraphrase it. Give an opinion if you wish, or say why you are too uncertain to give an opinion.

Body: Write two paragraphs which give examples or arguments which support your statement in the first paragraph.

Conclusion: Reach a decision and give a final opinion in the last paragraph.

You will note that the body of the essay contains arguments and supporting evidence rather than opinions. Your opinion may be expressed in the first paragraph and must be expressed in the last paragraph.

Now, write the essay. Be careful to use impersonal, academic language.

Agreeing/disagreeing with an argument

Candidates are not expected to agree with any argument, and are at liberty to disagree.

Useful language:

although	however	but	agree
disagree	concur	argue for/argue against	

When a writer agrees or disagrees with a proposition it may be necessary to express opinions as part of that agreement or disagreement.

47 Look at the essay question and the sample answer below.

> *Many of the diseases which afflict people who do office jobs are the direct result of a sedentary lifestyle. Do you agree?*

Glossary: a sedentary lifestyle is one where people spend most of their time seated, for instance at computer terminals, and get little exercise as part of their daily work.

Sample answer:

Although it is true that a sedentary life is not good for people's health, it would be far-fetched to suggest that doing an office job is directly responsible for the diseases which afflict office workers.

A sedentary lifestyle may indeed lead to high blood pressure and heart attacks, but people often balance the hours they spend sitting at a desk by joining fitness clubs where they can exercise or play sport. These clubs encourage their members to watch their diet and to take part in physical activities: for instance, a fitness club may be affiliated with another sporting body like a rowing club. People who do not want to join these clubs will often take walks during their lunch hour, or even jog. The very fact that they do these things means that they have a sedentary job, but not a sedentary lifestyle.

One might ask, what are the diseases which afflict office workers which do not afflict other people? It is very hard to think of an illness which is peculiar to office workers. They are prone to the same diseases as everyone else, and are protected from many of the hazards which afflict other workers. Working at a desk is far safer than mining or being a professional racing car driver, and is more comfortable than either.

It seems to be fair to say that, although an office worker spends a lot of time sitting down, he or she does not have to have a sedentary lifestyle. I cannot agree that the office worker is doomed to disease simply because he or she is an office worker.

271 words

In the example the writer disagreed with the proposition that many of the diseases which afflict people who do office jobs are the direct result of a sedentary lifestyle.

Work with your group and think of ways you would agree that the sedentary lifestyle of the office worker leads to disease.

Write an essay which agrees with the proposition.

Evaluating ideas, evidence or argument

Evidence is something which proves an idea or supports a belief or an opinion. An argument is a reason given to support or disprove something.

Evaluating something is assessing its worth. If you evaluate an idea you decide if it is a good idea or not.

When you challenge an idea or evidence you question its value or truth.

It is very difficult to prove ideas right or wrong, so it is important to have reasons for what you say.

48 Look at the argument set out below.

In the late twentieth century, the proportion of the world's population living in cities has increased substantially. People have moved in ever-growing numbers from rural to urban areas.

As migration from rural areas to cities continues, it is inevitable that the infrastructure in these cities will collapse.

Write a paragraph considering the value of the statement: is it a reasonable thing to say? Why? Why not?

Exchange your paragraph with another member of the class, and discuss your answers.

When a writer evaluates ideas it may be necessary to express opinions as part of that evaluation. We can say that one idea is more dangerous or sensible or foolish than another, but we must be able to explain why.

The language of comparison and contrast studied on page 110 of Academic Writing Task 1 can be used for ideas.

Comparing and contrasting evidence or opinions

Once again, the candidate is free to express their ideas provided they can be justified. You are not obliged to agree with the proposition.

49 Work with your partner and prepare a plan for this essay question. Compare your plan with others.

Some people say domestic animals, like cats, should not be kept in cities. Others say that such companion animals are beneficial to the community.

Which attitude do you believe to be correct?

50 Read the following essay question and the two sample answers.

These two essays answer the same question but in different ways. Remember that there are usually many acceptable ways to answer a question.

There has been a huge increase in the size of cities. Many cities have grown in a haphazard way.

Why is careful planning important in the development of cities?

Sample answer 1:

In all aspects of life planning has a role to play. It is especially important in major projects such as developing cities. This essay will provide some reasons why careful planning is important in the development of cities.

Careful planning is important in the development of infrastructure. For example, all cities need efficient water delivery services and hygienic sewage disposal systems. Planning can ensure that when services are built they form an integrated, efficient system. As well, public transport infrastructure needs to be carefully planned to ensure it provides a useful alternative to private vehicles.

Careful planning is also important in building developments. In most cities, more and more homes and industrial areas are being built as populations increase. Without planning, the results of this building boom could be disastrous, leading to a situation which satisfies no-one. Furthermore, planning the building of homes and factories can also allow for better integration of old and new, thus retaining the original character of the city while accommodating increases in population.

Lifestyle issues also benefit from proper planning. The provision of parks, open spaces and sporting facilities enhances the quality of life of the inhabitants of cities. However, these recreation areas need to be planned, otherwise urban sprawl will leave no room for them. In addition, with careful planning a clean environment can be provided more easily.

To sum up, careful planning is important in the development of cities as it can provide efficient and effective infrastructure, lead to better building practices and contribute to the quality of life of the city's inhabitants. Consequently, planning should be a high priority in all areas of development in cities.

274 words

Sample answer 2:

In order to answer this question, it is necessary to examine the problems experienced by unplanned cities, and then show how careful planning could have prevented those problems. Cities like Bangkok and Jakarta present typical examples of problems due to lack of planning.

The results of this are apparent – severe traffic congestion, an increase in respiratory diseases, and deaths caused by traffic accidents. The growth of Bangkok has been rapid and huge, resulting in more motor cars than the road system can support. Careful planning may have forecast this growth and measures could have been taken such as road building and traffic control systems. Other measures could have been the provision of better public transport such as a light rail system to discourage car buying.

An increase in population is usually associated with high urban growth. Planners should consider housing projects to cater for the needs of this growing population, served with good transport links to areas of work and shopping.

Another result of urban growth is pressure on sewerage and water supply systems. If more sophisticated sewerage and water systems were built, future problems could be prevented. With increased growth comes waste disposal problems and consequent damage to outlying areas where waste is dumped, as well as polluted waterways. Planners need to consider waste treatment and disposal.

Lastly, the quality of life suffers when planning fails to consider the urban environment. Open spaces, gardens and parks need to be preserved or created in order to prevent overcrowding.

In conclusion, planning measures must consider the needs and desires of the urban population to ensure a healthy, comfortable, safe and fulfilling urban environment.

272 words

Which of these sample essays is a problem/solution treatment of the question?

Is the other sample essay also a legitimate answer to the question?

How does it treat the question?

Which essay do you think would be easier to write? Why?

Checklist for essay writing

Audience
- Who am I writing for?

Answering the question
- Does the essay answer the question?

Introduction
- Does the introduction state the issue?
- Does the introduction preview the main ideas of the essay?

Paragraphs in the body of the essay
- Are there good topic sentences?
- Are all the points in the supporting sentences relevant?
- Are all the points in the supporting sentences clearly written and easy to understand?
- Do they need further elaboration?
- Is the essay the right length (at least 250 words)?

Conclusion
Does the conclusion:
- signal the end of the essay?
- summarize the main points?
- provide an interesting final comment for the reader to think about?

Language
- Is the essay written in the appropriate register? Check the use of personal pronouns.
- Is the vocabulary interesting and appropriate?
- Are there any grammar mistakes which make the essay difficult to understand?
- Are linking words used to connect the paragraphs and sentences appropriately?
- Are there any spelling or punctuation mistakes?

Further practice in Writing Task 2

There is a list of essay topics below. Consult your teacher about which topic to choose.

You may write each essay as though it were a class assignment if you plan to take the General Training Writing module and as an argument or case for an educated reader with no specialist knowledge if you plan to take the Academic Writing module.

 Talk with your partner or group, analyse one of the writing tasks and prepare a plan together. Follow these steps and recommended times.
   You may have **10** minutes to analyse and plan.
   Write the essay. You may have **25** minutes.
   Proof-read your work. You may have **5** minutes.
   After **40** minutes, exchange work with your partner.
Compare your essay with others.

Remember, there is no single correct answer.

Essay topics

a) *Raising children is the most important thing an adult ever does. Do you agree?*

b) *Students can become very tired both emotionally and physically when they are preparing for an examination. How can they look after their health while they are studying?*

c) **It is very important that children should study hard at school. Time spent playing sport is time wasted. Do you agree?*

d) *When students are in large classes it is very hard for the teacher to give every student individual attention. What can educational authorities do about this?*

e) **Can computerised data collection on individuals be justified even though it endangers the rights of individuals?*

f) **In the late 20th century, many cities are being rapidly redeveloped. In this process, the needs of special interest groups, such as people with physical disabilities, are sometimes taken into account.*

   How can society improve conditions for people with physical disabilities?

g) *Sometimes it is very difficult to learn the way people do things in a new culture. What can we do to make life easier for newcomers?*

h) *Children below the age of sixteen should not be allowed in public places after midnight unless they are accompanied by an adult who is responsible for them.*

   How far do you agree with this suggestion?

i) **In the late twentieth century, the proportion of the world's population living in cities has increased substantially. People have moved in ever-growing numbers from rural to urban areas.*

   As migration from rural areas to cities continues, it is inevitable that the infrastructure in these cities will collapse.

   To what extent do you agree or disagree with this statement?

j) **The high road toll is robbing our society of many people who could otherwise be leading useful and productive lives. How can society protect itself from these losses?*

k) *All children should stay at school until they are eighteen years old.*

* Some topics are marked with an asterisk. These topics have sample answers so you can see how another person has answered the question. Please do not read a sample answer until you have completed your own essay.

Sample answers

It may be helpful to analyse how these sample answers have been written.

Consider:

- how well the essay answers the question
- the introduction
- the way the essay flows from the introduction to the body
- the paragraphs in the body of the essay
- topic sentences and supporting sentences
- the conclusion, and the way it follows from the body of the essay
- language used
- length
- the best part of the answer
- the worst part of the answer.

c) *It is very important that children should study hard at school. Time spent playing sport is time wasted. Do you agree?*

We could argue that children go to school to study so that they may become fully productive adults and good citizens. We should ask whether playing sport helps children to become better people. If so, sport is not a waste of time.

No sensible person will deny that it is important that students study hard. The school day is broken up so that students can attend classes in different subjects in order to learn what areas they are most likely to enjoy and succeed at in later life. It is very important that the schools offer a wide range of subjects to cater to all the students in their care. After all, the school is preparing the students for life and for the workforce.

However, it is also true that students need more than the knowledge of a subject. They need to know how to work in groups to achieve a mutual goal, how to work as a team. Where better to learn those skills than on the sports field? Any of the team sports involve coordination with other players, understanding and adopting a team mentality. These skills are too useful to be ignored.

Furthermore, it is important that people be healthy, and good health is not so easily achieved in a sedentary society. Sport gets students outside and gives them good reason to run about, thus countering hours spent sitting still.

So, although school studies are undeniably important, we should regard time spent playing sport as time well spent.

250 words

e) *Can computerised data collection on individuals be justified even though it endangers the rights of individuals?*

Data collection is a fact of modern life. Some argue that data collection is endangering the rights of individuals, though others see it as a useful tool which increases efficiency. This essay will discuss both sides of this issue.

Data collection can violate the right to privacy. When data about a person is collected and stored in a computer then it is open to misuse. For example, the information may be sold to unauthorised persons such as credit agencies or insurance companies. Furthermore, some computer users who have no right to see the data may be able to gain access.

A further problem with data stored on computer is accuracy. Information stored in a computer may be out of date, or simple wrong. This can seriously affect a person's rights if decisions are made on the basis of false information.

On the other hand, databases provide a very useful tool. Large databases which contain information on many individuals can enable more effective decisions to be made. Institutions such as government departments and police rely on data collection in order to operate efficiently, and hospitals use computerised records to help in their fight against disease.

Databases stored on computer can also be very efficient. Information can be rapidly updated or added, and retrieval of information is extremely fast. Moreover, data which has been collected in one area can be sent anywhere in the world almost instantly. This means that those who have legitimate access to this data can work very efficiently.

In summary, although it is possible that unauthorised access or incorrect information may endanger the rights of individuals, the benefits far outweigh these risks. Consequently data collection on individuals can be justified, although all possible measures should be taken to minimise the risks.

293 words

f) *In the late 20th century, many cities are being rapidly redeveloped. In this process, the needs of special interest groups, such as people with physical disabilities, are sometimes taken into account.*

How can society improve conditions for people with physical disabilities?

Disabled people living in our cities daily face challenging and potentially difficult situations which society must consider. This essay will offer suggestions as to how conditions may be improved for people with a physical disability.

One of the most important ways in which life can be improved for disabled people is the provision of financial support. Some disabled people may have difficulties due to the cost of special equipment or care which they require. The government could offer assistance through a range of measures including tax deductions for equipment such as wheelchairs, or loan assistance for major purchases. Even such small measures as concession passes for transport or entertainment would assist in improving life for the disabled.

The special needs of people with disabilities must be taken into account by the education system and appropriate services provided. For example, the visually impaired would benefit from access to computers which convert text to voice. The hearing impaired may need special tutors skilled in sign language. The goal, however, would be the integration of the disabled into the regular school system while maintaining these services.

Employment is a third factor which must be considered. In order that disabled people can be given equal opportunity to work and contribute to society in every possible field, the government could establish quotas for disabled workers in large companies. Moreover, financial incentives such as tax rebates could be offered to smaller companies who hire disabled workers.

Thus, conditions for the physically disabled can be improved in a number of ways including providing financial support, adequate educational services and equal employment opportunities. Through the pursuit of these goals, society can ensure that life for the disabled is rewarding and fulfilling.

283 words

i) *In the late twentieth century, the proportion of the world's population living in cities has increased substantially. People have moved in ever-growing numbers from rural to urban areas.*

As migration from rural areas to cities continues, it is inevitable that the infrastructure in these cities will collapse.

To what extent do you agree or disagree with this statement?

Cities act as magnets to many from rural areas. A consequence of this migration is the strain placed on infrastructure in the cities. This essay will discuss whether or not the infrastructure will collapse.

A city's infrastructure is certainly put under pressure by continuing migration from rural areas. For example, as more and more people crowd into cities, water delivery and sewage disposal systems are often found to be inadequate to cope with demand. Moreover, unlicensed construction of dwellings usually leads to further problems for water and sewerage systems.

Roads and transport services also suffer when they are overused. As more and more people attempt to travel, the roads quickly become overcrowded and the traffic flow slows. Examples of this situation can be found in many cities throughout the world.

However, infrastructure problems are not inevitable. The water and sewerage systems can be effectively planned taking into account future projections of population growth, and systems can be put in place to deal with this increase.

Traffic infrastructure problems can also be dealt with. A regulatory system which limits the number of cars and trucks on the roads could be introduced. There are no doubt several ways in which this could be accomplished. In fact, such a system is already in force in Singapore.

In conclusion, infrastructure such as water, sewerage and transport is certainly under strain from rapid migration. Nevertheless, with careful planning many of these problems can be minimised. Consequently, it is not inevitable that the infrastructure will collapse, though action should be taken as early as possible.

259 words

j) **The high road toll is robbing our society of many people who could otherwise be leading useful and productive lives. How can society protect itself from these losses?**

Every day we see newspaper and television reports which give details of road accidents. We are saddened by the loss of human life and the pain of the victims' injuries, but we tend to forget the terrible cost to society of these events. This essay will try to suggest ways we can cut the road toll by considering the road, safety devices in the vehicle and, most importantly, people.

Prevention is better than cure: we should concentrate upon ways to prevent these accidents. Well-built roads are a great aid to calm and safe traffic flow. Imagine roads without blind corners or potholes, with excellent road signs and properly planned intersections. These roads reduce the risk to both motorist and pedestrian.

Pedestrians are frequently hurt on the roads. City roads should have enough well-marked pedestrian crossings so people are not tempted to wander across the road just anywhere. Ideal road management would segregate cyclists from motorists. A truly lethal combination is a road with a rough edge which makes bicycling difficult and tempts the cyclist toward the centre of the road and into the path of cars.

Inside the car, the seat belt does save lives. So does the baby's safety seat and the increasingly popular air bag. Cars can be designed to withstand impact from the side as well as from the front or rear. Helmets help protect cyclists and motor cyclists.

Good road design and well-planned safety devices will only work if people choose to use them properly, and the ultimate responsibility must come back to drivers, riders and pedestrians. One impatient driver driving through a red light can cause terrible damage: it is indeed up to everyone to use the road responsibly.

284 words

Correction Key

SYMBOL	MEANING	EXAMPLE
T	tense	She <u>studied</u> ^T at UTS next year.
VF	verb form	We like <u>eat</u> ^{VF} in the dining room.
VA	verb/subject agreement	He <u>like</u> ^{VA} listening to music.
A/P	active/passive voice	They <u>were</u> ^{A/P} read many books.
N	number (singular/plural/uncountable)	He lived in New Zealand for two <u>year</u>. ^N She makes a lot of <u>moneys</u>. ^N
Prep	preposition	He lived <u>on</u> ^{Prep} Canada for two years.
WW	wrong word (vocabulary)	I like <u>hearing</u> ^{WW} to music.
WF	word form (part of speech)	There are many steps in the production <u>to make</u> ^{WF} sugar.
Art	article	They like going to ^{Art} library.
L	linking word & reference	They bought a book. Then they read it. <u>Then</u> ^L they ate. They bought <u>it</u>. ^L Then they read it.
WO	word order	[Always I] ^{WO} listen to music on the bus.
Sp	spelling	<u>Loudon</u> ^{Sp} is too cold for me.
P	punctuation & capitalisation	They read many books they like reading. ^P
X	unnecessary word	Singapore it is too hot for me.
∧	word/s missing	Cities too noisy for me. _∧
//	new paragraph needed	
?	unclear expression	
✓	good	
⌣	join these sentences	

Unit 5
The Speaking Test

Introduction to the IELTS Interview

Like the Listening test, the Speaking test is taken by all candidates, whether they are taking the Academic or General Training modules. It is a one-to-one interview of 10 to 15 minutes and may be done on the day of the examination, or up to two days later, at the discretion of the examination centre.

There are five phases or stages to the interview. They will all run into each other, and candidates may not know when one has ended and another begun. The interviewer has been trained to guide candidates through the interview. The interview will be recorded.

Phase 1. Introduction
The interviewer will help the candidate to feel comfortable. The candidate will be encouraged to talk briefly about familiar topics such as their life, home, work and interests. The interviewer will ask for the candidate's identification and will look at the candidate's CV if it is used at the particular test centre. A CV (curriculum vitae) or resume is a brief account of somebody's personal details, for example, education, employment history and interests. The interviewer may also ask the candidate how to pronounce her/his name correctly. This part of the interview takes one to two minutes.

Phase 2. Questions and extended conversation on general topics
The interviewer will lead the conversation to a topic of general interest. This part of the test finds out whether the candidate can give general information, describe things, express opinions and preferences, describe events or describe how something works. This part of the interview takes three to four minutes.

Phase 3. Question-asking by the candidate
The interviewer will give the candidate a card which describes an imaginary situation and will ask the candidate to ask questions about it. The purpose of this section is to check whether a candidate can form questions and obtain information. This part of the interview takes three to four minutes.

Phase 4. Further conversation, especially on the candidate's future plans, or abstract discussion
Here the candidate may be able to talk about their future plans; things like what they plan to do, and what they plan to study, or they may be asked to speculate, or guess, about what the future holds. The interviewer may return to something said before which she/he found interesting. This part of the interview takes three to four minutes.

Phase 5. Closing comments
The interview ends, the candidate and the interviewer say goodbye and the candidate leaves. This part of the interview takes one to two minutes.

1 What is the role of the interviewer in the IELTS speaking module?

What skills do you think you will require to do well in this test?

In some test administration centres, candidates fill in a CV form before their interview. This form gives the interviewer some basic information about the candidate which the interviewer may use to begin the interview.

This activity may be photocopied

Fill in the sample CV form below.

SPEAKING TEST: SAMPLE CV FORM

To help the interviewer in the Speaking Test, please give some information about yourself.

Family name: _____

Other name: _____

Nationality: _____

First Language: _____

Occupation: _____

Work experience: _____

_____

How did you learn English? _____

_____

What are your personal interests? _____

_____

What are your future plans? _____

_____

Why are you taking this test? _____

_____

FOR CENTRE USE ONLY

(The candidate does not fill in this part of the form.)

Phase 1

In Phase 1 of the interview you are expected to:

• exchange greetings
• answer basic questions about ordinary topics
• give general information, including some personal details.

It is polite to wait until the interviewer invites you into the room. If you make a mistake and go into the room before you are called, apologize and leave quickly.

2 Why should you leave quickly if you enter the interview room too early? What could you say?

Suggest some polite greetings to use when your interviewer has invited you into the room.

Arrange the greetings you have suggested in order from most casual to most formal.

How can you tell if a greeting is too informal?

Check with your teacher to find what is appropriate in the country where you are doing the test.

Register 1: greetings

3 Which greetings are appropriate in an examination situation?

Register means using language which is appropriate to the situation.

Discuss with your partner what the interviewer may say, and work through the exercise below.

The interviewer will:

• greet the candidate and ask the candidate to sit down (What might the interviewer say?)

• introduce her/himself (How much personal detail is the interviewer likely to give?)

• ask for the candidate's CV, if used (How will the interviewer do this?)

• ask for identification (This identification must include a photograph. What might the candidate offer?)

• chat about everyday things (Like the weather, or anything which is very ordinary)

• chat about things on the candidate's CV, if used. (Why is it important to give personal details like educational qualifications, work experience, future plans, reasons for studying abroad, interests and hobbies, on the candidate's CV?)

Work with your partner and role-play the first part of the interview. The student playing the part of the candidate should respond, giving as much detail as possible. Students should exchange roles.

When you have both taken a turn at being the interviewer, consider these questions:

How much did the interviewer find out from the CV? Give details. How useful was it? Would you write more in future? Give reasons for your answer.

Body language

4 What do these words mean?

tense	confident	cold	relaxed	tentative
nervous	brash	familiar	unfriendly	shy
agitated	open	uncooperative	casual	over-confident

Arrange these words into a group which describes attitudes which will help you in the IELTS interview, and another group which describes words which will not help you.

Identify the words which relate to being confident. Arrange them in order from the strongest to the weakest. (Some will have almost the same meaning.)

Mime the way people sit when they are feeling tense, confident, and so on. Remember, the way people sit and move may mean different things in different cultures. For example, if you sit with your arms folded and your eyes cast down you may be sending a message of great respect in one culture and of defiance or indifference in another.

Role-play: Work with your partner or a small group and begin the interview. Have another student observe and decide which word describes the candidate's body language.

Posture: Check with your teacher about appropriate ways to sit during the interview. Should you:

- sit on the front of the chair?
- slouch?
- wriggle?
- sit with your knees rammed tightly together?
- cross your legs at the knee? At the ankle?
- kick your foot? Shake your legs?

Proximity: The interviewer will probably place a chair and ask you to sit down. How close to your interviewer should you be? (This is another issue which is different in different cultures).

Look at these diagrams of people at a table. **C** means Candidate and **I** means Interviewer. Which position would make you most comfortable? Why?

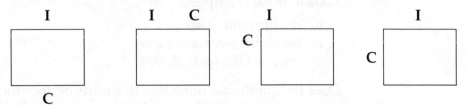

Check with your teacher about the way people use personal space in the country where you are doing this test.

Phase 2

Questions, and how they are asked

Questions can come in many forms. Here are a few beginnings to questions:

Whereabouts…?	Can you tell me some more about…?
How do you know that…?	What do you think of…?
How…?	What's your opinion of…?
How often…?	When…?
Do you have any information about…?	Do you know anything about…?
Do you have any views on…?	What do you know about…?
How do you feel about…?	How do you find…?

5 What other ways can you think of to ask a question?

Working in pairs, make up 10 questions for your partner using the words and phrases discussed above.

Possible topics:

- your partner's home town
- something in the news
- your partner's leisure activities.

Which questions signal that you are being asked to give an opinion?

Tag questions

Sometimes students find tag questions confusing.

Look at these examples:

    a) You like birds, don't you?
    b) You do like birds, don't you?
    c) You don't like birds, do you?

Does the questioner think you like birds or does the questioner think you don't like birds? In a) and b) the questioner believes you like birds, in c) the questioner believes you don't like birds. The meaning is in the first part of the question.

More rarely, the questioner may say something like: *You like birds, do you?* This is simply to confirm your liking for birds.

6   Answer these questions truthfully. Listen to the first part of the question.

Example: You like birds, don't you?
Response: Yes, I do. (OR, if you dislike birds) No, I don't.

1. You eat fish, don't you?

2. You don't drive a car, do you?

3. You like dancing, don't you?

4. You don't enjoy shopping, do you?

Register 2: questions

It can be rude to ask a very short question. Conversely, people sometimes use long question forms to be very polite, or they may even give polite instructions which you should answer.

For example, *What's your family like?* could be expressed as:

    I'd like to know about your family, please.
    Could you tell me about your family?
    Please tell me about your family.
    Would you like to tell me about your family?

If the candidate has to ask a question of the interviewer, he/she should use polite forms.

What to do when you can't understand something

Imagine you cannot understand a question. How should you respond?

Some possible responses are:

    I'm afraid I don't understand.
    I'm sorry. I don't understand.
    Excuse me. I didn't catch what you said.
    I'm sorry. I don't know what 'demystify' means. Would you explain?

7 Role-play with your partner. One person says something, but says *blah blah blah* in place of an important word. The other has to find out what the first person meant.

Examples:

    A. Could you meet me at blah blah blah o'clock?
    B. Sorry, what time?
    A. Two.

    B. I think we should meet at blah blah blah.
    A. Where did you say?
    B. The Town Hall.

1. **A.** Did you bring the blah blah blah?
    B. ...?
    A. ...

2. **B.** Have you got any blah blah blah?
    A. ...?
    B. ...

Make up as many examples as you can.

Extended discourse

In the interview, you should speak more than the interviewer, not less.

In the IELTS speaking test, the candidate should try to extend their responses to say more than just a few words in answer to a question by the interviewer.

To say more, not less, you can:

- develop an idea through several sentences
- use longer sentences
- vary the type of sentence used
- use several sentences in a reply.

When there is more than one sentence, the ideas should be organized by using connecting words.

Useful language:

although	but	so	in addition
however	first, second...	next	
then	afterwards	before	

Finally, there should be variety in the vocabulary. Try to find appropriate words and to use synonyms.

8 Look at this dialogue:

> **Interviewer:** I see you live near Main Street.
> **Candidate:** Yes.
> **Interviewer:** How did you come to the interview?
> **Candidate:** By bus.
> **Interviewer:** *(getting desperate)* Is it a slow trip?
> **Candidate:** Sometimes.

Work with your partner and think of ways these answers could be made longer. Make notes on what the candidate could say.

> **Interviewer:** I see you live near Main Street.
> **Candidate:** Yes. ...
> **Interviewer:** How did you come to the interview?
> **Candidate:** By bus. ...
> **Interviewer:** Is it a slow trip?
> **Candidate:** Sometimes. ...

9 Record the following exchanges in the language laboratory or on an individual cassette recorder.

Work with your partner and talk about the place where you are living at the moment. Give as much detail as you can. Your partner will ask questions about:

- the size of the place you live
- how you get to school or work
- the type of neighbourhood you live in
- the best/worst parts about living where you do

and any other questions that come to mind.

When you have finished, change roles and talk about a sport which is popular in your country. Give details about:

- the people who play
- the size of the crowds
- the degree of professionalism involved
- how children and new players come into the game.

Your partner will ask questions about all these things, plus any other questions.

Play the exchanges back and see how you could have improved your answers, and what else you could say. Record your exchanges again.

Outline of a response

This is a way to expand your response to a question.

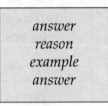

answer
reason
example
answer

For example, somebody might ask your teacher: 'Do you enjoy teaching?' The response could be yes or no, but that doesn't tell us much. People want to know why people feel as they do.

Here's a more interesting answer.

> **Interviewer:** Do you enjoy teaching?
> **Teacher:** Yes, I do *(answer)*. I find it very exciting to watch students learn *(reason)*. Sometimes I'm desperately trying to explain something, and I see that gleam in the eye that means the student understood *(example)*. That's why I really enjoy teaching *(answer)*.

OR

> **Interviewer:** Do you enjoy teaching?
> **Teacher:** I think I'll like it more when I'm a bit more experienced. I still find it hard to check that the class understands. Sometimes I think I've made them see something, and then when I test them they clearly have not understood. Still, I think I'll find it easier with a bit more experience.

10 Look at the two examples above. What questions could the interviewer ask the candidate after each response?

Practise responding to the questions below. Take it in turns to ask the questions. When you are the questioner, try to help your partner to speak more. When you are answering, answer as fully as possible and support your responses with reasons and examples.

- Is there one industry in your country which is more important than others?
- What was the best job you ever had?
- What did you enjoy most about your schooldays?
- Where would you most like to go for a holiday?

Topics for impromptu talks

In Phase 2 of the interview the candidate is expected to be able to:

- express likes and dislikes
- give directions and instructions
- describe and compare things
- narrate events or a sequence of events
- explain how something works or why something is the case.

Your teacher will ask you to speak for one minute about one of the topics below, or you may choose a topic of your own not on the list.

This activity may
be photocopied

After you speak the class should ask you questions.

Describe your family	**Tell us about the things you enjoy most in life**
Describe your home	**Tell us about things that annoy you, and explain why they irritate you**
Compare your home town/city with the city where you are now, or another city	**Talk about someone you admire**
Tell us how to cook something which is popular in your country	**Explain the best way to kick a ball**
Tell the story of an amusing experience	**Tell us why you came to study at this language school**

Checklist:

Check that you have:

- answered the question directly
- explained why
- given examples
- finished your speech properly.

Topics in Phase 2

Here are some topics the candidate may be asked to discuss:

- Festivals
- Pollution
- Family life
- Tourism
- Equipment in schools
- Income, distribution of wealth and poverty
- Marriage rites or wedding ceremonies

- Travel by air
- Education systems
- Leisure interests
- Industries and industrialization
- City life
- The teaching of Science/Arts in schools
- Style of architecture in the candidate's country

PREPARE FOR IELTS: The IELTS Preparation Course
Unit 5 The Speaking Test

11 Choose a topic with your partner, from the list above. What are ten words you would expect to be associated with this topic?

Role-play: one student is the interviewer, the other the candidate.

> **Interviewer:** Tell me about *(the topic chosen from the list)* in your country.
> **Candidate** speaks for about a minute.
> **Interviewer** asks a further question.

Record your interview and play it back. What more can you say about the topic? What sort of questions can the interviewer ask?

You may find it useful to write out your answer from the tape and discuss its structure, content and grammar with your teacher. Afterwards, record your interview again.

There are more topics for practice for Phase 2 on pages 188–190.

The unpredictability of conversation

Do not think you can just memorize a speech on each topic. If the interviewer says 'I'd like to know more about how you spend your free time', you should talk about your leisure activities, but the interviewer will control the conversation. Here's an example:

> **Interviewer:** I'd like to know more about how you spend your free time.
> **Candidate:** Well, back in my own country I seemed to go shopping a lot. I'd meet my friends and we'd go to the mall, and afterwards we'd often go to a party of some sort. I'm not sure we bought much, but we looked at a lot of things.

> **Interviewer:** What else did you do with your friends?
> **OR**
> What do you do in this city?
> **OR**
> What sort of parties did you go to?
> **OR**
> What could I buy in the malls in your country?
> **OR**
> How would you compare shopping here and in your country?
> **OR**
> Is the mall in your country like a mall here?

The candidate must then respond to whatever the interviewer has said. A candidate who goes on with what appears to be a prepared speech will score very badly.

> The interviewer may use the candidate's CV to decide what questions to ask.
>
> It's a good idea to learn the English words and phrases which refer to anything you have mentioned on your CV.

Phase 3

In this part of the interview the candidate is expected to:

- elicit (find out) general factual information
- express needs, wants, likes and dislikes
- get information about objects, events, and sequences of events
- find out opinions, attitudes and values
- find out how something works or why something is the case.

In Phase 3 the interviewer will give the candidate a card which describes an imaginary situation and will invite the candidate to ask questions about it.

For instance, your examiner may give you a card like this:

Candidate Card

You want to take the train to the city of Bridgewater on a weekend, for two days of sightseeing. Your interviewer is the Information Officer at the Railway Station Booking Office.

Ask about:

- cost of the trip
- frequency of trains
- length of the trip
- express trains
- platform the train leaves from.

We can describe the items under 'Ask about:' as 'cues'. A cue is a signal which tells people that it is their turn to speak or act.

What do the cues mean?

A cue tells you it is your turn to speak or act. In this case, it gives you an idea of the sort of question to ask. For example, if you see a cue like 'frequency of trains' this means the candidate might ask: *How often does the train depart?*

12 Match the cues (1-21) in the first column with the question forms (A-O) in the second column. There are many different possible matchings.

Ask about ...	Question form
1. duration	A. When...?
2. standard	B. How many...?
3. size	
4. reason	C. What is required...?
5. age	D. How much...?
6. length	
7. requirements	E. How likely is it that...?
8. number	F. How often...?
9. place	
10. probability	G. Where...?
11. time	H. Why...?
12. cost	
13. action to take	I. Whereabouts...?
14. destination	J. How long ago...?
15. dates	
16. means	K. How long...?
17. prerequisites	L. What should ... do...?
18. likelihood	
19. frequency	M. How big...?
20. possibility	N. How old...?
21. location	
	O. How good/bad...?

Think of similar expressions to add to the list A-O.

Choose ten of the question forms (A-O) above and write a full question for each.

13 Look again at the candidate cue card about the train to Bridgewater. Work with your partner and write some questions using the cues.

Candidate Card

You want to take the train to the city of Bridgewater on a weekend, for two days of sightseeing. Your interviewer is the Information Officer at the Railway Station Booking Office.

Ask about:

- cost of the trip
- frequency of trains
- length of the trip
- express trains
- platform the train leaves from.

The interviewer has this information, but the candidate cannot see it.

Information

Trains to Bridgewater:

      Three regular trains every day except Sunday
      One express train every day except Sunday
      The trip takes 2 hours on the express, 2½ hours on the regular train

Timetable:

      Monday to Friday: regular train leaves 8 am, 3 pm, 6 pm
      Express leaves 7 pm
      Saturday: Regular train leaves 12 noon, 6 pm; no express train
      Sunday: Regular train leaves 12 noon, 6 pm; no express train

Platforms:

      All trains leave from platform eight

Cost:

      First class: single - $24, return - $48
      Economy: single - $17.50, return - $35

The interviewer has enough information to answer your questions. It doesn't matter which order you ask your questions. The interviewer will do everything to make this seem like a realistic conversation.

It is your task to find out the important information by asking relevant questions. Look at the exchange below. (An exchange is part of a conversation).

> **Interviewer:** I'm going to give you a card to read. You may ask questions when you are ready.
> *Candidate looks at the card.*
> **Candidate:** How often does the train go to Bridgewater?
> **Interviewer:** There are three regular trains every day except Sunday, when there are two. If you want to take the express, it goes every day except for Sunday.
> **Candidate:** How long is the trip?
> **Interviewer:** The trip takes two hours on the express, two and a half hours on the regular train.
> **Candidate:** Which platform does the train leave from?
> **Interviewer:** They all leave from platform eight.
> **Candidate:** How much will it cost?
> **Interviewer:** If you want to go first class, a single ticket costs $24, and a return $48.
> **Candidate:** Thank you. *(Hands card back.)*

The candidate has asked good, well-formed questions, but they are very brief. The candidate needs to talk more, make comments, and ask more questions to follow up the interviewer's replies.

Think of polite ways to ask your questions. Discuss them with your partner and your teacher.

Look at the exchanges above. What comments could the candidate make? What other questions could the candidate ask? Here's an example:

Candidate: How often does the train go to Bridgewater?
Interviewer: There are three regular trains every day except Sunday, when there are two. If you want to take the express, it goes every day except for Sunday.
Candidate: No express on Sunday. That's a pity. I'd really like to go on Saturday and come back on Sunday, and the express would save me some time. Is there much difference between the express and the regular train? I mean, how long is the trip?

Add more to the other exchanges. You can express your own opinions and wants, and ask for the interviewer's opinion.

Interviewer: The trip takes two hours on the express, two and a half hours on the regular train.
Candidate: ...
Interviewer: They all leave from platform eight.
Candidate: ...
Interviewer: If you want to go first class, a single ticket costs $24, and a return $48.
Candidate: ...

This part of the test is meant to take three to four minutes.

GOLDEN RULES

Obtain all the essential information
Try to pretend you really are one of the people on the card
Ask questions arising from the interviewer's responses
Stay with the topic on the card

Obtain all the essential information

This is one occasion where curiosity is not only polite, it's expected. Ask as many questions as you can. Although it may be rude to ask a lot of questions in a social situation, here you are being rewarded for asking questions.

To practise asking questions, you can:

- look at a photograph in a newspaper and ask as many questions as you possibly can
- get a newspaper advertisement and ask as many questions as you can
- play 20 Questions, the game where somebody thinks of an object and the class may ask no more than 20 questions to find out what the object is.

You may ask direct or indirect questions.

Direct questions

Where is the information office?

Indirect questions

Can you tell me where the information office is?
Do you know where the information office is?

What do you notice about the word order in indirect questions?

The relationship between the people on the card

You will usually find from the information on the candidate card or from the interviewer's comments that the relationship between the candidate and the interviewer has been defined. For example:

> 'You have come into a new district. The interviewer is a friend.'
> 'You are a business student. The interviewer is also a business student.'
> 'You are a student. The interviewer is a Student Information Officer.'
> 'You want to buy a video. The interviewer is a salesperson.'
> 'You want to book a holiday. The interviewer is a travel agent.'
> 'You want to join a special group. The interviewer controls entry to the group.'

The relationship between the candidate and the interviewer will help you decide what questions are appropriate.

 How will you begin the conversation for each example above? Be sure you include a greeting, like: 'Good morning. I'd like to find out about the train time-table. Can you help me?'

How much could you tell about the relationship between the two people in each question?
Who was more powerful?
How much difference in power was there between the two people in each exchange?
Did that difference in power influence your response?
Should it have influenced your response?

Asking questions arising from the interviewer's responses

Look at this example of a Phase 3 task:

> The interviewer has been invited to a tennis party. You have to find out the details of the tennis party, and how the interviewer feels about going to the party.
>
> **Find out about:**
>
> > time
> > date
> > place
> > hosts

Example exchange:

> **Candidate:** I believe you're going to a tennis party. When is it?
> **Interviewer:** It's next week. I believe the club is strict about what people wear, and I haven't got any white tennis clothes.

The interviewer has answered the question, and has given the candidate an opportunity to ask more questions about clothes. The candidate might continue like this:

> **Candidate:** That's a bit of a problem! Are all the clubs strict like that?
> **OR**
> > Is it easy to find tennis clothes near here?
> **OR**
> > Are you sure? I often see people playing tennis in ordinary shorts and tops.

The candidate can then go on and ask more questions about the time of the party, and so on. It is up to the candidate to be inventive.

> Stay with the topic on the card. If your examiner believes that you are trying to twist the topic to a prepared speech you will score poorly.

15 Work with your partner and write as many questions as you can to ask about the suggested cues.

1. The interviewer says: 'I am a business student at university and a member of the International Students Business Council. You are also a student and you would like to join the Council too. Ask me questions about the Council.'

   Ask about:

   * membership
   * benefits
   * activities
   * meetings
   * speakers
   * cost.

   Look at the questions you have asked. What sort of answers would you expect? Work with your partner, and think of answers to the questions you asked above.

2. The interviewer says: 'You are new to the college and you would like to find out about the sports facilities for student use. I am a Student Information Officer. Ask me questions about sports facilities at the college for student use.'

Write questions and answers for each of these cues:

- type of facility
- location
- availability
- user's fee
- sports club membership
- injury insurance
- training.

Question-asking practice

Take it in turns to be the candidate and the interviewer in the next four practice cards.

The *Candidate* must see only the *Candidate card*. The *Interviewer* may see both sets of information. When you are the *Candidate* please cover the information at the bottom of the page.

Record your exchanges and play the dialogue back after you have completed each practice card. Decide how you could improve the *Candidate's* part of the dialogue.

Be careful to begin and end your conversation appropriately.

This activity may
be photocopied

Practice card 1

Candidate Card

You want to buy a video camera. The interviewer is a salesperson in a camera shop.

Ask about:

- the brands available
- the levels of quality
- the price
- the guarantee
- methods of payment.

Information

Brands, Prices, Quality and Guarantee:

Impressif: medium quality, $200, 3 months guarantee
Sonar: high quality, $300, 1 year guarantee
TVT: very high quality, $420, 2 years guarantee.

Methods of Payment:

Visa, Mastercard, American Express
Personal cheques not accepted
Cash
No lay-by or lay away

This activity may
be photocopied

Practice card 2

Candidate Card

You want to book a holiday in the capital city of your state. The interviewer is a travel agent.

Ask about:

- places to see
- accommodation
- things to do there
- hotel menus
- prices
- extra facilities
- special deals or conditions
- travel arrangements.

Information

Places to go:

> Museums
> Shopping, restaurants, theatres
> Sporting facilities
> Theme park

Things to do:

> Visit scenic areas around the city
> Walking tours of the city

Accommodation:

> Bed and Breakfast ranging from modern houses to old homes
> Youth hostels: inexpensive dormitory style accommodation; men and women sleep in different dormitories
> Large range of city hotels, one star to five star; five star hotels are luxurious and expensive

Travel arrangements:

> Local and international airlines
> Trains
> Daily bus services connect all towns

Practice card 3

Candidate Card

You want to enrol in a photography course. The interviewer is the Information Officer at the photography school.

Ask about:

- location
- dates of the course
- times
- length of the course
- equipment needed
- qualification given
- size of classes.

Information

Location:

Cultural Centre, Larwood

Dates of the course:

Courses commence 7th Jan., 23rd March, 4th May, 10th August, 23rd November

Times:

6 to 8 pm, Tuesdays and Thursdays

Length of the course:

5 weeks

Equipment needed:

Own camera only

Qualifications given:

Certificate in Elementary Photography

Size of classes:

Maximum 15 students

This activity may
be photocopied

Practice card 4

Candidate Card

You want to find out about shopping for furniture because you have to buy some furniture for your new home. The interviewer is a friend who recently bought furniture and other goods.

Ask about:

- best ways to buy furniture
- where to buy bed linen and blankets
- where to buy electrical goods
- opening hours of shops
- delivery arrangements.

Information

Best ways to buy furniture:

> Check advertisements for second-hand furniture.
> Go to Liberty Furniture Traders for desks to assemble yourself.

Where to buy bed linen and blankets:

> Department stores are very expensive; it's better to go to cheaper retail chains or even large supermarkets.

Where to buy electrical goods:

> Look around for bargains, as there is a great variety in prices.
> Look for electrical discount stores.

Opening hours of shops:

> Usually 9.00 am to 5.30 pm, but sometimes until 6.00 pm.
> Most stores open all day Saturday and many are open on Sunday between 10.00 am and 4.00 pm.

Delivery arrangements:

> Stores usually charge extra for delivery, between $15 and $25.

Phase 4

In this phase you are expected to be able to:

*   provide general personal and factual information
*   express needs, wants, likes and dislikes
*   express opinions, intentions, attitudes, moods, possibilities, values and emotions
*   describe and compare objects, events and sequences of events
*   explain how something works and why something is the case
*   speculate on future events and their consequences.

The last item on the list is a skill which has not been mentioned before. 'To speculate' means to guess about the future, for instance: *I wonder where I'll be in five years from now*. The interviewer may want to discuss your future plans, or he/she may return to something you've talked about earlier in the conversation.

16 Identify the words and phrases below which show the speaker is speculating:

Let's be definite about this...	I wonder...	I'm quite sure that...
I don't know, but...	It would be interesting to find out if...	
Make no mistake about it	Possibly	
It may be that...	I expect	I'm sure
Undoubtedly	Perhaps...	I'm quite sure that...
I imagine that...	I believe that...	
Maybe...	I'm not sure that...	
It's certain...	I guess that...	I hope that...

These words and phrases indicate different degrees of certainty. Arrange them in order of strength. (Some are very similar.) Put the most certain one at the top of the list.

I'm certain	it may be that...	I'd like to...	I suppose I might
I might	I hope to	I am sure I'll...	I've got a good chance
probably	I expect...	I'm likely to...	I most probably will

Make notes on what you might be doing in two months from now, in one year and in five years. Use the phrases above.

Show your notes to your partner, and look at your partner's notes. Ask your partner questions. Make your partner explain more and justify what they have written.

A speech in which you speculate

17 Think about the sort of job you have now, and the sort of job you would like. What do you most want to change? Write notes for a one-minute speech and tell the class. They will ask you questions after you have finished speaking.

The notes you write should only be headings to remind you what you will say. They should fit neatly on a business card.

The forgotten word and fillers

If you cannot think of exactly the right word, do what native speakers do, and use another word, or express the idea another way. It's all right to use fillers to give you time to think. People say things like: *Let me see; Let me think about that; Hmm…; Well…*

What other fillers can you think of?

Specialist vocabulary

The interviewer may ask you about your job. Let's say it's computer programming. Your vocabulary for computer programming may be excellent in your language, but very lacking in English.

Please be sure to learn the English words and phrases which refer to anything you have mentioned on your CV, if it will be used, or that relate to your own specialist area.

18 Share the special language of something you are interested in with a small group or the class. Be ready to explain what happens and what the words mean.

19 Group discussion: use these cue cards with your partner or in a small group. Choose one topic, talk together as long as you like, record what you say, and then listen to the recording. What other things could you have said?

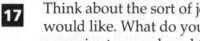

Move on to the other topic and discuss it as fully as you can.

> **If you could choose any city in the world, which city would you live in?**

> **How do you think living in 100 years' time will be different to now?**

Discussion with a speaker: one person will speak on each topic and the others in the group will ask questions.

Make notes while the speaker is talking and ask questions afterwards.

This activity may be photocopied

In the field of medical research, what should most money be spent on in the next ten years?	**What criticisms would you make of the education system in which you were educated?**
Will children's emotional and intellectual development be adversely affected by video games?	**Should environmental laws be applied equally to developed and under-developed economies?**

 Talk for at least 1 minute to answer the following question:

If you were...

- the president of the USA
- the Sultan of Brunei
- the Secretary-General of the United Nations
- the Minister for Health in your country
- General Manager of a large department store
- the best nuclear physicist in the world
- Minister for Education in your home country
- the Chief of Police in your capital city
- your favourite pop star
- a high school Principal

...what would be the first 3 things you would do?

This activity may be photocopied

21 Talk for at least 1 minute on the following topics:

What three things do you hope to achieve in your life?	**What is the most important medical discovery of all time?**
What will people value most in the year 2020?	**Why have you chosen your particular course of study?**
'Marriage is the most important event in a person's life.' How true is this statement?	**'Without a university degree, ambition alone will not allow you to achieve what you want.' Is this an accurate reflection of the current job market?**
What would be your perfect job?	**'In sport as in business, winning is the only result that matters.' How useful is this attitude?**

More topics for impromptu talks

This activity may be photocopied

22 Speak for one minute on any of these topics, and be ready to answer questions.

You do not have to agree with the statement or question in these topics.

❷ = suitable for practice for Phase 2 of the interview
❹ = suitable for practice for Phase 4 of the interview

A funny experience ❷	**Your feelings on sport** ❷
A strange experience ❷	**Your feelings on technology** ❷
A confusing experience ❷	**Your feelings on education** ❷

Speak for one to two minutes on any of these topics, and be ready to answer questions.

Explain why religion is important. ❹	**Why is studying abroad important for you?** ❷
How can we change our lifestyles to protect the environment? ❹	**Explain why development is important for countries in your region.** ❹
Describe the difficulties of studying another language. ❷	**Which social problem makes you feel most concerned?** ❷
Describe some effective ways to overcome stress. ❷	**Do you think modern technology only benefits developed countries?** ❹
Why are human rights important? ❹	**Why is family life important to you?** ❷
Tell us about your greatest achievements. ❷	**How can the world be a better place?** ❹
Are friends more important than family? ❷	**What are the qualities of a good citizen?** ❹

Describe your strategies for academic success. ❷	Do you think sport promotes good relations between countries? ❹
Describe any environmental problems your country has. ❷	Talk about someone who has made a great contribution to the world, or to your country. ❹
Tell the class about a funny or confusing incident that happened when you first visited a foreign country. ❷	Compare the benefits of a university degree from a foreign university to a degree from a university in your country. ❷

Phase 5

Ending the interview

How do you think the interviewer will signal that the interview is over?

What words might the interviewer use?

What body language or gestures might the interviewer use?

At the end of the interview, you say goodbye to the interviewer and leave. The interviewer cannot tell you how well you have done.

Unit 6
Listening Tapescripts and Answer Key

Tapescripts for the Listening Activites

1

Narrator: Activity 1: 'About the Listening Test'. Listen to this conversation about the IELTS listening test.

Candidate: Excuse me. You're teaching people how to sit for the IELTS listening test, is that right?
Teacher: Yeah, that's right.
Candidate: Can I ask you some questions about the test? I have to take it in two months' time.
Teacher: Sure. I'd be glad to help.
Candidate: First, I'd like to ask you about the length of the test.
Teacher: Okay. The test is usually about 30 minutes long, that's fairly standard, and it contains around 40 questions.
Candidate: Forty questions. Is that all one continuous conversation?
Teacher: No, no, it's divided into four sections.
Candidate: Are all the sections on the same topic?
Teacher: Each section is on a different topic and has different voices, and what you hear in each section could be in several parts of, I suppose, about a minute or two, or it might be all the one thing, say a conversation that goes for four or five minutes.
Candidate: Okay, and what about time in between each section?
Teacher: Well, between each section first of all you'll have the instructions, which are all given on tape, and then usually you'll be given, well always you'll be given, thirty seconds or so to read over the questions, then you'll hear the tape and answer the questions as you hear it. You only get it once so you have to listen very carefully. That's very important.
Candidate: Oh, only once.
Teacher: Yeah, only once, and then at the end of each section they'll give you 30 seconds to check over your answers, and again at the end of the entire test they'll give you some time to look back over the answers for the test.
Candidate: Right. What about the content of the test? What am I going to hear?
Teacher: Well, again it varies but it tends to be taken from two general areas. In the earlier sections, the first two, it's usually from survival kind of situations, I mean the type of experiences students would have when they arrive in a foreign country, like getting ready to start your course.

Candidate: Or checking in at a hotel or a dorm?
Teacher: Yeah, that's right, things like that, asking directions, arranging to meet people, that kind of thing, and then in the later part of the test, which is generally more difficult, the passages are usually taken from some academic kind of situation so it could be somebody ... part of a lecture, for example ... or it could be somebody introducing library facilities, or explaining how to get a student card. That kind of thing.
Candidate: Okay, and what about the accents? Do they have British accents?
Teacher: No, there could be British accents on it or there could be Australian or American or, say, Canadian. You could have quite a range of accents, although they wouldn't be too strong but you have to be ready for that. And they'll be male and female voices on the tape. It could be, also, a monologue if someone's giving a lecture, for example.
Candidate: What's a monologue?
Teacher: A monologue means just one person will be talking.
Candidate: Right.
Teacher: But it could also be dialogue ... a couple of people discussing what they're going to do that evening or something like that. Usually the first section is a dialogue, you know, a conversation between two people, and then you'll usually hear another conversation in Section Three.
Candidate: Okay. Well, the last thing I'd like to ask is about the type of questions you get.
Teacher: Okay. Here they've really tried to make a variety of different types of questions to test people. So there might be some questions which have a graphic format. There could be pictures to choose from, there might be a chart where you have to fill in information, or a table. You'll probably have some multiple choice in there somewhere. You'll almost certainly at some point have to write in some answers which could be single words, or a cloze test for example, where you have to fill in the gaps of a test, or it might be filling in a few words. You might have to fill in a form, for example putting down addresses or times or dates, or information like that. Or you might have to write down short answers to questions, but you never have to write more than three words.
Candidate: Do you always write down exactly what you hear on the tape?

Tapescripts for the Listening Activites

Teacher: Not necessarily. A lot of the pieces are organized so that you can't copy down exactly what you hear word for word. They're trying to check the candidates' understanding of meaning, so you have to listen carefully for the meaning, but when you're filling in a cloze test, a gap-fill for example, you might have to use other words which still convey the meaning of what you heard.

Candidate: Where do you write the answers? Can I write on the exam paper?

Teacher: Yes, you can. You have to write your answers on the paper and then at the end of the test you have to transfer your answers to the answer sheet. You get time to do this and the instructions are always clear. But you've got to be careful when you're doing it so you don't get the questions mixed up.

Candidate: Right. Okay, well, thank you very much. I feel more confident now about the listening part of the test.

Teacher: I'm sure you'll do well. Good luck.

Candidate: Thank you very much.

Narrator: Activity 2: 'Passenger Survey'.

Market researcher (MR): Excuse me, Madam, could I get you to answer some questions about Route 440?

Respondent (Resp): Will it take long? I have to get off soon.

MR: It should only take about 5 minutes.

Resp: Okay.

MR: Thanks. Hmm. Today's date is the fifteenth of May, isn't it?

Resp: Yes, that's right.

MR: Okay. Thanks. The first question is: how often do you travel on this bus route? Less than once a month, daily, twice a day, more than twice a day?

Resp: I use this route twice daily. Once on my way to work, and once on my way home.

MR: So are you going to work now?

Resp: No, I'm not. I'm going to the movies.

MR: Thanks. Now I have to ask you to rate the service on a scale of 1 to 4: 1 is very bad and 4 is very good. First of all, punctuality: is the bus on time? 1 is very bad...

Resp: It used to be good, but during the last few weeks it's been very unreliable. Say 1.

MR: What about the comfort of the bus?

Resp: Well, this one is okay, but some of the older buses on route 440 are very uncomfortable. I'd say 2.

MR: What about the cost?

Resp: I travel from the beginning of one section to the end of the other, so the cost is okay. I'd say 3.

MR: Is the bus clean?

Resp: Usually it's fairly clean in the morning, but it deteriorates during the day, and it's quite dirty on the way home. Can I give it two scores, one for the morning and one for the afternoon?

MR: Sorry. The computer can only read one score here.

Resp: I'll give it a 2.

MR: Last question: how do you rate the service from the staff?

Resp: Really good. Let them have a four. The drivers are always polite, and the passengers can be very difficult.

MR: Thank you very much for helping.

Narrator: Activity 4: 'Word endings'. You will hear 10 sets of three words. Circle the word you hear twice. For example, if you hear '18 80 18', you will circle '18'. Now we will begin:

1. 15   50   15
2. bend   bent   bent
3. led   let   led
4. word   work   work
5. 16   60   60
6. dish   ditch   ditch
7. bed   bet   bet
8. 13   30   13
9. seal   seal   seam
10. slim   slim   slip

Narrator: Activity 5: 'Numbers'. You will hear ten numbers in these conversations. Write these numbers down as you hear them.

1.
Speaker 1: Directory assistance, can I help you?
Speaker 2: Yes. I'd like the number for interstate directory assistance.
Speaker 1: Yes, it's 1175 *(double one seven five)*.

2.
Speaker: Please call me at home after 6. My number is 9555 6140 *(9555 614 oh)*.

3.
Speaker 1: What's the number for the snow report, please?
Speaker 2: It's 0055 12370 *(double oh double five, one two three seven oh)*.

4.
Speaker 1: Do you know the number for transport services?
Speaker 2: Yes, it's 131 500 *(one three one five hundred)*.

5.
Speaker 1: Could I have the number for the Accommodation Service?
Speaker 2: Yes, it's a 1 800 number, 1 800 666 9181 *(one eight hundred, six six six, nine one eight one)*.

6.
Speaker: His phone number at work is 672 3000 *(six seven two three thousand)*.

Tapescripts for the Listening Activites

7.
Speaker: The number for the translating service is 13 13 50 (*one three one three five zero*).

8.
Speaker 1: What was that fax number again?
Speaker 2: 973 7333 (*nine seven three seven triple three*).

9.
Speaker 1: What's your fax number in Vienna?
Speaker 2: It's 43 for Austria, 1 201 316 809 (*one two oh one three one six eight oh nine*).
Speaker 1: Was that 43 1 201 316 809?
Speaker 2: That's right.

10.
Speaker 1: The emergency number for the crime hotline is 1 800 025 121 (*one eight hundred, zero two five, one two one*).
Speaker 2: Thanks.

6

Narrator: Activity 6: 'Dates'. You will hear ten dates. Write the dates you hear.

1.
Speaker: Johan Sebastian Bach was born on the 21st of March 1685.

2.
Speaker: Omar Sharif's birthday is April 10th.

3.
Speaker: The enrolment date is February the 21st.

4.
Speaker: He was born sometime in the '90s.

5.
Speaker: Did you say the 30th of September?

6.
Speaker: The morning of the 8th of November will be fine.

7.
Speaker: How did people travel around in the 16th century?

8.
Speaker: It was finished in November 1853.

9.
Speaker: War broke out on December 1st, 1950.

10.
Speaker: The public holiday is on the fourteenth of July.

7

Narrator: Activity 7: 'Fractions, percentages, money and decimals'. You will hear ten numbers. Write every fraction, percentage, decimal number and amount of money you hear. You should indicate any currency you hear.

1.
Speaker 1: The recipe calls for two-thirds of a cup of rice.
Speaker 2: That's a pity. We're fresh out.

2.
Speaker 1: That's twelve and a half per cent, then.
Speaker 2: Correct.

3.
Speaker 1: Do you have $50? I've lost my money.
Speaker 2: OK.

4.
Speaker 1: A kilometre is five-eighths of a mile.
Speaker 2: Are you sure? I thought it was more than that.

5.
Speaker 1: Did you know that 38.65% of samples were affected?
Speaker 2: Are you sure?

6.
Speaker 1: That horse was sold for £750.
Speaker 2: That's not bad.

7.
Speaker 1: The average American family has 2.2 children.
Speaker 2: Is it the same in Canada?

8.
Speaker 1: On the map, only 0.3% (*point three per cent*) of the total area shows up as being in use.
Speaker 2: Is that all?

9.
Speaker 1: The government paid $530,000,000 for that.
Speaker 2: You mean the taxpayer paid!

10.
Speaker 1: How did you get on?
Speaker 2: I scored 85.5%!

9

Narrator: Activity 9: 'Spelling places and names'. Write every name or place name that you hear.

1.
Speaker: I'm going to Missouri. That's M-I-S-S-O-U-R-I.

2.
Speaker: The capital is Canberra, C-A-N-B-E-double R-A.

Tapescripts for the Listening Activites

3.
Speaker: Please send this to Harry Luske, that's H-A-R-R-Y L-U-S-K-E.

4.
Speaker: Write to me in Johannesburg. J-O-H-A-double N-E-S-B-U-R-G.

5.
Speaker: In your atlas, look up Vancouver, V-A-N-C-O-U-V-E-R.

6.
Speaker: Her name is Maria Strella. I'll spell the family name, S-T-R-E-L-L-A.

7.
Speaker: Bill McLean spells his surname capital M-small-C-capital L-E-A-N.

8.
Speaker: The restaurant is called Sammy's, that's S-A-M-M-Y apostrophe S.

9.
Speaker: We live near Runnymede, that's R-U-double -N-Y-M-E-D-E.

10.
Speaker: My teacher is Professor Kumar, K-U-M-A-R.

10

Narrator: Activity 10: 'Tasks which involve graphs'. Listen and write A B C or D to indicate the chart or graph being discussed.

1.
Lecturer: Please look at the graphs which show the types of waste we are dealing with in four different cities. Fortunately for us our city has the least toxic waste of them all.

2.
Teacher: The bar graph I want you to look at shows the largest column in the middle, with the smallest amounts at either end.

3.
Accountant: These figures show our sales for the year. As you can see, we did best in April and showed very little variation during the rest of the year.

12

Narrator: Activity 12: 'Listening for specific detail in descriptions of people'. Listen to the taped descriptions of the people in the illustrations A-H. Match the descriptions to the pictures.

Narrator: Person Number 1.
Speaker: The first person is John Edwards. John is 40 years old and works in an office. He is not very tall and he is of medium-build. His hair is thinning but he is not bald. He is clean-shaven. He likes to wear a bow-tie with his suit and usually carries an umbrella or a cane.

Narrator: Person Number 2.
Speaker: The second person is Gwen Charles. She likes to wear casual clothes that she can be comfortable in, but she always looks tidy and rather conservative. She has short, dark, straight hair and a pleasant face.

Narrator: Person Number 3.
Speaker: The third person is Sally Valdes. Sally has been married for two years; she married very young. Before her marriage she was a photographer, but now she only works occasionally in her profession. She dresses very casually and has short, curly hair.

Narrator: Person Number 4.
Speaker: The fourth person is Matthew Lee. Matthew is 17 and still in high school. He doesn't enjoy school very much and looks forward to the time when his studies will be finished. He prefers to dress in very casual clothes like jeans and T-shirts.

Narrator: Person Number 5.
Speaker: The fifth person is William Poinkin. Mr Poinkin retired from his job when he reached the age of 65. He still dresses very conservatively, and enjoys wearing a suit. He is almost bald but is very proud of his moustache.

Narrator: Person Number 6.
Speaker: The sixth person is Teresa Blake. Mrs Blake has been a school teacher for the last thirty years. She dresses in very practical clothes because she says there is no sense in wearing fashionable clothes or good jewellery to work because they just get ruined. She has had to wear glasses for some years now.

Narrator: Person Number 7.
Speaker: The seventh person's name is Margaret Connors. Margaret is a university student. She is studying politics at the moment but hopes to change to law. She likes to wear loose, casual clothes and is very tall with long hair. She also likes to wear jewellery.

Narrator: Person Number 8.
Speaker: Andrew Janacek is the eighth person. Andrew is a bus-driver, aged 23. In his spare time he plays a lot of soccer. He plays several other sports as well because he tries to keep as fit as possible, but soccer is what he really loves. He wears his hair fairly long and has a short beard.

Tapescripts for the Listening Activites

Narrator: Activity 13: 'Completing forms'. Listen to the dialogue and fill out the application form while you listen.

Interviewer: I need to ask you some questions so I can fill out this form. Could I have your name, please? I need your family name first.
Applicant: My family name is Calvi. You spell that C-A-L-V-I. My first name is Mario, that's M-A-R-I-O.
Interviewer: Any other names?
Applicant: No.
Interviewer: What's your nationality?
Applicant: Italian.
Interviewer: So your first language is Italian?
Applicant: No, actually it's not! My first language is German.
Interviewer: Thanks. How long have you studied English?
Applicant: Quite a long time. About ten years.
Interviewer: How much education have you had? Have you finished high school?
Applicant: Of course. I've completed a graduate diploma in nursing.
Interviewer: That's good. When would you like to do the test?
Applicant: Is there a test available in August?
Interviewer: August 13, 19 and 30 are all test days. You have to nominate two.
Applicant: Then I'd like to do it on the 13th, and if that can't be done, make it the 30th.

14

Narrator: Activity 14: 'Moving to a new campus'. The speaker is explaining the process of a move to a new campus. As you listen, answer questions 1-7 by marking T for true and F for false.

Manager: Good morning, ladies and gentlemen. I've called this meeting to discuss our new campus which is opening fully next year. We plan to move our students to the new facilities in groups, so please listen carefully. The Agricultural Science students won't move at all. As you know, their new facilities were opened last year, and they are well placed for both laboratory and classroom space. The Arts students, however, are a different case. Students of History will now attend lectures in the newly opened Grenfell Hall. This applies to all the students: the whole faculty will teach in the Grenfell Complex, and, as I said before, major lectures will be in the Grenfell Hall.
History students are all moving, but unfortunately their teachers will be left in the old building as the new office accommodation isn't yet ready. We hope to move some staff from the History Department within three months, but it will depend upon the availability of space.
Better news for the engineers. Your faculty, staff and students, are already in the process of moving to the new campus. The structures lab is already in

operation. The move for the engineers should be complete next week.
The old engineering building will be taken over by the Philosophy department. The old structures lab has been gutted, and will be a small lecture hall. Work should be complete next summer in time for the new university year.
The Faculty of Law has been moved downtown. As you know, this has been an on-going process for some time and it is now complete. The last books from the law library were put on their new shelves at the weekend. This leaves the premises previously occupied by the lawyers vacant. The planning committee is accepting suggestions for the way the building could be used. We'd like, if possible, to keep it as a public space: there has been a suggestion that it might be used as an art gallery or museum.

15

Narrator: Activity 15: 'Listening for distinguishing features'. Listen and write A, B, C or D to indicate which picture is being discussed.

1.
Teacher: I want you to look at the triangles and find the one where both the inner and outer triangles are drawn with broken lines.

2.
Man: Which flower do you like?
Woman: They're all pretty, but I like the one with four petals best.

3.
Lecturer: Now here we have four excellent specimens of cactus. They're all fine and healthy, but the best of them is the one with the single stem which divides into three branches.

4.
Police Officer: The missing girl is young. She has long hair, and when she was last seen she was wearing it in one pigtail falling over her shoulder.

5.
Woman: Oh dear! I think Mr Lee has broken his glasses! They're lying here with one lens badly cracked.

17

Narrator: Activity 17: 'Swallow Life Insurance'. You will hear a conversation between a representative of an insurance company and a person who wishes to apply for life insurance. While you listen to the conversation, complete the person's application form.

Interviewer: Now, to process your application I need some details about you and about your medical

Tapescripts for the Listening Activites

history. Could you tell me your name, please?

George: Yes, my name is Rowlands, that's R-O-W-L-A-N-D-S, George Rowlands.

Interviewer: Thank you. And your address, Mr Rowlands?

George: I live in Strathfield, at 52 Green Street. The postcode for Strathfield is 2135.

Interviewer: Strathfield 2135. Thank you. How old were you at your last birthday?

George: I was 35 on September the 10th.

Interviewer: How tall are you, Mr Rowlands?

George: Um, I think I'm about 170 or 175 centimetres tall. Let's say one metre seventy-five.

Interviewer: And is your current weight your normal weight?

George: Oh yes, my weight doesn't change much. I suppose I'm lucky, really. I've never had to worry about putting on weight. I'm always about the same, around 80 kilos.

Interviewer: Fine. Are you married at the moment, Mr Rowlands?

George: Actually, that's one of the reasons I wanted to sort out some insurance. I'm planning to get married quite soon. I guess when you settle down you start to think of things like that.

Interviewer: Yes, we often find people take out life insurance when some major change happens in their lives, like getting married or changing their job. Now, I've got some questions relating to health matters. We will of course be requiring a full medical examination but I need some basic details from you now.

George: That's OK. I expect you need to know that I'm healthy, don't you?

Interviewer: That's right. Have you ever had a serious illness at any time of your life?

George: What would you describe as a serious illness?

Interviewer: Oh, not childhood things like measles, or a bad cold, but a kidney disorder, say, or pneumonia, or a cancerous growth.

George: Oh no, I've never had anything like that. I've always been healthy, never been in hospital.

Interviewer: I'll just write 'none' then. And I'll put the same thing, 'none', for major operations too, if you've never been in hospital. Do you have any medical conditions requiring medication?

George: No, not really. I take aspirin for a headache at times, but that's all. Oh, I guess you had better mention hay fever. I get bad hay fever in the early summer, and I take anti-histamines then.

Interviewer: Yes, I'd better note down 'hay fever'. Now, what about your parents? It's usually relevant to a person's medical history. Can you tell me if your parents are still alive?

George: My mother is still living, and she's healthy, but my father was killed last year in a car accident.

Interviewer: I'm very sorry to hear that. It must have been a shock to you.

George: Yes, it was a bad time for the whole family. He had just retired from his job and was looking forward to doing all sorts of things. He was only 67.

Interviewer: It's terrible the way these things happen, isn't it? I've just got one last question, Mr Rowlands. Do you smoke?

George: No, I don't smoke now. I used to, but I gave it up about 5 years ago.

Interviewer: Well, I think that's all for now. Thank you, Mr Rowlands. We'll let you know the date and time of your appointment for the medical checkup, and after that we can finalize your application.

George: Thank you very much. I'll wait to hear from you.

Narrator: Activity 18: 'Earthquakes'.

Newsreader: An earthquake struck Mexico's Pacific coast yesterday, killing at least 34 people and injuring more than 100. The destruction was greatest in the state of Colima, where a hotel collapsed in the earthquake. Last night it was confirmed that eight people had been killed in the collapse of the hotel and more were still trapped in the rubble. Emergency workers were using cranes and earthmoving equipment to try to locate hotel employees and guests still believed to be in the wreckage.

Communications with the area were difficult as most services were cut by the quake, but telephone services were re-opened late last night, and electricity supplies are slowly returning. Many roads were cut in the north part of the state where the damage was most severe. Hospitals in the area are believed to be coping with the emergency, and medical teams are being flown in by helicopter from Mexico City to assist in the disaster.

The earthquake measured 7.6 on the Richter scale. Officials said that had the epicentre of the quake been closer to a more populated area such as Mexico City, the toll in lives would have been greater. Mexico City itself suffered a series of earth tremors several days earlier.

21

Narrator: Activity 21:

1. 'Sydbourne earthquake'.

Newsreader: An earthquake measuring 6.5 on the Richter scale caused widespread damage to the northern areas of Sydbourne last night, striking around 10.30 pm, Eastern Standard Time.
Fire Department officials said that three thousand buildings were completely demolished, while hundreds of fires started when electricity cables were brought down, causing short circuits.
A State of Emergency was declared in Sydbourne as gas mains throughout the northern suburbs ruptured, causing massive explosions and fireballs that could be

Tapescripts for the Listening Activites

seen 80 kilometres away, illuminating the city horizon. Authorities reported that by this morning most of the fires had been brought under control. However, damage to buildings is so severe that hundreds and possibly thousands of people are still trapped under tons of debris. Emergency crews say there is a shortage of heavy rescue machinery and they are powerless to rescue the victims of the quake.

Some sections of major highways have been damaged, to the point where they are all but impassable. A witness who survived the collapse of her house said that it was the worst earthquake in living memory. Other residents in her area were not so lucky. At least ninety per cent of the downtown area resembles the scene of a nuclear disaster.

The latest quake followed a series of minor tremors reported last Friday by the Centre for Seismic Research. A spokesperson for the Centre said that despite the repeated warning issued by the Centre to government authorities, the government failed to inform the media, with the result that warnings to evacuate the city were not issued. The spokesperson said that this negligence would now be paid for in human lives.

Hilary Hughes, reporting from Sydbourne Emergency Co-ordination Centre, Sydbourne, for ILTC RADIO NEWS.

2: 'Storm lashes Sydney'.

Newsreader: Severe storms hit the western areas of the city last night, leaving scenes of destruction and at least a hundred homes without power or running water. Dozens of families were left homeless when the roofs of their houses were ripped away.

Many of the areas hit were the same ones badly affected by hailstorms last week. In Macquarie Street, the council car park was completely flooded. A Toyota Corolla was badly damaged by floodwaters which carried the car across the carpark and into a large stormwater drain. A separate storm raced through the Federation Botanical Park. It uprooted at least fifty trees; many of them were over a hundred years old. In Menai, several trees were found lying on parked cars, causing an insurance bill that will run into the tens of thousands of dollars. Winds were recorded at speeds of over seventy kilometres an hour.

People were trapped in cars for up to an hour because the floodwaters had left them stranded in swollen creeks, amidst a sea of debris. There were reports of cars being piled one on top of the other. In Lucas Heights a tree fell on a mini-bus that was taking the local soccer team to training. Luckily all but the driver escaped serious injury. The driver is in a satisfactory condition in Westmead Hospital.

For tomorrow, weather reports predict improved conditions, with clear skies and an expected maximum temperature in the city of 14.

Helen Brookes reporting for ILTC RADIO NEWS.

22

Narrator: Activity 22: 'Enrolment Day'. You will hear part of an introductory talk by a Student Information Officer. As you listen, answer questions 1 to 7. Circle the correct answer.

Speaker: Welcome to the Orientation Program. I hope you are all settling in to your new residences and starting to feel at home here.

This Orientation Program is designed to familiarize you all with some of the essential information about the University and about what it is like to be a student here, but before we begin I'd like to say a few words about enrolment day because I know that many students ... many of you are unsure of the procedures. There are two enrolment days, for different categories of student. Local students, or students who are permanent residents will enrol on the 16th of February. Overseas students will enrol two days later, on the 18th of February, in one of two sessions. First of all, all students doing undergraduate studies must come and enrol in the morning session. That morning enrolment session, for people enrolling in undergraduate courses, will be from 9.30 to 12.30 on Level 6 of the Walsh Building, in Room C 658. The Walsh Building is the one where the Faculty of Law is located. So that's for undergraduate students. Postgraduate students must also come to the same place, Room C 658 on Level 6, from 1.30 pm on the 18th, and that enrolment session finishes at 4.30 pm.

When you come to enrol, and this applies to all students, please bring your passport or some other identification, that's really essential, and also bring the letter of acceptance from the Faculty you will be enrolling in. For overseas students we'll also need proof of your English proficiency level, that is, your IELTS test results, that's if you're an overseas student, and your health-care cards for health insurance, plus the receipt from the Student Admissions Office to show you have paid your fees.

If there's anyone who hasn't paid their fees for this semester yet, please go to the Student Admissions Office and pay the fees as soon as possible. Your place at the university is not guaranteed until you've paid your fees and you cannot enrol. Just a word of advice: it's best to get a bank cheque to pay your fees. The thought of carrying $10,000 in cash in your pocket is terrifying. You could easily lose it or have it stolen.

On Enrolment Day you'll all be issued with your Student Cards. You don't have to bring a photo for these. The enrolling officer will take an instant photo, and put it on the card with your student ID number and then laminate the card, so it's all done at once. You use this student card to borrow from the library, to use student services like the medical centre, and even get discounts at the cinema and bookstores. By the way, the library hours are from 9.00 to 4.00 at the moment, but when the university term begins on the 21st of February

Tapescripts for the Listening Activites

the library opening times will be from 8.30 in the morning until 9.00 at night. It's also open at weekends. Okay? So, if you're all ready, we'll begin our tour of the campus now.

23

Narrator: Activity 23: 'Heathrow Airport Information'. Listen to this information about London Heathrow Airport. Write no more than three words for each answer.

Speaker: This information about London Heathrow Airport is provided by British Airways. There are four terminals at London Heathrow. Terminal One deals with all domestic flights within the United Kingdom. British Airways do not use Terminal Two. British Airways flights to Philadelphia use Terminal Three. All other British Airways intercontinental flights use Terminal Four. This includes the service on Concorde. If you are connecting flights with an airline other than British Airways, please ensure you follow the signs to your correct terminal. Travelling time between terminals is ten minutes by coach. A moving walkway connects Terminal One to Terminal Two.
You should allow between 45 and 75 minutes between flights. On arrival, follow the signs to Flight Connections. Passengers who do not hold a boarding pass should report to the Flight Connections Centre. The Flight Connections Centre is located between Terminals One and Two. It contains a lounge of 600 seats, a children's play area, and, for a small charge, an executive-style lounge has secretarial support, shower facilities and sleeper seats in a quiet area. Central London is 15 miles to the east of the airport. There are several ways to travel there: taxi, bus, London underground and the Heathrow Express. A taxi will cost approximately 35 pounds, and is licensed to carry four passengers. The journey will take approximately 40 minutes. If you prefer to use the bus, Airbus Heathrow Shuttle has twenty-three Central London stops. The fare is six pounds for an adult travelling one way. Or you may take the London Underground served by the Piccadilly line. The trains depart approximately every five minutes, and the journey takes about fifty-five minutes. Or the Heathrow Express travels non-stop to London Paddington every fifteen minutes. This journey takes approximately fifteen minutes, and there are check-in facilities for customers with hand luggage only.
We hope you enjoy your stay in the U.K., and look forward to serving you again.

24

Narrator: Activity 24: 'Student Counsellor's Talk'. Listen and complete the sentences below. Write no more than three words for each answer.

Speaker: Good morning everyone. This is the second of my three introductory talks as Overseas Student Counsellor at the university. In the first session you will remember we talked about the services offered in the Overseas Students' Unit at the university, and in this session I'd like to talk to you briefly about some of the problems, the most common problems that overseas students encounter when they come to study with us. After all, it's no secret that you may not find everything as easy as you would like, and we are here to help you.
Firstly I'd like to talk about the transition experienced by many students from euphoria to doubt and depression. When students arrive they are usually excited by being in a new city with lots of attractions. Many students also enjoy the personal freedom of being in a foreign country, of meeting new friends and so on. But then when classes start and the student feels under pressure to hand in assignments, complete all the reading, understand the differences in learning style and everything else, they may begin to feel very unsure of their ability to cope and even wonder if they have made the right decision to come and study here. This depression phase that many students experience can be put down in the first place to simply being away from everything you are accustomed to. Being homesick is a natural thing to experience. Even students from this country whose family live in other cities experience homesickness. As part of missing home, many students find it hard to look after themselves, cooking, cleaning, shopping, paying bills, doing the laundry, things they might never have had to do before. It's part of learning to be independent, and to overcome it try to make friends with other students from your own country and also with students in your classes; you'll be in class with them for a very long time so it's worth developing friendships here to make you feel more at home.
The second factor that may be at the heart of depression is one that needs to be looked at carefully. Many students achieve low marks at first, low grades for academic work, and this is a problem that all students might experience, not just overseas students. Students often come to university with very high expectations; they are used to being high achievers, to doing very well at school, so their expectations are too high when they move to a completely different learning environment. In fact, this new learning environment should not be underestimated as a cause of low grades. Students may be using a different language, they may be required to work independently for the first time. Many of you will have to present seminars, something you may never have done before in academic studies, and to do independent library research. You have to develop skills for this different style of learning, before you can achieve good grades.
So, to cope with this possibly huge swing in your emotional state from excitement to very low morale,

Tapescripts for the Listening Activites

my advice in this first semester of your academic life is: be realistic about what you can achieve. If your expectations are too high you may become very depressed if you do not receive the grades you expect. A realistic approach is more sensible.

Narrator: Activity 25: 'Library Tour'. Listen to the guided tour commentary and label the places marked. Choose from the box below. Write the appropriate letters A to J on the diagram.

Librarian: Welcome to the library tour. We'll begin our tour of this level of the library here at the entrance. Then we'll go in a clockwise direction.

So, first of all, over here on the left, next to the entrance, is a touch-screen information service; these computers can be used at any time to get general information about the library and how it works. In front of the touch-screen information service are the catalogues. As you can see it's a computerized catalogue system and it's very easy to use. The catalogues are linked up to the other libraries at the university, so make sure you check which library a book is in when you are trying to locate a particular item.

Next, along here on the left, we have the Circulation Desk for borrowing and returning books. The Returns Area, the place for returned books and other items is at the end of the Circulation desk near Closed Reserve. Closed Reserve, as most of you probably know, is a collection of books that are in high demand so they are on restricted circulation. If a book is on Closed Reserve you can only borrow it to use within the library for three hours at a time.

Over there in the corner are the shelves for newspapers. The library has an extensive collection of local and international English-language newspapers. They are kept on those shelves for one month and then stored elsewhere.

As we continue our tour around to the right this large central section is the Reference Section. Reference texts cannot be borrowed for use outside the library; they must be used within the library. All these shelves in the centre of this level are the Reference Section.

Now, the stairs here on the left lead to Level 2 only. On Level 2 are most of the Law books. To go up to the other levels of the library you have to use the lifts. Beside the stairs are the restrooms for this floor.

Now, as we walk around this corner to the right, this large room on the left is the Audio-Visual Resource Centre. You can come in here if you wish to listen to a tape or watch one of the library's videos. Next to the Audio-Visual Resource Centre is the photocopying room. There are 15 copiers for student use, and we've recently added a colour copier. The system for copying uses cards not coins. You can buy a photocopy card from the technician in charge of the photocopying room, or from the information desk if he isn't here at

the time. On our right, these work tables are for student use, especially for small groups to work together, or you and your colleagues can use the conference room, which is that small room there next to the lockers. You can work on group projects in the conference room without disturbing anyone, and there's a conference room on each level of the library. The round desk in front of the lockers is the Information Desk. If you need help using the catalogues or you need to organize a loan from another library the information desk is the place to come. And finally, here, beside the exit doors, these two shelves contain current magazines and journals. Like the newspapers they are kept here for a time and then stored elsewhere.

Okay, that's the end of the tour of this level of the library. I'll leave you to look around yourselves now, and if you need any further help please ask at the Information Desk.

Narrator: Activity 26: 'The Video Shop'. Robert has just bought a video recorder, and wants to hire movies from the local video shop. The manager is asking him for personal details to fill out the application form. Listen, and answer Questions 1 to 10.

Manager: Ok, could I have your full name, please?
Robert: Yes. My first name is Robert, R-O-B-E-R-T, Wutherspoon, W-U-T-H-E-R-S-P-O-O-N.
Manager: Could you repeat your surname, please?
Robert: Sure. Wutherspoon, W-U-T-H-E-R-S-P-O-O-N.
Manager: Good. Now, where do you live?
Robert: My address is 9809 Richmond, Apartment E 66, Houston, Texas, 77042.
Manager: Richmond is spelt R-I-C-H-M-O-N-D, right?
Robert: That's right. And it's Houston, Texas, 77042.
Manager: Right. Your contact number?
Robert: Yes, it's 795 (pause) 5183.
Manager: Is that at home or is it your work number?
Robert: That's my home number. My work number is 743 (pause) 3027.
Manager: And your date of birth is ...?
Robert: December 6, 1979.
Manager: Good. Now I'll have to see some proof of identity. Do you have a driver's license or a passport with you?
Robert: Yes, I've brought my driver's license.
Manager: Thank you. Okay, I'll just record your license number: 1361 7844. You need to give me a password to authorize borrowing as well. What would you like as a password?
Robert: 'Horace'. It's my cat's name so I'll remember it easily.
Manager: Okay. Well, here's your license, and if you'll just wait a few minutes I'll laminate your membership card.

Tapescripts for the Listening Activites

27

Narrator: Activity 27: 'The bicycle pump and tyre valve'. Listen to the tape and label the parts of the bicycle pump and tyre valve. Write no more than two words for each answer.

Man: Why are these things always harder to describe than they are to use?
Woman: What do you mean?
Man: Well, I bet you know how to use a bicycle pump.
Woman: Of course. You use the bicycle pump to push air into your bicycle tyre.
Man: That's right. But I have to label these parts for an advertisement.
Woman: Let's have a look. Hmm. You could start with the handle. You could say something like 'The handle is easy to grip'.
Man: That's good. Now the pump body, which is drawn cut away so we can see inside it.
Woman: Maybe you could say 'The cylindrical pump body is made of durable material.'
Man: And then I could go on: 'The plunger in the centre of the pump body has a disc at the end of it...'
Woman: Hang on. You mean that big piece at the bottom of the plunger that looks as though it takes up all of the space inside the pump body? You could talk about how neatly the disc fits.
Man: That's right. Then I could go on about the air hose. You can see it connects the screwed hole at the bottom of the pump body and goes to the tyre valve.
Woman: I see. The air goes through the air hose into the tyre valve – that's that whole thing between the hose and the tyre.
Man: It's bracketed together on the diagram.
Woman: Yes, but there's one little piece that's labelled separately. Is it important?
Man: Hmm. Oh, oh, I see. It's the valve core. That's where the air goes before it's forced into the valve. You can see where the rubber sleeve keeps the air in the tyre.
Woman: It's a really neat, simple design, isn't it?
Man: Yeah. Been around a while, too.

28

Narrator: Activity 28: 'Book Sales'. You will hear a talk about book sales in the University Book Stores. As you listen, answer questions 1 to 6 by completing the table showing the type of books sold in greatest numbers at the different University Book Stores.

Manager: Today I want to give you a breakdown of our sales in the different university bookstores across the campus. We've had some interesting results. We've used figures which show the number of books sold, not their dollar value. This is to screen out those very expensive technical books.
Let's start in 1997. The bookstore in the Humanities Building sold hundreds of novels, but the major sales, by far the greatest number, were of general interest books. This result was probably to be expected. On the other hand, we were very surprised by the results we obtained in the Engineering Building, where we fully expected that most of the sales would be in technical books, and then found that they were in fact selling more novels than any other category. The question had to be asked: why is this so? We found there was a heavy trade among the students in second hand technical books, and also there was serious competition from a cut-price bookseller who supplied from a van just off the university campus, so those two factors would have kept our technical book sales down, but they don't explain why novels were the top seller. The bookstore in the School of Nursing in 1997 also mainly sold novels, with technical books a distant second. The Sports Centre sold marginally more general interest books than anything else.
And so we come to 1998. The bookstore in the Humanities Building sold more novels than ever before, edging out the general interest books two to one. The Engineering Building bookstore is still not selling as many technical books as one would wish; their main sales in 1998 were in general interest books. The store in the School of Nursing once again sold novels and very little else. The Sports Centre saw a return to the technical books—80% of their sales in fact—with a popular series of Sports Medicine books which came out early in 1998.
These results from 1997 and 1998 have taught us that we have to be competitive in technical books. Now, as to the future....

29

Narrator: Activity 29: 'Matching to illustrations'. Listen and write A, B, C or D to indicate the illustration being discussed.

1.
Speaker 1: These graphs show the grain sales in this state. The graph for our particular area shows that we sold almost equal amounts of corn and barley—large amounts, in fact. We also sold equal amounts of wheat and rice, but we sold much less of these grains.

2.
Speaker 1: The house I want you to look at has two stories and five windows downstairs.
Speaker 2: Does it have a chimney?
Speaker 1: Yes, it does. There's a little bit of smoke coming out. And it has six windows upstairs.

3.
Speaker 1: Have you seen my mug?
Speaker 2: What does it look like?
Speaker 1: Well, it's a mug, it has no saucer.
Speaker 2: Does it have a lid?
Speaker 1: Yes. I left the lid sitting next to it.

Answer Key

Notes for teachers

Answers to activities are printed in a regular font, with acceptable alternatives indicated by /.

The text in italic provides suggestions and advice for teachers. These suggestions have been made by teachers who have used the material, and by their very nature are neither complete nor prescriptive.

Unit 2: The Listening Test

There is a Listening Activities answer sheet at the end of Unit 2: The Listening Test, that may be used to record answers to the activities.

1

Accept any reasonable suggestion to fill the gap before the students listen to the tape. Encourage discussion.

1. 4
2. 1 or 2 minutes; 4 or 5 minutes
3. 30 seconds (to read over the questions); 30 seconds (to check); you only hear the tape once
4. getting ready to start a course/checking in at a hotel or a dorm/asking for directions/arranging to meet people ('survival situation'); part of a lecture/(introducing) library facilities/(explaining about) getting a student card ('academic situation')
5. British/Australian/American/Canadian
6. 1 person talking; 2 people talking/conversation between two people
7. choose pictures/use graphic information/fill in table, chart, short answers, form/write in answers/cloze (gap-fill)/multiple choice
8. meaning
9. Answer sheet

2

1. 15/5 or 5/15 or 15th May etc. *(accept any correct form of the date)*
2. twice a day
3. recreation
4. 1
5. 2
6. 3
7. 2
8. 4

3

Make sure students understand the wide variety of listening situations they may encounter.

4

This exercise may be regarded as a diagnostic test to identify students' problems.

1. 15
2. bent
3. led
4. work
5. 60
6. ditch
7. bet
8. 13
9. seal
10. slim

5

This exercise may be regarded as a diagnostic test to identify students' problems.

1. 1175
2. 9555 6140
3. 0055 12370
4. 131 500
5. 1 800 666 9181
6. 672 3000
7. 13 13 50
8. 973 7333
9. 43 1 201 316 809
10. 1 800 025 121

6

Ensure students use either US or British system, not both at the same time.

1. 21/21st March 1685 or 21/3/1685 or 3/21/1685
2. 10/10th April or April 10/10th or 10/4 or 4/10
3. Feb./February 21/21st or 21/2 or 2/21
4. '90s or nineties or 90's
5. 30/30th Sept./September or 30/9 or 9/30
6. 8/8th Nov./November or 8/11 or 11/8
7. 16th century or C16
8. Nov./November 1853 or 11/1853
9. Dec./December 1/1st, 1950 or 1/12/1950 or 12/1/1950
10. 14/14th July or 14/7 or 7/14

7

This exercise may be regarded as a diagnostic test to identify students' problems.

1. 2/3 or two-thirds
2. 12½% 12.5%
3. $50
4. 5/8 (five-eighths)
5. 38.65%
6. £750
7. 2.2
8. 0.3%
9. $530,000,000
10. 85.5% or 85½%

Unit 2: The Listening Test

8

This exercise may be regarded as a diagnostic test to identify students' problems.

9

1. Missouri
2. Canberra
3. Harry Luske
4. Johannesburg
5. Vancouver
6. (Maria) Strella
7. (Bill) McLean
8. Sammy's
9. Runnymede
10. (Professor) Kumar

10

Be sure students understand what the term 'distinguishing features' means.
1. B
2. D
3. A

11

Direction exercise. Encourage students to give clear directions. If there is time, get students to direct each other around the school.

12

By now the students should be anticipating and identifying distinguishing features. They should be able to do this exercise quickly.
1. C
2. H
3. B
4. G
5. E
6. A
7. F
8. D

Encourage the students to use as many kinds of questions as possible when creating the questions to get information needed to complete a form. Listen for the correct question forms being used.

13

1. Calvi
2. Mario
3. Italian

4. German
5. more than 7
6. Post-graduate
7. 13/8 or 8/13 or 13th August *(accept any accurate form)*
8. 30/8 or 8/30 or 30th August *(accept any accurate form)*

14

Encourage discussion. The students should recognize the key words which alter meaning. Remember that True/False questions are not used in the IELTS Listening module.
1. T
2. T
3. F
4. F
5. T
6. F
7. T

15

1. D
2. B
3. B
4. A
5. D

16

This is a typical paired practice activity. Make sure Student A does not see the answers to their questions given on Student B's card. Encourage the students to give more than single word answers to their partners' questions.

17

1. George Rowlands (surname must be spelt correctly)
2. 52 Green Street, Strathfield 2135
3. 175 centimetres/1 metre 75 (cm)
4. 80 kilos
5. Single
6. None
7. None
8. Hay fever
9. Mother: yes; Father: no
10. Father: 67; Cause of death: car accident
11. No

Using the 'Cue cards for further practice', follow-up practice could be done in a language laboratory, or taped and played to the class as listening practice.

18

Encourage students to think of as much vocabulary as possible. This is a useful board exercise.

Unit 2: The Listening Test

19

Once again, encourage students to think of as much vocabulary as possible. They should listen to news programs as often as possible. If there is time they can listen to the news at home and report what they hear to the class.

20

Encourage students to recognize the great number of appropriate responses possible. All these prediction activities are to encourage students to think ahead.

21

There are two broadcasts in this exercise. This exercise is not an IELTS-type task; it is designed to activate prediction as a listening skill. Encourage discussion. The taped broadcasts can be used for confirmation of the students' guesses.

22

Do not let students look at the text of the question items for more than 30 seconds. They must learn to anticipate quickly.
1. D
2. B
3. C
4. A
5. B
6. B
7. C

23

Do not let students look at the text of the question items for more than 30 seconds. They must learn to anticipate quickly.
1. (Terminal) 3
2. ten (10) minutes
3. Flight Connections Centre
4. four (4)
5. fifty-five (55) minutes

24

Do not let students look at the text of the question items for more than 30 seconds. They must learn to anticipate quickly.
1. excited
2. homesickness/being homesick
3. (receiving/achieving) low grades/marks
4. high expectations/different learning environment
5. realistic

25

Do not let students look at the text of the question items for more than 30 seconds. They must learn to anticipate quickly.

1. B
2. F
3. H
4. G
5. C
6. I
7. E
8. J
9. A
10. D

26

Do not let students look at the text of the question items for more than 30 seconds. They must learn to anticipate quickly.
1. Robert (must have correct spelling)
2. Wutherspoon (must have correct spelling)
3. 9809 Richmond (must have correct spelling)
4. E 66
5. Texas
6. 795 5183
7. 743 3027
8. 6/12/1979 or 12/6/1979 or 6th December 1979 or December 6, 1979
9. (driver's) license (US)/licence (Brit.)
10. 1361 7844

27

Do not let students look at the text of the question items for more than 30 seconds. They must learn to anticipate quickly.
1. handle
2. pump body
3. plunger
4. disc
5. screwed hole
6. air hose
7. tyre valve
8. valve core

28

Do not let students look at the text of the question items for more than 30 seconds. They must learn to anticipate quickly.
1. N
2. N
3. G
4. N
5. N
6. T

29

Do not let students look at the text of the question items for more than 30 seconds. They must learn to anticipate quickly.
1. C
2. B
3. A

Unit 3: The Reading Test

Introduction to the IELTS Test

Explain to students that good time management is critical in the IELTS test. There will be reminders throughout the reading section.

a) No. The Academic and General Training Modules of the test run concurrently (the word 'or' appears in the diagram between both the reading and writing tests). This indicates that students must decide which Module they want to take when they apply to sit the test.
b) The Listening and the Speaking test are common to both Modules.
c) 9 bands
d) Band 9
e) *Students should indicate which Module they intend to take. They should read the General Training test description if taking the General Training Module, and the Academic Test description if taking the Academic Module.*
f) By referring to the heading.
    Encourage students to check titles.
g) Listening test; Reading test; Writing test; Speaking test
h) The Reading and Writing tests are different.
i) A candidate must wait 3 months before taking the test again.
j) Academic reading texts are taken from magazines, journals, books and newspapers.
k) General Training reading texts are taken from notices, advertisements, official documents, booklets, newspapers, instruction manuals, leaflets, timetables, books and magazines.
l) The General Training Reading test includes an extra question type, true/false/not given.
m) Duration of test, number of questions, positioning of questions, description of instructions, information about question sheet and answer sheet.
Focus on gleaning as much information as possible in a short time from the text. The work may be done orally to save time.

A Walk in the Woods

Other sentences support the topic sentence by referring to time and place, by giving examples, and by describing what the forest looked like.
Accept any answer which indicates that the student recognizes the support given by detail, discussion of time and place, examples, etc.

Topic sentence of first paragraph: first sentence: 'Through the end of the 19th century, Vancouver was the centre of British Columbia's logging and sawmilling industry.'
The other sentences give examples and details, and refer to time and place.

Topic sentence of second paragraph: second sentence: 'Although temperate rainforest has given way to high-rises and highways, manicured lawns and suburban sprawl, vestiges of the region's original ecology remain.'
The other sentences state facts and figures, describe the area and give examples to support the topic statement.

Paragraph beginning: 'For decades the civil engineers…':
The second sentence supports the topic sentence and gives detailed information. The third sentence describes the destination. The final part of the text is a direct quote giving further information and an opinion about the destination referred to in the topic sentence.

Paragraph beginning: 'Obstructions in the vicinity of an airport…':
Topic sentence: first sentence: 'Obstructions in the vicinity of an airport, whether they be natural features or man-made structures, may seriously limit the scope of its operations.'
The second sentence describes an ideal situation for an airport, the third discusses the expansion of airports, the fourth discusses the influence of high-rise buildings, the fifth, new structures and the final sentence describes the effect of combined obstacles.

Bird Hazard

The topic sentences are the first sentences in each paragraph.
Encourage students to see that the topic sentences contain all the important information of the essay. All other sentences serve purely to give more detailed information thus supporting the topic sentence. We can often predict what the supporting sentences may say, and this should help students to be able to guess meaning even when faced with vocabulary not previously met.

Theatre in the West End of London

Encourage students to guess the meaning of unknown words. Dissuade them from wasting time trying to work out the meaning of words which are not crucial.

Unit 3: The Reading Test

Theatre in the West End of London

Accept any reasonable summary. Encourage brevity.
Paragraph 1: London's West End; home of theatre; connection with Shakespeare
Paragraph 2: theatres not comfortable; themes still relevant today
Paragraph 3: actors all men; Sarah Siddons made female actors respectable
Paragraph 4: opulence of London theatres

Cultivating a Passion for Learning

This activity is best suited to group or class discussion, to encourage reading for understanding that is not halted by unknown vocabulary. In the paired activity to write a title, accept any reasonable title for each paragraph that refers to its content.

The Bamboo Organ

Paragraph 1: The organ was made of bamboo.
Paragraph 2: Wind is pumped into pipes to produce sound.
Paragraph 3: Bamboo was inexpensive and available locally.
Paragraph 4: The bamboo was buried under sand for about a year.

The Bamboo Organ (2)

Accept any reasonable points, provided the students can explain why they are important.

1. C
2. A
3. B

---

4. C, D
5. A, C
6. C

11

The words and phrases in brackets do not occur in the passage under study but may be discussed with the class.
Adding an idea: moreover; not only … but (also)
Giving an alternative idea: whether … or; while; but
Explaining: because
Giving an example: such as
Ending, summarizing: (in conclusion; finally; to sum up)
Giving a result: (as a result; consequently)
Repeating for emphasis: indeed

12

Local Bus Guide

1. Citizens' Advice Bureaux; Libraries; Police Stations; Main Post Offices
2.
a) Blackheath Village Library: 54, 89, 108, 202
b) St Catherine's Library: P12
c) Sydenham Post Office: 75, 194, 202
d) Sydenham Citizens' Advice Bureau: 122, 176, 202, 312
e) Greenwich Police Station: 177, 180, 199, N77
f) Lee Green Post Office: 21, 122, 178, 202, 261

Information was organized in alphabetical lists under the four headings.

3.
a) Catford Citizens' Advice Bureau: 120 Rushey Green
b) Manor House Library: Old Road
c) Penge Police Station: 175 High Street
d) Downham Post Office: 488 Bromley Road

4.
Encourage the students to use the headings and other organizational devices in the text to find the information they need.

13

Laundry list
Note that some pieces of required information are not available, e.g., there is no dry-cleaning price for slips.

Item	Laundry	Dry cleaning
1 x Sport shirt	4.00	6.75
1 x Slip	2.50	not given
1 x Vest	not given	3.50
1 x Swimsuit	3.50	not given
1 x Tie	not given	3.75
1 x Blouse	6.75	7.00

Unit 3: The Reading Test

1. To eat oysters, go to The Oyster Bar or the Gallery. To watch TV, go to Schooners.
   To eat Italian food, go to Andiamo Presto.
2. 12 noon
3. 3333

General Information about New Zealand

1. New Zealand
2. by taxi, shuttle or bus
3. different in different parts
4. informing; describing

16

General Information about New Zealand

1. 15 km
2. in the (drier) eastern regions
3. 9.30 am – 4.30 pm Monday to Friday except public holidays

Accept any reasonable suggestions for reading advice, but make sure the students understand they should:

- *skim first to understand the gist of the passage*
- *scan to find the specific information they are looking for.*

17

The Efficient Reader

1. D
2. C
3. D
4. A
5. A
6. B

18

1. multiple birdstrike
2. Sydney airport
3. failed fan blade
4. dumped fuel*

Remind students of the three-word limit. Thus the quantity of fuel is deleted.

In the first instruction, 'USING NO MORE THAN THREE WORDS taken from the passage', candidates have to use words or phrases that appear in the passage. In the second, 'Answer the questions using NO MORE THAN THREE WORDS', candidates can use their own words.
Encourage students to recognize the significance of word limits in the test.

Medicare Benefits Wealthy Most

1. Medicare beneficiary
2. upper income brackets
3. supplemental insurance coverage
4. Paragraphs 2 & 3

Accept any reasonable paraphrase.
Suggested answers:
Paragraph 2: Wealthy Medicare enrollees get more out of Medicare than they pay in, because they live longer and use more medical services.
Paragraph 3: Skinner and McClellan conducted research to find out how much Medicare spends, over a lifetime, on a variety of elderly people.

20

Japanese Schools, Foreign Students

1. Japanese
2. commitment
3. inability
4. limited
5. teaching
6. creativity
7. society
8. size
9. generally
10. secondary

Encourage discussion of words chosen.

Choosing your answers from a box eliminates many possible but erroneous choices.

In this passage the writer was describing as well as discussing the Japanese education system, and explaining why foreign parents do or do not use it.

Unit 3: The Reading Test

21

Top Marks for Singapore Schools

A. ii
B. x
C. i
D. iv
E. xi
F. vii
G. ix
H. iii
Encourage discussion.
This exercise may be done on OHTs to facilitate an exchange of information.

22

The West and American Unity

Accept any reasonable heading, and encourage discussion.

23

Cleaner Industrial Production: Why?

1. No
2. Yes
3. Not given
4. Yes
5. Not given

24

Small Change, Big Deal

1. A
2. A
3. B
4. A
5. A
6. C
7. A
8. C
9. C

25

Personal Communication in the Age of the Internet

1. B
2. B
3. D
4. E
5. C, D
6. D, E
7. A
Whether students prefer to read the questions before or after reading the passage is a personal choice. The most important skill in answering any type of comprehension question is that students can quickly find the relevant information they need.

26

How Safe is a Cup of Tea?

1. D
2. A
3. B
4. A
5. C

27

Art Lovers Enjoy New, Decorative Lights

1. D
2. A
3. B
4. A
5. C

28

Cape Town and Peninsula Region

1. J
2. B, C (must have both)
3. G
4. E
5. B, D, F, K (must have four)
Encourage students to work quickly.

Unit 3: The Reading Test

29

Oral Communication Skills

1. B, C, D, F (must have four)
2. C
3. D, F (must have both)
4. E
5. D
6. F

Encourage discussion of ways to get information quickly.

30

Nesting Habits

1. 100 days
2. a (small) slit
3. fold of skin/skin fold
4. eight (8) weeks

Whether students prefer to read the questions before or after reading the passage is a personal choice. The most important skill in answering any type of comprehension question is that students can quickly find the relevant information they need.

31

Bondi and Bay Explorer Bus

1. closures/works
2. busy/crowded
3. responsibility
4. not responsible
5. early

32

The West and American Unity

1. US Constitution
2. George Washington

33

A Good Night's Sleep

A. vii
B. ix
C. iii
D. i
E. iv
F. viii
G. v

34

The West and American Unity

Accept any reasonable heading, and encourage discussion.

35

Culture in Action - Table Manners

1. YES
2. NO
3. NOT GIVEN
4. NOT GIVEN
5. NO

Encourage discussion. It can be especially difficult to choose between a 'NO' answer and 'NOT GIVEN'. Remind students that information can only be drawn from the passage.

The last part of this exercise (creating Yes/No/Not Given questions on the last three paragraphs of the passage) may be done on OHTs so that students can compare the questions they formulate.

36

The University of Hong Kong Museum Society

1. True
2. False
3. Not Given
4. False
5. True

Unit 3: The Reading Test

Staff Value a Career Path Above Salary

1. True
2. False
3. True
4. True
5. Not Given
6. Not Given
7. False

Safety Information for Guests

1. A
2. C
3. C
4. B
5. B
6. B
7. C

The headings act as markers, directing the reader to the section of the passage containing the relevant information needed to answer a particular question. *Students should be reminded not to waste time reading the whole passage again and again when the relevant passage can be located by quickly scanning the headings.*

39

Smoking a Problem for Occupational Health Nurses

1. H
2. E
3. G
4. F
5. D

Unit 4: The Writing Test

1

Encourage students to note the limits on time and word count; it is often very difficult for them to fulfil the task in the time allowed.

1. table
2. coal production in Australian states
3. coal production by state
4. comparing state by state and increased production over time
5. All states show increased coal production with the exception of South Australia (SA) which shows a decrease between the years 1970–71. Queensland (Qld) shows a dramatic increase in production.

Encourage students to discuss organizing the information shown in the table before they write.

3

Sample answer (1): focuses on the most popular destination for each age group in turn.
Sample answer (2): focuses on each destination in turn, and what percentage of each age group visited this destination.
Recommend to students that they follow an equally systematic approach.

4

Check that students have used the correct tense. Accept any reasonable answer.
1. declined/fell/dropped sharply/steeply/dramatically
2. has reached its lowest point/bottomed out/has reached an all-time low
3. will remain constant
4. will begin/is predicted to rise steadily
5. reach/achieve/arrive at a peak/high/new high

remain constant →	plunge ↓	remain unchanged →
fall ↓	climb ↑	rise ↑
increase ↑	even out →	drop ↓
decline ↓	go down ↓	go up ↑
level off →	remain stable →	decrease ↓

Better: recover; pick up; improve
Worse: deteriorate; slip back

Accept any reasonable answer for the explanations of 'reach a peak' etc.

Unit 4: The Writing Test

Check all the verb forms in the exercises for their past participles.

Noun forms: plunge; climb; rise; increase; evening out; drop; decline; levelling off; decrease; recovery; deterioration; improvement; reach (as in 'The book was on a high shelf, beyond his reach', but not used in the context of graphs and charts); fluctuation

Adverbs: gradually; slowly; steadily; quickly; substantially; considerably; dramatically; noticeably; negligibly

If we say '10% of the students ate bread for breakfast', we don't know how many students are being referred to, just that one in ten ate bread.
If we say '10 students ate bread for breakfast', we know that exactly 10 students ate bread for breakfast.
A percentage identifies a portion of a group.
A number identifies the total of people or things in a group.

Academic Writing Task 1: Practice 1
Encourage students to discuss the information before writing. The answer should be in the present simple because it is describing facts.

Academic Writing Task 1: Practice 2
If your students are ready to work alone, let them do so. However, many students are more comfortable discussing the information in groups. When they start to write, remind them they should only spend 20 minutes on Writing Task 1, and that this will include planning time.

8

The problems with this answer are that the vocabulary is boring and repetitive, the language is too simple, the same sentence structure is used again and again, the sentences are all approximately the same length, and they are all in the active voice.

Rewriting the passage on air and sea travel may be done on OHTs to facilitate comparison. Accept any reasonable answer. Encourage students to use conjunctions, to vary sentence structure and sentence length, and to use vocabulary of an appropriate register.

9

Simple sentences
The underlined words are verbs.
Each simple sentence contains only one finite verb (a verb that can stand alone).

Compound sentences
Each compound sentence contains finite clauses joined by a connecting word (if you take away the connecting word the clauses can stand alone).
Because, but, and, when and *while* are conjunctions. Other words used to make compound sentences include: *yet, so, for, as, nor, or, otherwise.*

Possible rule: a simple sentence contains only one finite verb, while a compound sentence is made up of more than one finite clause connected by a conjunction.

The sentences are interesting to read because the sentence structure and word order are both varied and each sentence contains a lot of information.

Complex sentences
a) My favourite teacher has left the country (main clause)
   who is an expert in Arabic literature (dependent clause)
b) The bank clerk has retired (main clause)
   who usually works here (dependent clause)
c) Simple
d) Complex
e) Simple
f) Simple
g) Compound
h) Complex
i) Complex
j) Complex
k) Compound
l) Complex

10

Sentences should be in the in order: 3 // 6 5 // 7 4 // 8 1 // 2 (the // indicates a paragraph break).

Information in the answer is more clearly presented if it follows the same order as in the graphs.

Academic Writing Task 1: Practice 3
If the students are ready, make them do the whole exercise in 20 minutes. The checklist is for guidance when they are checking their work.

12

An acceptable order could be: infinitely, many times, a great deal, far, very much, a lot, much, a little, slightly, not very much, hardly, scarcely, barely
Encourage students to discuss subtleties of use. Accept any reasonable order.

Unit 4: The Writing Test

 13

The differences between a mug and a cup might include that a cup is used with a saucer, a cup might be tapered at the base, a mug is often more stable than a cup, and a cup is usually made from finer china or porcelain than a mug.

14

Encourage discussion. Students should aim to organize their ideas logically/systematically. Accept any reasonable description.

To describe how you make a bicycle move, one way would be to use the present simple imperative, i.e. 'First you...', although this would be less acceptable in a written text, where the passive would be preferable: 'To make a bicycle move, the pedal must be pushed downwards by the rider's foot...'.

15

Remind students to use illustrations if they are available to help them guess meanings of unfamiliar words. Dissuade them from spending too long puzzling over unfamiliar words in the Writing Task.

16

Drawing A is described in the text.

17

Be sure students observe the time allowed.

18

Encourage students to discuss subtleties of use. For example, over and outside could arguably be used in reference to both time and direction.

Time: before; since; after; prior to; later

Read diagrams or cartoons in English left to right, and from top to the bottom.

19

Encourage discussion of ways to organize the information. For the comparison, one way would be to describe the similarities then the differences.

Academic Writing Task 1: Practice 7

Topic words: 'sewage', 'sewage treatment unit'
Task words: 'write a description of the process'
Dimensions: pictorial diagram. Reader must follow the arrows.
Striking features/general trends: orderly progression through plant; different end points

Passive verbs in sample answer: is removed, are taken; is removed; is taken; (is) trucked; are added; is transferred; are sent; (are) trucked; is released

Words and phrases in the sample answer which express the order in which things occur: firstly; then; then; subsequently; meanwhile; then

Advise students that one sentence for a conclusion is sufficient.

The paragraphs describe the stages in order.

To determine the best things about the answer, encourage discussion. For example, the answer was methodical, clear, well paragraphed, the right length.

20

1. The letter is to the manager of the hall. Probably the writer does not know this person well, or they may have never met. He/she is probably known only through business.
2. The subject of the letter is to explain the writer's concern at the rising rent of the hall.
3. The main point/points might deal with the writer's need to continue renting the hall and why, but that the group cannot afford this increase in rent, and what effect the increase will have on the group.
4. *Encourage students to use their imagination. For example, candidates may invent details of the type of group and its importance to the members. Encourage invention within the framework of the writing task. This exercise may be done on OHTs to facilitate comparison.*
5. An appropriate ending would be 'I hope that you will seriously consider our problem. Yours sincerely/faithfully, ...'.

23

a) I do hope you can find room at your school for a boy with Andrew's interests.
Encourage discussion. Students should be aware that as an ending the final sentence must convey 'conclusion', which sentence 2 does not. Sentence 3 is irrelevant in regard to the purpose of the letter, and inappropriately introduces new information in the conclusion.

Unit 4: The Writing Test

24

Paragraph breaks should be inserted after: '...at his school.' '...very successful.'
Point out to students that the first sentence is an introduction, that the greater part of the letter is taken up by the body in which the writer expresses his feelings about the concert, and that the conclusion summarizes the body of the letter.

25

Familiarity and friendliness would be more likely found in a personal letter, precise information and respect in a business letter, although a friendly tone may also be appropriate in a business letter.

Endings for personal letters: Affectionately; Yours sincerely; With love
Endings for business letters: Yours truly; Yours faithfully; Yours sincerely

Requests suitable for the end of a letter: 'I look forward to your reply'; 'Please advise me as soon as you can'; 'I would appreciate an urgent reply'

Use of the imperative or 'I want' sound too demanding and are not polite enough for a formal letter.

Inappropriate phrases in the business letter: 'a shocker of a time'; 'horsing around'; 'running like wild things'; 'a solitary person'

Students should be advised not to use colloquial English or slang in a formal letter.

GT Writing Task 1: Practice 1
Encourage students to discuss this orally as a class or in small groups before beginning any written work. Some points that may arise are:

- *the question requires a formal letter*
- *the letter should include all the important facts, such as when and where the bag was left*
- *the letter requires a response so it should conclude with an appropriate phrase.*

This exercise is perhaps best done with students working in pairs to discuss the situation first, before making notes. Accept any reasonable answers. This exercise may be done on an OHT to facilitate comparison. Students should realize there are many different responses.

26

These activities are open-ended exercises to practise extracting and reporting general factual information.

GT Writing Task 1: Practices 2, 3, 4
Encourage students to stay within the time and word limit. If it is suitable for your class some or all of these exercises may be done on an OHT to facilitate comparison.

27

Needs: require; must have; need
Wants: want; wish; wish for; desire
Likes/dislikes: hate; appreciate; dislike; value; enjoy; loathe; love; detest; admire

28

Students should avoid overusing personal pronouns in formal letters. The passive is a useful alternative.

29 30

These activities may be done on the board.

31

Topic words are:
a. the safety of workers
b. to eat meat (in a world where) food resources are (growing increasingly) scarce
c. violent TV ... influences behaviour
d. smoking in places where people gather (to eat and to drink)
e. an ideal television show for children below school age
f. children (watch only) suitable material on television
g. (the) major achievement (of the) twentieth century
h. twentieth century development
i. the problems of people with disabilities
j. responsibilities at home and in the workplace
k. students have to absorb a great deal of information
l. the responsibility of a government to protect its citizens from natural disasters

Task words are:
a. What can be done (to ensure workers' safety as described)?
b. Write a report for an association which sells meat. *Ensure that students recognize the bias of this question.*
c. Do you agree (that violent TV influences behaviour as described)?
d. What is your opinion (on smoking in the places described)?
e. What are the features of (an ideal television show as specified)?
f. How would you ensure (that children watch television as specified)?
g. What do you consider (to be the major achievement...)?
h. What evidence can you offer to support this statement (on twentieth century development)?

Unit 4: The Writing Test

i. How can society reduce (the problem specified)?
j. What advice would you give (to people in the situation described)?
k. Describe quick and efficient ways to do this (that is, for students to do what the statement describes).
l. How far do you agree (with the opinion stated)?

32

Ensure that students' answers relate to the question.
Topic words: access to electronic services (personal computers; Internet)
Task words: How can access (to the services specified) be controlled?

Topic words: employee ... to smoke ... leave the building ... time away from work
Task words: How could this problem (of time away from work being break time or wasted employer time) be resolved? Give reasons ....

34

Ensure students do not introduce new information into the essay at this point. Remind them of the word target.

36

Encourage discussion of words and phrases like 'may', 'might, 'sometimes', tend to', 'it is possible that', and accept any reasonable answers.

37

More information is added: also; as well as; for example; furthermore; similarly; and; while
A cause and effect relationship is shown: as a consequence of; because of; then; therefore
Time is indicated: final; now; recently; subsequently; then; when; while
General and particular statements are linked: also; for example; furthermore; in the case of; such as; similarly; and
Information is compared or contrasted: although; despite; however; similarly; such as; while
This list is not exhaustive, nor are the categories mutually exclusive. Accept any reasonable answer. If a student can produce a sentence which shows a word can go in another category, accept it.
1. such as; for example
2. then; subsequently
3. as well as; and
4. as a consequence of; because of
5. although; while
6. when
7. and; while
8. therefore

9. however
10. for example
11. however
12. despite

38

Words which show the order in which things occur: all the dates, which are in sequence, and also: first; was followed; following; next; next; until; followed by

39

To follow the four steps, encourage students first to identify the topic. Make sure they understand what the question is asking them to write about. They should note down as many ideas as possible before attempting to arrange them in a logical order. Encourage discussion and accept any reasonable plans for the essay. Make sure they have enough points to form an introduction and a body, and that new ideas are not introduced in the conclusion.

Encourage students to write as neatly as possible and to pay attention to the time allowed and the word limit. In checking their work they should think about grammar, spelling and punctuation.

This exercise may be done on OHTs so students can see how many legitimate approaches are possible.

40

Encourage discussion among the students aimed at increasing their awareness that an essay may be approached in more than one way, as long as the chosen approach answers the task requirements. For example, topic 1 on the rising road toll asks the candidate to 'agree/disagree with an argument'; the candidate may, in answering, also 'give and justify an opinion' and 'provide general factual information', or 'examine cause and effect'. She/he may even 'compare and contrast evidence and ideas'. Discussion of these approaches should lead the students to the realization that what is not acceptable in an IELTS-type essay is an unstructured, badly organized collection of random ideas.

43

Encourage students to express the problem clearly and to make relevant, pertinent suggestions.

44

Suggest students complete steps 1 to 4 before reading the sample essay.

Unit 4: The Writing Test

45

Ensure students use language which is appropriate to the strength of their opinions.

46

Ensure students recognize that they do not have to agree with the proposition expressed in the essay question.

47

Ensure students recognize that they do not have to agree with the proposition expressed in the essay question.

48

Encourage discussion. Students may be asked to evaluate the strength of the supporting evidence presented in another student's paragraph.

49

Encourage discussion. If there is time, have students compare their essay plans.

50

Sample answer 2 answers the question by using a problem/solution approach, first stating the problems evident in large cities and suggesting ways in which careful planning could have prevented or solved them. Sample answer 1 gives a clear opinion on why careful planning is important by systematically describing the aspects of city living which benefit from careful planning and supporting each statement with examples. Both approaches are legitimate answers to the task, and the question of which essay would be easier to write can only be answered individually.

This exercise may become clearer for the students if they extract a plan for each Sample answer, working backwards.

Unit 5: The Speaking Test

In all speaking activities, please be sure that the students' responses and body language are appropriate to the country where they are doing the test.

The speaking test is an interview, so it is important that the candidate responds as fully as possible.

Most of the work in Unit 5: The Speaking Test is designed for open discussion, with the result that there are no absolutely right or wrong answers. For this reason answers are not always given, but we have indicated where information may be found.

1

Encourage students to see that the interviewer is a guide (see the section 'Introduction to the IELTS interview', paragraph 2) and that they will succeed by talking as freely as possible. Although pronunciation and grammar are important, the test is concerned with the ability to communicate.

Specific skills being assessed in the Speaking module are listed in the section 'Introduction to the IELTS interview', in the information on Phase 2, Phase 3 and Phase 4. *Encourage students to discuss what all these skills actually mean.*

Encourage students to give a lot of detail on the sample CV form.

2

By entering a room too early, students may inadvertently interrupt an interview. They should excuse themselves, leave quickly and compose themselves.

Check the polite greetings suggested by the students for register.

3

This activity is meant to demystify the opening of the interview.

4

Encourage students to explain why they feel a particular posture will or will not help them.

5

Check that students recognize the opinion questions: 'Do you have any views on...', 'How do you feel about...', 'What do you think of...', 'What's your opinion of...', 'How do you find...'.

8 10

Encourage students to enlarge upon the topics as much as possible.

Unit 5: The Speaking Test

 11

*The student playing the part of the Interviewer should try
to encourage the student playing the Candidate to speak
as much as possible.*

12

1. J K
2. C O
3. M
4. H
5. N
6. K
7. C L
8. B F
9. G I
10. E
11. A F J K
12. D
13. C L
14. G I
15. A J K
16. C
17. C
18. E
19. F
20. E
21. G I

*These matchings are far from exhaustive. Accept any matching
which the students can put into a well-formed question. For
instance, probability could be indicated by a question like
'How many times would you expect this to happen?'.*

13 15

Practice will make this part of the test far less formidable.

16

*Be sure the students understand the nature of speculation
and that you cannot be right or wrong when speculating,
although what is said should be justifiable/plausible.*

Words and phrases that show the speaker is
speculating: I wonder; I don't know, but...; it would be
interesting to find out if...; possibly; it may be that...;
I expect...; perhaps; I imagine that...; I believe that...;
maybe; I'm not sure that...; I guess that...; I hope that...

19 21 22

*These activities may be photocopied and cut up so the
students can draw the topics at random.*

Acknowledgements

Bird Hazards reprinted with permission from Federal Airports Authority Town Planning for Airports 1993; *Chihuly's neon orbs beckon art lovers to Bute Street* by Janet Smith reprinted with permission from Westender April 2 1998; *Composition of exports of Papua New Guinea* (graph) reprinted with permission from 'Recent developments', The Papua New Guinea Economy, Te'o Ian Fairbairn, AIDAB, Commonwealth of Australia 1993; *A Comprehensive Guide to Heathrow and Gatwick Airports* reprinted with permission from BA Inflight magazine Highlife October 1998; *Course Calendar* reprinted with permission from North Shore Continuing Education (Vancouver) January to July 1998; *Cultivating a Passion for Learning* reprinted with permission from NIACE (The National Organization for Adult Learning), Titus Alexander and Marian Young, Adults Learning February 1998; *Holiday Planner* reprinted with permission from NZ Holiday Planner © 1998 New Zealand Tourism Board; *Hong Kong University Brochure* reprinted with permission from the University of Hong Kong Museum Society; *Hotel Sofitel Safety Instructions* reprinted with permission from Hotel Sofitel, Washington DC; *The IELTS Handbook* extracts reprinted with permission from *UCLES* 1998; *Investor Sentiment* (graphs) reprinted with permission from JLW Advisory Corporate Property Services, Australian Property Digest #38; *Local Bus Guide Information Service Booklet* timetables reprinted with permission from London Transport, August 1991; *Medicare Benefits Wealthy Most* reprinted with permission from NBER Digest, September 1998; *PNR Periodical* 25 October 1997 pp. 5 and 6 reprinted with permission; *Sheraton Towers Information Brochure* reprinted with permission from Sheraton Seattle Hotel and Towers 1996; *Small Change Big Deal* by Jay Teitel reprinted with permission from *enRoute* magazine, April 1998; *Smoking test case poses dilemma for OH nurses* reprinted with permission from Occupational Health, June 1998; *South African Arts, Culture and Heritage: 1997 Calendar* reprinted with permission from South African Tourism Board; *Staff Value a Career Path Above Salary* by Ruth Prickett reprinted with permission from People Management, 16 April 1998; *Sydney Explorer* Brochure, March 1998 reprinted with permission from State Transit; *Table Manners* reprinted with permission from the author, Victoria Strutt, first printed Boomerang, February 1998; *Top Marks for Singapore Schools* by Andy Green (TES August 1997) reprinted with permission from Times Supplements Limited 1997; *UNIDO, Cleaner and Safer Industrial Production: The National Cleaner Production Centre Programme, 1997* reprinted with permission from United Nations Industrial Development Organization; *A Walk in the Woods* Brochure reprinted with permission from Forest Alliance of British Columbia 1998; *The West and American Unity* from Frontier America © 1988 the Buffalo Bill Historical Center, Cody, Wyoming, United States of America, reprinted with permission.

Every effort has been made to contact holders of copyright in all materials used. If you feel that your rights are unacknowledged, please contact the publisher, who would be delighted to hear from you.

The publishers take no responsibility for the opinions expressed in the reading and listening texts and sample answers in this publication, nor for the accuracy of facts and events described.

This book has been the product of much consultation. The author would particularly like to thank Dr Joyce Merrill Valdes of Houston, Texas, for her insights and observations on the developing manuscript. Thanks are also due to the staff and students of Insearch Language Centre at the University of Technology, Sydney, and at the University of New South Wales Institute of Languages, through the good offices of Simon Tancred and Brett Doyle. The teachers' time and expertise in trialling the materials and their subsequent comments were invaluable, as were the insights provided by the students. Special thanks are due to four Insearch Language Centre teachers: Thomas Wyld for Writing Activity 34, Lyndal Bruce for Writing Activities 42 to 44, Samantha Milton for preparing the answer keys and Diane Hoggins for her work on the Speaking unit.

This coursebook is a direct descendant of *The IELTS Preparation Course*, a 100-hour syllabus with lesson guides for teachers which was produced by the Department of English for Academic Purposes and the Publications Department of Insearch Language Centre, with annual upgrades, from 1994 to 1996. The original *IELTS Preparation Course* was produced and edited by Mary Jane Hogan, and designed by Deborah Lewis, Paul Vaughan, Diane Hoggins and Sue Emonson with contributions from Adam Aitken, Michael Jacklin and Simon Moore.